730.92 MIC
D

£ 40 00.

209164

THE
SISTINE
CHAPEL

MICHELANGELO
REDISCOVERED

THE SISTINE CHAPEL

MICHELANGELO REDISCOVERED

FOREWORD BY:
CARLO PIETRANGELI
DIRECTOR GENERAL OF THE PAPAL MONUMENTS MUSEUMS
AND GALLERIES

MULLER, BLOND & WHITE

A NTV-Co-Publication

First published in Great Britain in 1986
by Muller, Blond & White Ltd.,
55 Great Ormond Street,
London WClN 3HZ.

British Library Cataloguing in Publication Data

The Sistine Chapel: Michelangelo rediscovered.
  1. Michelangelo   2. Vatican Palace (Vatican
City) – Sistine Chapel   3. Mural painting
and decoration, Italian – Vatican City –
Conservation and restoration
I. Chastel, André
759.5   ND623.B92

ISBN 0-584-11140-1

Editorial Director: Masashi Azuma
Production Manager: Franz Gisler
Picture Researcher: Rosaria Pasquariello
Translator and editor
of the English edition: Paul Holberton

Photolithography by: Hego, Littau,
Switzerland

Phototypeset in Garamond by:
Fotosatz Stückle, Ettenheim, GFR

Printed by: BDV, Basler Druck- und Verlags-
anstalt, Print Medien, Basel-Liestal

Bound by: Maurice Busenhart SA, Lausanne

Printed and bound in Switzerland

Preceding page:
*Portrait of Pope Sixtus IV in a miniature from
Platina's* Liber de vita Christi ac omnium
pontificum *(Cod. Vat. 2044).*

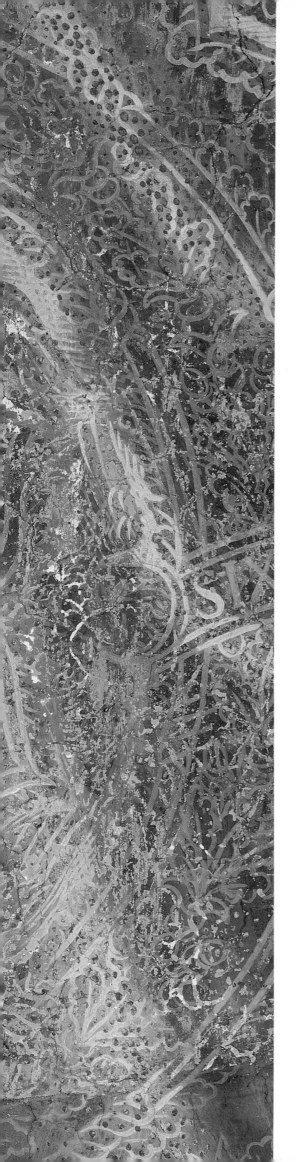

THE AUTHORS

ANDRÉ CHASTEL
MEMBRE DE L'INSTITUT DE FRANCE
FORMER PROFESSOR AT THE COLLEGE DE FRANCE
PARIS

JOHN SHEARMAN
CHAIRMAN, DEPARTMENT OF ART AND ARCHAEOLOGY,
PRINCETON UNIVERSITY
PRINCETON, NEW JERSEY

JOHN O'MALLEY, S.J.
PROFESSOR OF HISTORY
ACTING DIRECTOR, WESTON SCHOOL OF THEOLOGY
CAMBRIDGE, MASSACHUSETTS

PIERLUIGI DE VECCHI
ASSOCIATE PROFESSOR OF ART HISTORY
UNIVERSITA' STATALE OF MILAN

MICHAEL HIRST
PROFESSOR OF ART HISTORY, COURTAULD INSTITUTE OF ART
UNIVERSITY OF LONDON

FABRIZIO MANCINELLI
CURATOR OF BYZANTINE, MEDIEVAL AND MODERN ART
PAPAL MONUMENTS, MUSEUMS AND GALLERIES

GIANLUIGI COLALUCCI
HEAD RESTORER, LABORATORY FOR THE RESTORATION OF PAINTINGS
PAPAL MONUMENTS, MUSEUMS AND GALLERIES

PHOTOGRAPHS BY
TAKASHI OKAMURA

CAPTIONS THROUGHOUT BY
FRANCO BERNABEI,
ASSOCIATE PROFESSOR OF HISTORY OF ART CRITICISM,
UNIVERSITY OF PADUA

CONCEPTION AND DESIGN BY
EMIL M. BUHRER

EDITED BY
MASSIMO GIACOMETTI

CONTENTS

FOREWORD

Goethe wrote in his diary for 16 February 1787, when he was staying in Rome:

On 2nd February we went to the Sistine Chapel to witness the ceremony of the blessing of the candles … I thought … it is precisely these candles that over three centuries have blackened these splendid frescoes; this is the incense that … has not only with its smoke covered over the sun itself of art, but with every year continues to dirty it and will finally engulf it in darkness.

Even making allowances for the rather polemical tone of the German poet, little appreciative of the forces behind Catholic religious ceremony, we know now that the deterioration of the Sistine frescoes has been the result not only of candle and incense smoke, but also of the gradual darkening of the varnishes which were spread over them in the futile hope of returning them to their original splendour.

On the other hand the Sistine Chapel is still today not merely the most prestigious room of the Vatican Museums, it is also, happily, a living and functional papal chapel, a vital part of the papal organization, and it continues to be used for the ceremonies for which it was created five centuries ago – this in itself is obviously a fact of some importance.

We may gather from Goethe's words that already in his time the frescoes of the Chapel were growing darker and darker, until eventually in the minds of some critics the notion became rooted that Michelangelo had no interest or feeling for colour. But this idea can hardly be squared with such other works of the artist as the Doni *tondo* in the Uffizi, which has just now been superbly well restored to its original pure, bright and enamel-like colours. Nevertheless we had become habituated to the dull, lifeless colour of the Sistine Chapel frescoes, misled particularly by colour reproductions that were not faithful enough to reveal the deterioration of the frescoes, or even to give a hint of it. Their deterioration, and the extent of the loss of the original colour, could only be appreciated – with considerable dismay – by study of the original 'face to face'.

As I made my way down, not so long ago, from the scaffold where the restoration of the vault is still proceeding, my eyes still dazzled by the new

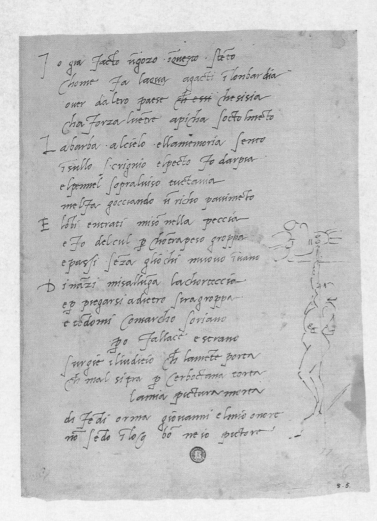

Michelangelo's sonnet describing in burlesque fashion and in plentiful detail the sufferings that the artist had to face painting the Sistine Chapel (Corpus 174 recto).

selves, to their head, Gianluigi Colalucci, and to his assistants, master restorers Maurizio Rossi and Piergiorgio Bonetti, for their expertise was undoubtably essential to the successful outcome of the restoration.

But our thanks must also be extended to all those – historians, art historians, critics and restorers from all parts of the world – who visited the work in progress and gave us the benefit of their advice and support. Recognition is also due to the artists who brought a different sensibility from that of professional critics or restorers, and who in various ways criticized our enterprise: their opinion was important in so far as it spurred us to an even greater punctilio (if that were possible) in the documentation of the restoration, so that a full report of the criteria adopted and the methods used should be available for all those interested either in the present or the future.

Particular mention is due to the Direction of the Technical Services of the Vatican State, for all their support and labour during the restorations, and in particular during the construction of the scaffold, inspired by the one used by Michelangelo, from which the restoration of the Ceiling was conducted. We would like also to express our gratitude to NTV of Tokyo, with whom the contract for exclusive pictures of the restored frescoes agreed with the Direction of the Vatican Museums indirectly facilitated the funding of the project, as well as providing a complete and thorough cinematographic record, and making possible this present publication.

Simultaneously with the restoration there were also undertaken two continuing projects of importance for the scientific examination of the present state of the Chapel, a photographic survey of the ceiling and a study of the micro-climate of the Chapel.

Heartfelt thanks are due to the generous benefactors who made it possible for us to begin and continue with this costly project: they have made it possible to assure a longer life for this extraordinary masterpiece of human genius, which continues daily to arouse the enthusiasm of thousands and thousands of people who come to visit it from all over the world.

CARLO PIETRANGELI
Director General of the Papal Monuments, Museums and Galleries

splendour of the frescoes that had been cleaned, I looked up to the ceiling proper, on which work had not yet started, still grey and dull, and I wondered how Michelangelo's masterpiece could possibly have been left to sink to such a state over so many years. Paradoxically enough, our very reverence for Michelangelo was partly to blame for the inaction; but it is still extraordinary that so little awareness had been shown of the importance of the colour to the full enjoyment of the Ceiling. It was even more extraordinary that this monotonous grey could ever have been mistaken for the authentic effect intended by Michelangelo.

So certainly we should praise the day on which the courageous decision was taken to undertake the restoration, and I would like take this opportunity to give public recognition to the people involved in this certainly exceptional enterprise: above all to the director of operations, Dr Fabrizio Mancinelli, Curator of the Department of Byzantine, Medieval and Modern Art of the Vatican Museums; to Dr. Nazzareno Gabrielli, head of the Vatican Scientific Research Laboratory, responsible for all the technical analyses required during the work; to Professor Pasquale Rotondi, former director of the Italian Institute of Research and consultant for the restoration on behalf of the Director General, for his assistance and counsel, the fruit of long experience; and finally to the restorers proper them-

From a report to Mantua made in 1472 Ludwig von Pastor quoted the representative words: "ad ogniuno pare vedere principio d'un novo mundo" – "It seemed to everyone that they were witness to the beginning of a new world". Sixtus IV Della Rovere (1471–84) had no intention that his pontificate should pass unregistered. Among his several decisive steps may be included that of constructing the building in which we are interested, the Sistine Chapel.

No sooner had he become Sixtus IV, than Cardinal Della Rovere made the decision to restore the Capitol to its honourable position by "restitution" to the Roman people of the famous statues that embodied its prestige – or, as the accompanying text of the donation has it, "the outstanding bronze statues [that are] proof of the historic excellence and capability of the Roman people who created them". These were very well-known and loved works such as the *Spinario,* and the suckling *She-wolf,* which was placed plumb in the middle of the façade of the new palace of the Conservatori. They had previously all been in the Lateran palace, the seat of the Bishop of Rome. The

ANDRÉ CHASTEL

ROME IN THE RENAISSANCE
1480–1540

Detail of a view of Rome by an unknown artist taken from Hartmann Schedel's Liber chronicarum, *Nuremberg 1493.*
At the bottom is the Porta del Popolo with the church of Santa Maria del Popolo nearby; then the bridge over the Tiber leading to the massive Castel Sant' Angelo. Old St Peter's is not in view, but only (at the top on the left) part of the old Vatican palace complex; at the top on the right, standing free, is the Belvedere villa built between 1485 and 1487 by Pope Innocent VIII. Later the Belvedere would be joined with the rest of the complex by a system of courtyards and buildings designed by Bramante. Significantly enough, this view was later used for the woodcuts of the Protestant attack on the Church of Rome, for instance by Lucas Cranach, though in these the palaces are shown in ruins or razed, expressing the characteristic Protestant identification of Rome with Babylon.

"restitution" had considerable political significance: it was intended to please and re-assure the citizens, and it affirmed the joint destiny of historic and modern Rome to those who saw their new setting. Further, it became legitimate, even desirable, that all public ceremonies, entries, festivals of the *rioni* or districts, including also public speeches and the exercise of oratory, should be modelled on antique precedent. A notary of the Ponte district reports that on 25 December 1483 the people of Rome, to manifest their joy, held a procession from the Capitol to the Vatican with their children dressed and with torches lit *all' antica:* "con fiaccole all' antica come quelle che stanno colpite de marmo" – "with torches like those which are carved on the marbles". Symbols of "Rome" became visible everywhere. It may be that the growth of papal power and the international character of the Curia had very little in reality to do with the old Rome, but the veneer, the trappings, the style was all classicizing. The entry of the Pope now resembled an antique triumph, thanks to the installation of arches under which he might pass. So it did for Alexander VI Borgia and especially for Julius II Della Rovere, in December 1503: "da castello Santo Aguilo fino in campo de fiore foro fatti sette archi trionfali i più belli che fossero fatti a Roma" – "between Castel Sant' Angelo

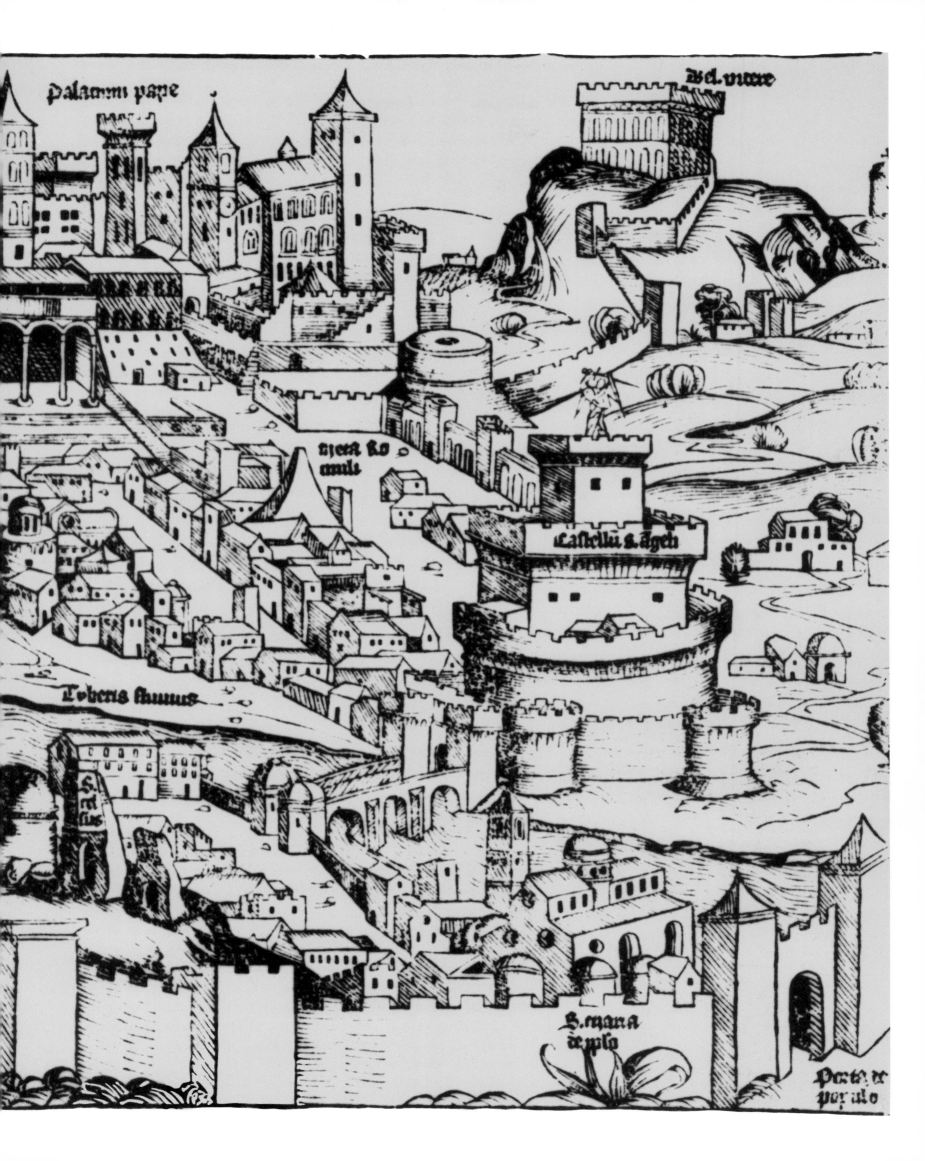

and the Campo de' Fiori there were erected seven triumphal arches, the finest ever erected in Rome".[1]

Of course these *all' antica* structures, of which the design was overseen by Giuliano da Sangallo, architect and intimate of the Pope, were a new variation on well-established medieval procedure. This was obvious to all, and was essential to the success of the idea, which, repeated in Florence in 1515, soon became standard throughout Europe.

Sixtus IV's foundation of the Vatican Library is familiar to us through the fresco now in the Vatican Gallery by Melozzo da Forlì, in which its librarian, Platina, is presented to the Pope; its Greek section was decorated by the workshop of Ghirlandaio with busts of the Fathers of the Church and of classical philosophers. The ideal of the "grand style" was pervasive. Another notable commission of Sixtus IV, though unfortunately it was dismembered and is difficult to reconstruct, was the ciborium installed about 1480 over the Altar of Confession in St Peter's, the work of Mino da Fiesole and Giovanni Dalmata, whose reliefs of the *Martyrdoms of Sts Peter and Paul* (in the traditional scheme) derived certain elements directly from those of Trajan's Column and the Arch of Constantine.

The papal ideology was propagated not least in book illustration. A miniature in a *City of God* of St Augustine in the Ste Geneviève Library in Paris[2] shows this 'synthetic' Christian Rome, conjoining classical ruins with modern churches; above, a fictive bronze medal is meant to represent Rome *ante gratiam*, the pagan city. But one notices straightaway that all its elements – Column, towers, Hadrian's Mausoleum – have also been incorporated into the modern city.

Interest in classical remains had its crudely commercial side; the appetite for them of cleric collectors was fuelled by considerations of prestige, and enthusiasm for things antique was a kind of self-advertisement. In some cases, however, there was shown a reverence for antiquity that deserves the word "pietas". It was directed towards the great names of the ancient world who had also been accepted into Christian culture – for instance Marcus Aurelius.

The fragments of a monument dedicated to Marcus Aurelius had long rested in Santi Luca e Martina by the Forum: in 1525 they were transferred to the courtyard of the Palazzo dei Conservatori (thus consolidating the role of the palace as a museum of antiquities). These reliefs were of some importance for the history of Christian Rome, which explains their popularity with artists charged to represent the legend of Marcus Aurelius as the founder of certain pontifical procedures and traditions. They showed a triumphal entry on a chariot, a sacrifice outside the temple of Juppiter, and the submission and pardon of conquered peoples, and they stood for grandeur, piety and magnanimity.

The transfer of the equestrian statue of Marcus Aurelius from the Lateran to the Capitol in 1538 was the culmination of the "restitution" to modern Rome of the *mirabilia* of pagan Rome by the Christian authorities. It is hardly possible to enumerate or to analyse satisfactorily the quantity of remarks made about, derivations from, analogies made with this remarkable statue in the course of the centuries. It was, as is very well known, the chief prototype of the form of the equestrian statue that fascinated the 15th century. It was transformed into a *Constantine*, and so protected from any harm. Sometimes even it was endowed with magical powers, making it into a kind

The fresco by Melozzo da Forlì (1438–1494), which is now in the Vatican Gallery, shows Pope Sixtus IV Della Rovere, founder of the Sistine Chapel, conferring the directorship of the Vatican Library on the humanist Bartolomeo Sacchi, known as Plátina. Plátina was the somewhat non-conformist and critical author notably of a biographical history of the popes, Liber de vita Christi ac omnium pontificum (1474). Melozzo's fresco is indebted to Piero della Francesca for the solemnity and harmonious proportions of its architecture, but shows a rather different taste for elegant refinement and decoration in the detail of its pilasters and their capitals, of the coffered ceiling, of the dress of the Pope and the chair in which he sits. This idiom became widely diffused in north and central Italy in the latter years of the 15th century. Solemn, august perspective and rich, classicizing detail both were eminently suitable for the commemoration of such an important moment for humanism. The Latin inscription beneath the fresco proclaims Sixtus's "restoration" of ancient Rome and concludes: "The library that long lay hidden in squalor is now raised to view on this glorious site."

TEMPLA DOMVM EXPOSITIS VICOS FORA MOENIA PONTES
VIRGINEAM TRIVII QVOD REPARARIS AQVAM
PRISCA LICET NAVTIS STATVAS DARE COMMODA PORTVS
ET VATICANVM CINGERE SIXTE IVGVM
PLVS TAMEN VRBS DEBET NAM QVAE SQVALORE LATEBAT
CERNITVR IN CELEBRI BIBLIOTHECA LOCO

of palladium. In order to restore to it its correct identity, humanist historians had to proceed in the manner of the philologists, as if they were re-establishing a correct text. By their acceptance of the new identification, the authorities established its validity in the minds of all. But before it could be placed on the Capitol, reinforcing its character as an emblem, the Capitol itself had to be made suitable for it. That did not become a priority until after the entry of Charles V in 1536, when everybody was made aware of the inadequate condition of the historic site.

The Pope who had strikingly revived the glamour of *Roma antiqua* by the "restitution" of the Lateran statues was the founder of the new chapel later adorned with Michelangelo's frescoes. The decision to build was taken in 1473. Its position in the immediate vicinity of St Peter's, the cradle of Christendom, is testament enough to its importance. It was also a building of exceptional size, as it needed to be in order to accommodate, among other things, the conclave of cardinals. Sixtus IV and his architect Giovannino de' Dolci fulfilled the need of the Church for a venue of a kind that was lacking: this was no private chapel, like the oratory which Fra Angelico had decorated for Nicholas V, and which indeed remained in service, but an immense hall for solemn ceremony. It has been observed that the proportions

"How many Popes, Holy Father, who possessed the same Office as Your Holiness, but not the same intelligence or greatness of mind and spirit – how many Popes, I repeat, have permitted the ruin and destruction of antique temples, statues, arches and other buildings redounding to the glory of their founders? ... I would even go so far as to say that this new Rome, in all its present manifest greatness and beauty, with its palaces, churches and other buildings, was created from the mortar to which its ancient marbles had been reduced ... But so may Your Holiness seek the more urgently, accepting the challenge of antiquity, to equal and surpass the ancients, as indeed Your Holiness is doing with great buildings, by nurture and favour to the arts, by arousing men's intellects, by rewarding meritorious effort, by spreading the most holy seed of peace among the Christian princes." (Letter of Raphael and Baldassare Castiglione to Pope Leo X).

of the Chapel have certain analogies with those of the Temple of Jerusalem as described in the Old Testament. We do not know, however, whether the decoration of the walls, completed in record time between 1481 and 1483, was intended from the beginning. It is likely enough, but at the time painters of the calibre to carry out such an enterprise were not available in Rome. A team of Florentine painters (Perugino was Umbrian, but with a practice in Florence) had to be summoned, which it was not possible to do until after the conflict between Sixtus IV and Lorenzo the Magnificent had been resolved, until after the unpleasant affair of the Pazzi Conspiracy. It has often been pointed out that the despatch of a team of the best Florentine artists of the time was in effect the seal of the peace that had been made. The walls were painted in a total of 17 frescoes disposed symmetrically in a broad frieze running all round the Chapel like a girdle.

The "istorie" represented were, on the nave wall to the left of the altar, the *Life of Moses* and on the right wall the *Life of Christ:* the parallellism was spelled out by inscriptions, although it is only recently that all the implications of the scheme have been been worked out.[3] Above the "istorie", between the windows, was a cycle of standing *Popes*. The ceiling was decorated in the usual way as a plain blue firmament adorned with gold stars. Thus the Chapel was a solemn, clear, programmatic representation of the history of the Papacy and a statement of its legitimacy, its priority (Moses the forerunner of St Peter) and its absolute rights.

The programmatic message was worked out in great detail — the seven frescoes of the *Life of Moses* in fact contain 25 biblical episodes[4]. The inclusion of several scenes from Scripture in one continuous narrative threatened to obscure the clarity and impact of the whole; Botticelli resolved the problem brilliantly, by developing the composition in every case round a strong axial element — the well in the *Youth of Moses,* the façade of the papal Hospital of Santo Spirito in the *Purification of the Leper,* and the Arch of Constantine in the *Punishment of the Sons of Corah.* The presence of this last building, symbol of imperial power and monument to the first Christian emperor, was certainly not fortuitous — especially since it is directly opposite the

These five commemorative medals represent the humanist Popes most closely bound to the architectural development of Renaissance Rome. On the left, Nicholas V, born Tommaso Parentucelli da Sarzana, was Pope from 1447 to 1455. He was the founder of the programme for the renewal of Rome, in which he was aided by a large number of artists and men of letters, notably by Leone Battista Alberti and by Fra Angelico, who frescoed the Pope's private chapel in the Vatican palace for him. Next is Paul II, the Venetian Pietro Barbo, Pope from 1464 to 1471. His most important monument is the Palazzo Venezia beneath the Capitol, with its attached church of San Marco. Third, Julius II Della Rovere, nephew of Sixtus IV, was Pope from 1503 to 1513, and, most famously, commissioned Michelangelo to paint the ceiling of the Sistine Chapel. Julius's successor Leo X Medici, Pope from 1513 to 1521, was perhaps the greatest artistic patron of the Renaissance but his pontificate was also, in

centrally planned temple before which Perugino on the right wall painted the *Giving of the Keys to St Peter.* There was a firm consistency in the messages behind the narratives of the new chapel. The primacy of St Peter and the apostolic tradition were not simply asserted, but were buttressed by analogies with the history of the Old Testament legislator and leader of the people of Israel out of their exile, Moses. And the site in which the theocratic principle that was hereby proclaimed was to be put into execution, the site chosen by history, or rather by Providence, was Rome.

It is a conspicuous fact of the history of the Renaissance papacy that its great initiatives were taken every 20 or 25 years. There were intervals during which the project undertaken 'sank in', and during which it was not clear what should be done next. When Giuliano Della Rovere was elected to the papacy, his state of mind was quite different

significant contrast, witness to the first signs of the most serious and damaging crisis the Western Church had yet faced, the reforms championed by Luther and the eventual destruction of Western Christian unity. It was the task of Paul III Farnese, Pope from 1534 to 1549, to find remedies for the crisis with the convocation of the Council of Trent, 1542. He was an artistic patron of the stature of his predecessors, and commissioned from Michelangelo the painting of the Cappella Paolina in the Vatican, after having him carry out the Last Judgement *commissioned by the previous Pope, Clement VII.*

from that of Sixtus. But, though he developed them along new lines, he set about impatiently putting into action his uncle's projects.

Looking up at the vault of the Sistine Chapel, he can only have been dissatisfied with the very ordinary decoration – which was in any case marred by defects in the construction.[5] One of the reasons given for putting Michelangelo to work was, according to Vasari, respect for the memory of Sixtus IV. As it turned out, the decorations of the Sistine Chapel were destined to register at each point of their progress the hopes and reality of the papacy and of Rome. Or so it must have been felt on All Saints 1512, when the entire ceiling was laid open to view. The "triumphal" style for which the first Della Rovere pope had striven was here achieved under the second. Another 20 years later,

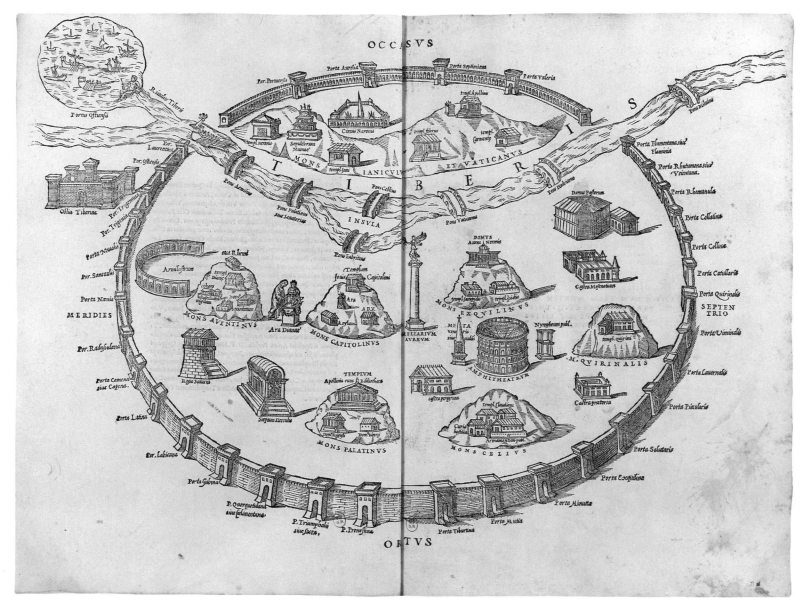

matters were very different. After the humiliation of the Pope and the disasters of 1527, necessitating an entirely new direction to papal policy, there was felt the need for a third decorative series (or more exactly a fourth, but this is not to include the tapestries designed for Leo X by Raphael). There is little room for doubt about the message of the *Last Judgement:* it was painted by Michelangelo on the altar wall for Paul III, though the idea had been suggested by Clement VII after his reconciliation with the artist. Directly behind it lay a period of desolation and despair after a humiliation of the papacy without precedent.

It took time for the new city to take shape from the chaos of makeshift and ruin in which it lay in the mid 15th century, though the guide-lines of the new arterial roads were there. The effort was made, in continuing scholarly investigation, to chart the structure of imperial Rome, though the work did not come to fruition until the famous archaeological maps of the mid 16th century appeared. The researches of Fabio Calvi, commissioned by Leo X and broken off most regrettably in 1527, had led him to the thesis that classical Rome had made possible, indeed had prepared and assisted the spread of the Christian religion. Thanks to Rome, the Faith of which the Pope was custodian had been enabled to circulate through Western civilization. This was always the conviction of the Curia; however, a notable portion of Christendom had begun to doubt it.

In truth, this grand vision had to contend with various problems. Besides the opposition, already mentioned, of the Romans themselves, who had not forgotten the "tribune" Cola di Rienzo and who resented papal autocracy and its "imperial" pretensions, there was the alienation of northern Christendom consequent upon what looked to them like paganism. There was also the rather thorny question of the attitude to be taken towards classical remains. These were not merely scattered throughout the city and its surrounding countryside, they served as shelters and had been transformed into houses, sometimes for the nobility, like the Theatre of Marcellus on Monte Savello. These remains could hardly be recovered, and every day the wave of excavations brought to light new ruins, and in them lucrative relics – vessels, coins, statuary. Rome pullulated with dealers and their traffic. And all the while there was a continuing demand for the marble that could not be otherwise sold to feed the lime kilns.

The purists pointed back to Gregory the Great and to the destruction of these idols, which is what these statues now celebrated as wondrous really were. Had the world gone mad? For some people there was a real moral danger in the rehabilitation of these statues of Juppiter or Venus or of sensual youths which were now crowded in the Belvedere museum. Hence the diatribe by Giovanni Francesco della Mirandola, nephew of Pico, with the title *De Venere et Cupidine Expellendis* – "That Venus and Cupid must be driven out". Driven from where? From the Pope's garden or, more seriously, from the minds of the beholders? The same protest appeared in more subtle form but animated by equal feeling in Erasmus's pamphlet directed against "Ciceronians", published without tact in 1528, just after the lansquenets of Charles V had driven the Roman humanists from their homes and destroyed their books. It is not then so surprising that the Dutch Pope Hadrian VI should have talked a few years earlier of demolishing the indecent ceiling of Michelangelo.

The situation was increasingly complex. In 1516, after his publication of the New Testament in Greek and Latin in Basle, Pope Leo X could consider making Erasmus a cardinal. In 1515, Filippo Beroaldo published a Tacitus from a newly discovered manuscript at Corvey. This work bore the *imprimatur* of the Pope together with an encouragement to bring other such unknown texts to the notice of his Holiness. The letter, drawn up by Sadoleto, in which new privileges were awarded to Beroaldo has a remarkable preamble:

> Since God called us to the great dignity of the Pontificate, we have dedicated ourself to the governance and increase of the Church. Among other concerns, we have realized our duty to the patronage

The Holy Face, or Veil of Veronica, from the anonymous Mirabilia Romae *of 1475.*
The Veil was perhaps the holiest relic of the city, the object of the particular veneration of pilgrims, and the particular care of the popes. The rumour that the Veil had been profaned during the Sack of 1527 had repercussions throughout Christendom.

Sympathetic to these laudable aims, Erasmus praised the Pope for restoring piety, letters and peace.

In other words, individuals selected what suited their own convictions from the irresistible campaign of the "restitutio antiquitatis" – a campaign that, like any campaign, could get drunk with its own rhetoric. It had created fine architecture, beautiful statuary, exquisite epigraphy (a department in which Bramante saw fit to school himself), the graceful Carolingian script in which manuscripts were written, the elegant ornament by which their elegant texts were surrounded. It did not occur to Raphael that there might be anything problematic in transferring directly – or almost directly – to the Vatican Logge the facile, copious decorative style of the corridors of the Golden House of Nero, discovered about 20 years before (although it is true that the identification of the "grotte" of the Esquiline with Nero was at that time not so clear; however that may be, Nero at that time stood for the ideation of the Colosseum, not for the persecution of St Peter). For Michelangelo, the design of the tomb of Julius II in 1505 inevitably had to resemble a four-fronted temple, bearing a digest of all antique sculpture.

It would be an interesting exercise to chart the history of the successive popes, and of the changing concept of what was "modern" in Rome, by their tombs – one could see their ideology "crystallized in the form". It is almost enough to consider just these, their inscriptions and the respective funeral orations. The monument to Innocent VIII in St Peter's by Antonio and Piero Pollaiuolo (1492) showing the Pope seated above the *gisant* below is timid in its iconography compared to the monument by the same artists to Sixtus IV (1484), consisting of a highly effective slab of bronze on which the *gisant* is surrounded by the Virtues and the Liberal Arts representing his mind and will. But the difference is vast when the comparison is to the tomb of Paul III by Giacomo della Porta (1549), realized according to the monumental principles of Michelangelo and in a pyramidal form that recalled the great monument that is missing in St Peter's, the ideal tomb conceived for Julius II, ideal because never realized and perhaps because unrealizable.

Having entered the service of Julius II in order to design and carry out a tomb without precedent, Michelangelo could not have imagined in 1505, in the enthusiasm of his youth, that this project would occupy him, or rather dog him, all his life. Forced to abandon the work hardly after it had been started, driven back to it periodically under pressure from the heirs of the Pope, he had to resign himself in despair to successive reductions of the design and to its eventual mutilation, devoting himself instead to the dome of St Peter's.

Before Innocent and Sixtus, few popes had received monumental commemoration at St Peter's. Even fewer had been preoccupied during their own lives with the form and iconography of their tomb. The enormous bronze in which Sixtus was enclosed is token of the self-consciousness in Rome of a new grandeur, civic and ecclesiastic. But Julius's project of 1505 on shows the tomb becoming a building, and its members and decoration, deriving from antique models, organized

Michelangelo's second project for the Tomb of Pope Julius II (in the copy by J. Rocchetti).
After the death of Julius II, who had himself commissioned Michelangelo to create his tomb, the artist was forced to scale down the original, enormous project, which was to display not less than 40 life-size statues, arranged around a free-standing mausoleum crowned by a reclining effigy of the pontiff. In the

second project, of 1513, the tomb was instead set against a wall, though even so it was to have three sides on which statues were to be displayed. Both the reclining effigy of the Pope and the Slaves *have been held over from the first design. The* Moses *that was eventually included in the final version of the Tomb, in San Pietro in Vincoli, and the two* Slaves *in the Louvre were executed for this, 1513 project.*

in a symbolic hierarchy, taking on a universal significance. This project, conceived early on in Julius II's pontificate, aimed at the fusion of the classical realm and the Christian realm, the first providing the style required for the glorification of the second. This is an important perception, especially in so far as so many of the ingredients invented for the tomb – indeed the very idea of a crowd of figures inhabiting a powerful architectonic framework – ended up on the Sistine Chapel ceiling.

The pontificates of Julius II (1503–13) and Leo X (1513–21) seem to us now from the perspective of centuries complementary: one, that of Julius, under the sign of politics and power, the other, Leo's, under the sign of peace and the arts. In less than 22 years, the city of Rome emerged free from hesitations and half-measures, and the enterprise of making it a modern capital could not be halted. Everywhere prestigious buildings were being built by the cardinals, that distinguished body known sometimes as the "Pope's Senate". Although the new St Peter's was no more than an enormous arcade, while the old church was reduced to the Constantinian nave and still without a façade, the rate of new building and the look of the entire city had altered. As far as the master idea associating the progress of the Church with a cultural renewal was concerned, the pontificate of Pope Hadrian VI, which turned against it, first revealed some fundamental points of weakness. Worse ones emerged in the next pontificate, that of Clement VII (1523–34). Into these we need not enter: but there was doubt and questioning in every aspect of the ideas we have been examining, and the pontificate of Paul III inherited them in the fraught atmosphere of crisis, in which the contradictions reconciled under the ideal of "Rome" stood forth plain.

THE GENIUS OF THE PLACE

In the report which he prepared for Pope Paul III after he had been appointed architect to St Peter's in 1547, Michelangelo with great vision had made clear the necessity of returning to the original project of his old adversary, Bramante. He dismissed the plans of Antonio da Sangallo conclusively: darkness would reign in the church, which needed on the contrary plenty of light inside if its massiveness was to impress; the many nooks, recesses and hollows required by the numerous subdivisions and compartmentalizations were absurd and dangerous and, Michelangelo added, the lateral expansion of the building would probably bring in its train the destruction of the Sistine Chapel. Neither the Pope, who had set so much store thereon, nor Michelangelo, who had only recently finished the *Last Judgement,* in 1542, had any desire to see the frescoes which were its glory disappear. Michelangelo, having lived through all the vicissitudes and success of the previous half-century, could hardly have avoided being aware that he had contributed considerably to the status, to the prestige or, as we would say today, to the "myth" of Rome in European culture.

Rome was at that time, as it would be again in the 18th century, the most visited, discussed, drawn, admired and condemned city in the world. The wealth of report is uncountable. The city never ceased to encourage "myth". But, surveying these books and chronicles, one realizes that later judgements often do no more than develop or echo the essential outlook which we have sought to establish here.[6]

The sight of the ruined, unkempt town of Rome in the Trecento had

View of the courtyard and terraces of the Vatican Belvedere, by G. A. Dosio, 2nd half of the 16th century (Florence, Uffizi, Gabinetto dei disegni e delle stampe).
Bramante was commissioned by Julius II in 1504 to incorporate the Villa Belvedere built by Pope Innocent VIII into the Vatican palace complex. He designed a series of terraces in a long rec-

tangle rising from the old buildings in progressive steps upwards to the villa in the north. The prospect he planned was blocked off by the construction of the Vatican Library, dividing the courtyard of the Belvedere proper from the Cortile della Pigna: the first building built inside the space dates from the late 16th century, the second (the Braccio Nuovo) from the 19th.

occasioned in Petrarch a twofold reaction. One was melancholy, at the spectacle of the degeneration of what had once been great, the extraordinary vision of a dead civilization. Another was bitter criticism of the Romans of the present, carrying out their business without any apparent conception of the Rome of the past: "Nusquam Roma minus cognoscitur quam Roma" – "Nowhere is Rome understood less than at Rome". Petrarch's shaft, sharpened by his dislike of the Curia, took on, when the papal administration once again returned to Rome in the following century, even more point, in the actual presence of all the intrigues and so on that went on in the Vatican. Petrarch's phrase, repeated by one humanist after another, became virtually a proverb. The progress of philology and history, the congress of the learned might – particularly under Leo X – be led from Rome, still the stigma of the unfitness for the task of the ecclesiastics composing the Curia persisted, though the accusation had shifted now to one of paganizing playacting and frivolous pomp. In his *Ciceronianus* Erasmus repeated the charge: "Roma Romae non est" – "Rome is not to be found at Rome". The true Rome of the sensitive and the learned, the Rome of the ancient philosophers and of the earliest Christian Church, was noble and pure. It could not be the Rome of these palaces, of these superstitious mobs, of these processions of cardinals, resembling a masquerade, a lie. But how could the achievement of Michelangelo square with this view?

The experience of Rome has always been disconcerting and mesmeric. One very well-known and very typical example is that of Joachim de Bellay, who arrived in the 1540s to stay with his uncle the cardinal, and found himself victim of the same fascination for its antiquity and repulsion for its reality. He meditated among the ruins and wrote his *Antiquités,* a bitter satire, and his *Regrets*. But he recognised that there was more to it than that, writing[7]:

> ... *le démon du lieu* ...
> *nous y tient attachés par une douce force*
> ... *the genius of the place holds us here by some gentle power*

Michelangelo must count for something in this "douce force". The range of visitors and 'tourists' was such that they could not all have seen the matter so clearly, and besides it is the poet's part to strike sentimental chords. But we know that in 1548 the fame of Michelangelo was great in France, where, admittedly, a Florentine queen kept alive the interest for the latest Rome creations. For those whose interest lay towards art, antique and modern, the argument over present corruption and past greatness was really of secondary importance. The Reformation had obviously enough checked the advance of the master idea of a Roman "rinascita". The pope's attempt to bolster his prestige had not convinced the adherents of a religion unadulterated by any "paganism", though it had succeeded in transforming old Rome and building a new one.

We can see this more clearly today thanks to studies which have served to lay bare this "ideology" of Rome. Scanning the "manifestoes" of the popes' funeral orations, analysing the terms of the official speeches of the time, gleaning what we can from the excited but sound treatises of theologians such as Egidio da Viterbo, General of the Augustinians, who opened the Council of 1512 in a famous speech, scholars have come better to understand on what those responsible founded the legitimacy of the action of the popes, still following out the imperatives formulated by Nicholas V. The embel-

The Campidoglio before and after Michelangelo. (Above) An anonymous drawing of the later 1550s (Paris, Louvre, Cabinet des Dessins); (below) an engraving of Michelangelo's design for the top of the Capitol, 1569.
Though Michelangelo's project was hardly started within his lifetime, and was subsequently altered, the engraving of 1569 preserves his ideas accurately. Comparison of the two images gives some idea of the transformation involved. In the background the Palazzo Senatorio was now set off by the two flanking palaces and the large oval inscribed on the pavement round the recently installed equestrian statue of Marcus Aurelius. The palace on the right, the Palazzo dei Conservatori, was already there, but received a new façade; the palace opposite, the Palazzo Nuovo, was created anew and for the sake of the scenography.

lishment of the papal city was an urgent requirement, a real need. The glorification of *Roma antiqua* was for the sake of the Church. The prestige of the two together was thus conjoined in the creation of a *plenitudo temporalis* of universal significance.

This utopian and contradictory vision was persuasive despite its weaknesses. It was the vision that created Rome and in more than one sense made the Sistine ceiling possible. Though the circumstances in which it was created were trying and giddy, in the end this masterpiece emerged as the watershed from which modern times began. Applicable is a remark about Bramante, whose great ideas for St Peter's could be brought to fruition only by Michelangelo, to be found in the

papers of Gugliemo della Porta, in a draft of a letter to Ammanati, of about 1560:

> The architect Bramante used to say that anybody who came to Rome to practice architecture must be ready to slough off like a snake its skin all he had learnt elsewhere.

Michelangelo would have liked to have heard the same thing being said about his Ceiling — at least before he had been induced to paint his tragic pendant of the *Last Judgement*. This unanticipated counterpart destroyed the equilibrium of the Chapel, but also revealed its unique place in the history of the papal city and of Christian art.

Maarten van Heemskerck: St Peter's under construction *(Florence, Uffizi, Gabinetto dei disegni e delle stampe). Heemskerck's drawing shows in its bare bones the powerful construction envisaged by Bramante (1444–1514) and laid out within his lifetime.*

Jacob Binck, Tourney held in the San Damaso courtyard.
Looming over Bramante's Belvedere courtyard on the right is the dome of St Peter's, then in construction. The holding of tourneys had a long Renaissance tradition; this one, held at this time in this place, indicates the continuity of the courtly, secular aspect of the papacy even after the opening of the Council of Trent (in 1542).

Monstra della giostra fatta nel Teatro di Palazzo
ridotto in questa forma dalla S.tà di N.S. Pio 4.º come
si vede nella stampa della pianta, con le sue mesure.

The building that we know today principally as the setting for the frescoes of Michelangelo is not lightly to be compared with any other that survives. Every part of its eventual painted and sculptured decoration must be seen as an element in a unity evolving with the architectural structure itself; and every element, above all its architectural form, must be understood in the first place as the product of practical decisions made in response to function, broadly interpreted. Function will include the accommodation of a liturgy peculiar to the place, but it will also include the no less singular expression of the *majestas papalis,* the Papal Majesty; and that is, among other things, a special form of that expression of magnanimity which motivates so much of the most spectacular building and decoration of the Renaissance.

Functionally the Sistine Chapel is the receptacle of a body known as the Papal Chapel. This is the title both of a corporate entity and of a building. The Papal Chapel in the corporate sense is a permanently existing but continually evolving body which convenes ceremonially

JOHN SHEARMAN

THE CHAPEL OF SIXTUS IV

The face of Pope Sixtus IV appears in this medal by Antonio Guazzalotti da Prato (1435–1495) in almost exactly the form it had been portrayed by Melozzo da Forlì (see page 11); it appears again, now much thinner and more craggy, in the effigy on the monument created by Antonio Pollaiuolo, now in the Grotte Vaticane of St Peter's – a tomb in bronze of unprecedented scale, reflecting the high ambitions of the builder of the Sistine Chapel and of a new Rome.

with the pope on prescribed occasions, and in prescribed patterns adaptable to variable locations; for often it will convene in a space which is not, like the Sistine Chapel, built for the purpose – for example when the pope travels. The Papal Chapel in the architectural sense, however, is properly a palace-chapel, one of a number, of different dimensions, required according to the varied devotional and ceremonial needs of the pope, and to the prescriptions of the calendar of the papal court. These needs and prescriptions also continue if the pope travels, and they evolve out of custom. But evolving custom is subject to a number of constraints, principal among them tradition and precedent which, in the setting of the papal court, are not so much a kind of inertia as an expression of the continuity that is the foundation of papal authority. The needs and prescriptions in question had become virtually stabilized by the end of the 15th century, but probably not by the 1470s when the Sistine Chapel itself was conceived; on the contrary it seems probable that the new chapel was more a contribution towards than an expression of a stable pattern.

The corporate Papal Chapel was a remarkably large and diverse body, and it was not, as is often supposed, exclusive of laity. In addition to the pope and the College of Cardinals (in the 15th century there would be about 20 in residence), senior churchmen attached to the Chapel would include generals of the monastic and mendicant orders,

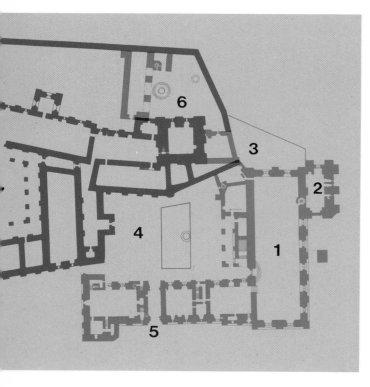

the patriarchs, and visiting archbishops and bishops. Qualifying members of the papal household or of the curial bureaucracy would include the Master of the Sacred Palace (the resident theologian), the sacristan, the major domo, chamberlains, secretaries, notaries and auditors. Accredited laity included the Senator and Conservators of the City of Rome, the diplomatic corps, visiting princes, and a few officials such as the captain of the Swiss Guard. Three further groups of some size were the servants of the cardinals, the papal choir (usually about twelve), and those engaged in the service itself (the celebrant, deacons and acolytes, the Master of Ceremonies, and so on). In so far as this Chapel was a bureaucracy it was natural that it had a tendency to expand. We cannot say precisely how numerous it was in the pontificate of Sixtus IV (1471–84), but something of the order of 200 would have to be accommodated, most with seating, in an enclosed space separated by a screen from a considerable further crowd of unaccredited laity who could get past the first door of the palace (additional servants, pilgrims, and spectators of substance). The scale and complexity of this need is important in the evolution of the architectural papal chapel.

The somewhat idealized information on these matters transmitted by ceremonials of the period needs some commentary. The corporate Chapel was in many respects an élite, not least in its theological expertise. Moreover it had time on its hands, time to be filled by wandering eyes and minds, for the services were often of great length. These facts bear upon the interpretation of the decoration of such a purpose-built space. Also, ceremonial theory was distorted in practice, so that (for example) an outsider with a little influence such as Erasmus had no difficulty in finding a place near the pope. Diplomatic correspondence of the period reveals that much secular business was done during the Office, and questions of precedence, notably among ambassadors, threatened indecorous chaos. A group of secretaries, who had to sit on the floor, was not naturally a tidy one. A proposal for the reform of the Papal Chapel, written about 1460, tells us that "on the floor of the chapel the papal household and others wander around and make so much noise during the Divine Office and sermons that one can scarcely hear what is being said." It is no wonder, then, that imposing order should have become a function both of architecture and of Masters of Ceremonies.

The Papal Chapel in the architectural sense must be understood within what might be called the three-chapel system, which had become stabilized long before Sixtus IV. The pope is to assist at the mass daily, and for this purpose he is provided with a small oratory (not accommodating the corporate chapel) adjacent to his intimate living-quarters, and it is known as the Daily Chapel *(Capella quotidiana)* or Private Chapel *(Capella secreta)*. Sixtus would have used the Chapel of Nicholas V (1447–55), decorated by Fra Angelico with stories of Sts Stephen and Lawrence, on the third level of the Vatican Palace.

In addition to the daily mass, however, the calendar of the papal court prescribed 50 occasions during the year when the whole Papal Chapel should convene; these occasions, of which 35 were masses, may be divided between those eight which require a basilica and the rest which require a large chapel within the papal palace. Thus, the Christmas and Easter masses, at which the pope is the celebrant, would in Sixtus's pontificate take place in Old St Peter's, where the Papal Chapel would assemble in the apse of the Constantinian basilica behind the high altar, the ciborium, and the double screen. But on the contrary the greater number of these services, for example matins on Christmas Eve, vespers on the eve of Corpus Christi, or the mass on Palm Sunday, were properly set in the large palatine chapel. These 42 celebrations, to which individual popes might add others of personal significance from time to time, were of obvious importance for the Pope's position in the living church, as the principal public demonstrations of his spiritual authority and majesty. For these Sixtus provided a permanent theatre within the papal palace at the Vatican. And a later Master of Ceremonies, Paris de Grassis, described this building in 1518 as 'the first chapel in the world, both for its majesty and for its structure.'

THE GREAT CHAPEL

The chapel built by Sixtus IV stands on the site of an earlier Great Chapel, the functions of which had been essentially the same. Information on this earlier building is very incomplete, yet enough is known to confirm the expectation that it was in many respects a model for its replacement; Sixtus, in fact, used it for the first six years of his pontificate before he pulled it down.

The Vatican Palace inhabited by Sixtus, still the nucleus of the present palace, was principally a construction of the 13th century, and the most important builder-pope of that period was Nicholas III Orsini (1277–80), a man of great personal wealth. An inscription records that in 1278 Nicholas "built the palace, the great hall, and the chapel"; the Latin is oddly imperfect,[1] but cannot be construed to mean that he built a Great Chapel. The chapel that he did build, and indeed dedicated to St Nicholas in 1278 or 1279, survived until the pontificate of Paul III (1534–49), who replaced it – not on the same site – with the Pauline Chapel. The Sistine Chapel, the Pauline Chapel, and Nicholas III's Chapel of St Nicholas all opened off the first great hall on the second level of the palace, the Sala Regia. The Chapel of St Nicholas, subsequently known as the *Capella parva* to distinguish it from the Great Chapel, was of modest dimensions (16.7×8.2 m), of irregular design widening towards the apse, and it opened off the Sala Regia to the east. When first built it was probably the principal public chapel of the palace. In the Renaissance it had a number of minor functions outside the three-chapel system: it served for the conservation of the Host for masses in the Sistine Chapel, it was every day the site of the papal choir's canonical Hours, and it was the chapel for conclaves for papal elections.

There is no reason to suppose that Nicholas III built, in addition, the Great Chapel; indeed that is very unlikely. The question is whether the Great Chapel first recorded in 1368 was built in the period immediately before the long exile of the popes in Avignon (1305–67), or immediately after it – a date during the exile is rather unlikely. The evidence is about equally balanced. On the one hand it may be argued that liturgical and architectural practice evolved in the papal court at Avignon appear to be the precedent for, not the sequel to, those of the Great Chapel at the Vatican; but on the other hand the Great Chapel was furnished and in use before the end of January 1368, which is to say in less than four months after the return of Urban V (1362–70) to Rome.

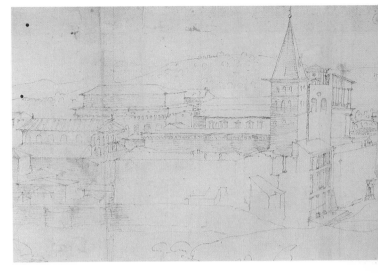

Maarten van Heemskerck's view of St Peter's in construction (Berlin, Staatliche Museen, Kupferstichkabinett) dates from the early 1530s. The Dutch painter and engraver (1498–1574) was in Rome between 1532 and 1535, and made a series of drawings and views of Rome at that time that have proved invaluable. Here St Peter's is seen from the side, showing the old Constantinian building and the new Bramante choir in course of construction. In the distance is the Sistine Chapel.

The drawing (below) is a plan attributed to Bramante of the Vatican palace and his Belvedere complex for Julius II (Florence, Uffizi, Gabinetto dei disegni e delle stampe). At the top is a rectangle representing the Belvedere courtyard, and to its left the papal apartments

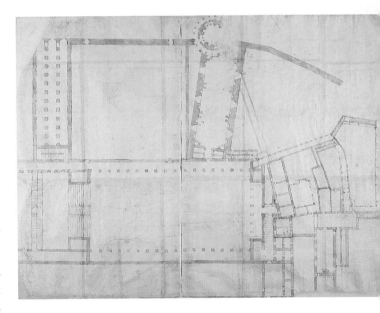

round the Cortile del Pappagallo. (Immediately to the left again, but not on the plan, is St Peter's.) The Sistine Chapel is the small rectangle up on the left.

Detail from Piero di Cosimo's Madonna adoring the sleeping Child in the Museum of Art, Toledo, Ohio. Amidst these buildings overlooking an expanse of water, the large building furthest away may show the original appearance of the Sistine Chapel, when it was fortified; it is beside a building of Early Christian form which could reflect Old St Peter's.

The palace built by the popes at Avignon became in the end a very much more splendid residence than the one left behind in 1305 at the Vatican. The first pope to live permanently at Avignon – in an existing bishop's palace – was John XXII (1316–34); he adapted a parish church, St Etienne, on the south side of the Cathedral, to serve as the palatine chapel. It was doubled in length by his successor, Benedict XII (1334–42), by which time it measured 38×9 metres and was on two levels, the upper level with a wooden roof being the principal chapel; it was provided with a sacristy. Within a third phase of expansion in the Avignon palace, the Palais-Neuf, Clement VI (1342–52) built the superb chapel we see today, 52×15 metres, with stone vaults 19.5 metres high; this too stands on the upper level of the palace, over a great audience hall; below that, again, was a basement. Its fortified exterior aspect was remarkably like that of the Sistina as first built, and the interiors of the two had a number of features in common: the lower walls hung with tapestry, the two tall, widely-spaced windows on the altar wall, the screen drawn right across not quite at the half-way point, a step or steps at the door of the screen which led to a symbolically higher level inside, and a sacristy with a door to the left of the altar (eventually at Avignon there were two sacristies). The supposition that Sixtus IV should have imitated the Clementine Chapel directly is as reasonable as the alternative, that both buildings shared such features with the Great Chapel in the Vatican. But probably these are false alternatives, which is to say that all three chapels (the sequence of the first two being unclear) had important features in common.

The scale of the Great Chapel is as uncertain as its date. Three indistinct views before its destruction show a tall, imposing structure with a straight western altar wall; this latter feature is not necessarily derived from the Clementine Chapel at Avignon, for it is already to be found in the Sancta Sanctorum in Rome, which was the palatine chapel at the Lateran built by Nicholas III about 1277–78. The strange irregularity of the ground-plan of the Sistina – it narrows towards the altar wall, which is itself not parallel to the entrance-wall – this irregularity is peculiar in a construction of the mature Renaissance, and it strongly suggests that Sixtus used the foundations of the medieval Great Chapel; indeed the irregularity looks old-fashioned even in comparison with the second chapel at Avignon, the Clementina. It may also be deduced that the Great Chapel was about as big as the Sistina, that is to say about 40.5×14 metres, from the fact that about as many cardinals' cells were erected there for conclaves as were subsequently fitted into the new building.

Scattered documents on the repair or use of the Great Chapel in the century after 1368 yield some significant details. A substructure had its own door and windows. The main chapel-space, approached on the upper level through double doors from the Sala Regia, was divided by a screen, which was provided with a second set of double doors and at least six candlesticks on its entablature. The choir, at first placed on its own step and bench, was given a gallery in 1421. Over the altar hung a textile canopy. Next to the altar was a small room, probably for the sacristan, and a wall-tabernacle for the reserved Sacrament. The lower part of the walls was hung with tapestries on great occasions. Documentation of a campaign of decoration in 1369, by painters of great distinction such as Giottino and Giovanni da Milano, suggest that the vault was panelled (like the earlier of the two Great Chapels at

Avignon) and the walls frescoed; the only subjects recorded are the *Four Evangelists.*

Many features of the medieval Great Chapel, then, were indeed repeated in the new chapel of Sixtus. Nevertheless it is not the case, as has recently been suggested, that the Sistina is nothing more than a refurbishment of the Great Chapel. On the one hand even the mezzanine floor below the present chapel is vaulted throughout in a manner that cannot be earlier than the late 15th century; on the other hand texts from the period praising the new chapel leave no doubt that Sixtus demolished the Great Chapel comprehensively. Why did he do so? A previous pope, Nicholas V (1447–55), had already conceived a plan to replace it with a new Great Chapel, vaulted. Aurelio Brandolini, in a poem on the Sistina, said that the new rises where the old "had become squalid through decay and from its position, and was scarcely worthy of the name 'temple', the place scarcely worthy of the gods;"[2] and Andreas of Trebizond reminded Sixtus that he had demolished to the foundations "the previous chapel, of which the walls were leaning, the roof and floor (or, the flat roof) in a state of collapse."[3] Whether it was about one or about two hundred years old it was not an ancient building, and its state ominously foreshadows problems that will follow on this site with the Sistina itself.

The celebrations prescribed for the Great Chapel are last recorded taking place there on the Feast of the Purification of the Virgin, 2 February 1477; on that day Sixtus's nephew the Cardinal Giuliano Della Rovere, later Julius II, made a marginal note in his copy of a taxation-list of dioceses that the Pope, after mass in the Great Chapel, invested him with the archbishopric of Avignon.[4] The new chapel, said explicitly to be unfinished, is already mentioned in a poem of the same year, 1477.

Detail from an engraving by the Master of the Die, showing the Sistine Chapel in the background.

The Master of the Die, so called from the device of a dice that appears on his engravings (and possibly to be identified with one Bernardo Daddi or Dado, 'dado' meaning 'dice') was a follower of Marcantonio Raimondi, and was active in Rome between about 1530 and 1550. His other works include a portrait of Pope Julius III.

THE BUILDING OF THE CHAPEL

Some time during 1477, then, Sixtus began a new Great Chapel; it is indicative of continuity of purpose that the new building was referred to in the same way as the old in innumerable ceremonial documents for several decades, and the attribution to Sixtus was uncommon before about 1513. Remarkably little is recorded of this, as of the many other architectural projects of this energetic pope. In fact the next clear indication of progress comes in the contract with four fresco-painters for the decoration of the walls of the chapel, 27 October 1481, which provides for ten out of 16 equal vertical sections and seems to refer to at least four sections already complete at that date. In other words the construction had reached a stage allowing decoration to begin several months before October 1481.

Sixtus IV was "an old man in a hurry", and his remarkable haste in the erection of the chapel, together with its tapestries, gilding, and sculptured screen, during the war with Florence, is mentioned by Andreas of Trebizond in a preface to be dated no later than May 1482. Andreas was the pope's secretary, and what he says deserves to be read with care. The Florentine war to which he referred might be taken to have begun as early as the spring of 1477, when Lorenzo the Magnificent's policies first threatened the integrity of the Papal States, or as late as April 1478 when Sixtus connived in the Pazzi Conspiracy; this war was effectively ended, however, with the lifting of the Interdict from Florence in December 1480. Andreas comments further that it was scarcely to be believed that such a large structure and its decoration could be finished, as it had been, in every part, during such a period of financial stringency. But it seems clear that in 'decoration' he did not include painting, which he comes to next, saying that Sixtus has added the cycles of the Old and New Covenants; and finally he admires the mosaic floor. Painting and floor, therefore, are implicitly dated after the cessation of hostilities with Florence late in 1480. This chronology is broadly consistent with two incidental remarks of a diarist, Jacopo Gherardi of Volterra, whose concern is with the observance of the curial calendar; on 11 March 1481 Jacopo notes that the chapel has been rebuilt, with construction work going ahead daily, while on 24 December of the same year he remarks that the chapel is still unfinished, with work proceeding on its painting and decoration, apparently in the sense of relief sculpture or mosaic. And as we have seen the painters had in fact been at work for some time by the autumn of 1481.

Andreas of Trebizond's text should not be taken as proof that the painting and the floor were completed by the Spring of 1482, only as confirmation of what is natural, that he knew what they were to look like; for panegyrists, like writers of guide-books, have a habit of anticipating the completion of work in progress. There is, as we shall see, good reason to believe in an interruption and a delay in the completion of the frescoes, and it is not altogether surprising that the first record of the chapel in use, which is also rather clearly the first occasion when Sixtus was present there at a service, was as late as 9 August 1483 – not a casual date, for it was the anniversary of his election; on that day, as an exception to the rule, vespers on the eve of the feast of St Lawrence were celebrated in the new Great Chapel. The last occasion upon which the regular calendar had not been observed, because the chapel was not available, had been on 29 July. Even in August, however, the chapel was not finished in every detail, for payments for minor furnishings, for painting the doors and gilding the ironwork, extend from May 1483 to August 1484. Two stained-glass windows with the arms of Sixtus, presumably the two in the altar wall, which were paid for in 1485, must have been made before the Pope's death on 12 August 1484. The papal treasury was often dilatory in settling its debts, and it was not until February 1486 that Cristoforo, son of Giovannino de' Dolci, received part-payment for "the building of the Great Chapel" by his father, by then dead. The case for Giovannino as the architect of the Sistina seems overwhelming.

To stand beneath the Sistina in one of the later courtyards around it is to be struck, like Andreas, by the immensity of the building accomplished structurally in about three years, for this is like a cliff of brick – indeed it is a construction in brick unparallelled in Rome since ancient Imperial structures such as the Mausoleum of Hadrian, the Curia Julia, or the Pantheon. Heemskerck's drawing reminds us how it towered above both the Vatican Palace and Old St Peter's. And when one stands in the chapel-space itself, its vaults rising nearly 19 metres, it is hard to remember that there are two levels below and yet another space above.

The lowest level was originally largely below ground level on the north side, and could have been entered from the outside only on the south; rebuilding has occurred where there might have been such an entrance. Steps down from the space below the Sala Regia on the east

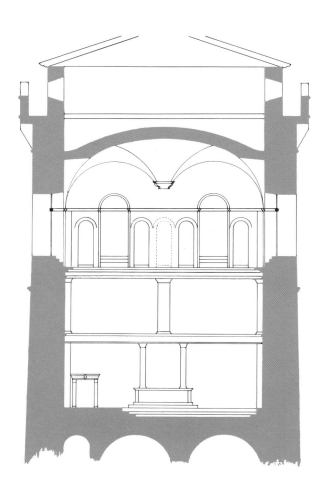

The Sistine Chapel seen in section, showing its three levels. Below, there are three ranges of barrel-vaulted rooms, of unequal width; there was access between them. Above these is the Sistine Chapel proper, which has something of the design of a fortress, with its high windows. Above, there are rooms in the attic below the roof, which give on to the gangway for the guard, machicolated and pierced with firing slits.

once led, it seems, to a low vaulted corridor running the whole length on the south; off this corridor there opened nine long rectangular spaces running north to south. The function of this lowest level, with no access originally from above, is unknown, but minimal fenestration, on the north side only, suggests storage of some kind. The next level, a kind of mezzanine, is a different matter. It is familiar now to those who penetrate to the modern collections of the Vatican Museum, unlikely as they may be to realize that the fairly regular and quite airy double file of small vaulted rooms through which they pass is beneath the Sistina. These rooms were grouped in three suites, one large and two small, generally well lit on the north side and connected again by a corridor on the south. Some of the rooms originally had fireplaces. The entrance to one of the smaller suites had an inscription identifying it as the apartment (or office) of the Masters of Ceremony, who certainly needed a library. The larger suite of rooms to the east probably always led, as it does now, to the broader vaulted space

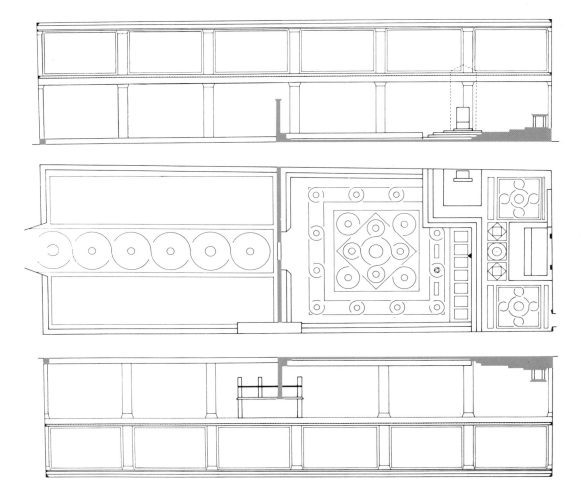

The interior of the Sistine Chapel: in the centre, a plan of the marble floor and its decoration, with the altar wall on the right; above and below, the lower part of the right and left walls.

On the walls the height and width of the choir screen is also marked: on the right-hand wall facing the altar (the lower wall on the plan) it bisects the cantoria or singing gallery, which is raised up above floor level. This was the original position of the choir screen, dividing the chapel into two almost equal parts, before it was moved to its present position, taking in more space for the choir, to include the first of the circles on the floor originally beyond it. The old arrangement, before practical and liturgical reasons occasioned the move, was complemented by the floor decoration; the line of circles outside the choir clearly indicated the processional route, leading into or up to the closed-off section of the choir, where the floor decoration indicated instead fixed positions for the functionaries. Immediately around the altar to the far right the floor decoration alters character again; against the left wall (upper wall on the plan) was the papal chair.

beneath the Sala Regia, where almost certainly the stables of the 13th-century palace had been. At this level the walls of Sixtus's building are three metres thick.

The chapel itself gives the impression that it is a rectangular space about three times as long as it is wide, about half as high as it is long; its slight irregularity of plan has already been mentioned. The interior shape may bring to mind that of another palatine chapel, the Arena Chapel in Padua, built just after 1300. The comparison serves to make the point that although both were clearly designed to be painted, the integration of architecture and painted decoration in the later building is so perfect that the articulation of the decoration, at least, must have been conceived from the beginning. Around the bottom of the walls of the Sistina, continuous save for the raised area supporting the altar, there is a stone bench, a feature already to be found in the palatine chapel of Nicholas III in the Lateran, the Sancta Sanctorum; and as in that building again the lowest of four zones in the painted decoration consists of non-figural, fictive tapestry. The first cornice, which is unassertive, is decorated with a string of rosettes each enclosing a hook from which real tapestries were to be hung on great occasions. This tapestry-zone was symmetrically interrupted on the short walls at one end by a great rectangular entrance door, now framed only on the side towards the Sala Regia, and at the other end (originally) by the frame of the altarpiece; and it is interrupted on the right, or north, wall by the hanging gallery for the choir.

The second zone of the chapel is crowned by a much more substantial cornice, which supports a vertiginous passage essential for cleaning and maintenance. Below it runs the sequence of narrative frescoes to be discussed in the next section; originally there were 16, divided like the tapestries below by painted pilasters. Above this cornice rise, by contrast, real pilasters and tall window embrasures, six on each side of the chapel. A third cornice, at the level of the springing of the arches of the windows, breaks forward over each pilaster so as to form a set of pseudo-capitals from which spring the flattened pendentives of the vault. The vault itself, when considered from the inside, is of a type frequently found in the late Quattrocento, for example in another Sistine Chapel built by the same pope as the mausoleum for his parents in the cathedral at Savona. It is essentially a slightly flattened barrel-vault with the curvature returning on the short walls, and interrupted all round by lunettes over the windows. These lunettes cut into the basic form of the vault so as to produce not only the 'pendentives' but also spherical triangles in the coves of the windows. And the lunettes of this fourth zone were also decorated by Sixtus's painters, although we cannot say how, for Michelangelo extended his commission to repaint the vault to embrace these vertical fields. The window-zone below, the third zone, was provided with a series of painted niches, in each of which was placed one of the early popes, in such a manner that in each bay the niches flanking the larger round-headed windows make a repeating pattern like that of a triumphal arch.

The vault of the chapel has, on its inner or lower side, a rich and complex three-dimensional shape. When looked at from above, however, it is rather surprisingly simplified, and in some ways more impressive. Its curvature is much flattened and there is no projection corresponding to the interruptions of the lower surface by the windows and lunettes. In other words the vault structure at points corresponding to the twelve 'pendentives' is of massive thickness, and these tremendous supports sustain a relatively thin shell down the centre (85 cm) and over the lunettes (50 cm). In the space above the vault, under a simple roof, was the fourth usable level of the building; this space was provided not only with a floor but also with interior walls dividing it into apartments; in these rooms a rebellious member of the Roman aristocracy was detained in 1503. Around the main walls at this height, originally outside the roof, was a machicolated passage exactly like the one at the top of the chapel of Clement VI at Avignon, and like that one it gave more than a defensive air to the whole edifice. The 15th-century popes, who contributed in other ways to the defences of the Vatican, could never forget that the Papal Palace at

Inside the choir of the Sistine Chapel, the symmetry of the floor decoration is disturbed by the raised platform on which the papal chair is located, at the same level as the platform on which the altar stands. This change was introduced at the same time as the movement outwards of the choir screen (see previous page).

This kind of marble floor decoration belongs to a long-standing tradition going back to Early Christian times. It had also undergone a notable revival in Rome in the 12th and 13th centuries, in so-called Cosmati work. The strongly geometric scheme is characteristic, and so is the alternation of large flags of marble with smaller elements mostly of mosaic, marking out divisions and compartments round them.

Avignon had twice been besieged in the first years of the century. Indeed the whole construction of Sixtus IV amounts to a powerful bastion for the western side of the Vatican.

MODIFICATIONS, DAMAGE, AND REPAIR

Several important changes have been made to the chapel built and decorated by Sixtus, some almost immediately, and these must be recounted not only so that we can visualize his legacy more accurately but also so that we can understand better the contributions of later popes. The building we visit today is the product of a continued sequence of modifications, and some of those that affect the structure, not just the decoration, may be mentioned now. One of the most immediate concerns the sacristy. It is usually said that Sixtus built a chapel without a sacristy, and indeed it was said as early as 1509 that the one then existing was built by the next pope, Innocent VIII (1484–92). However, the architect who extended it in 1582 called it the Sacristy of Sixtus, and in fact the existence of the suite of three rooms then in question is attested by a description of the conclave immediately after Sixtus's death, and in the same way repeatedly in the next few years. Sixtus therefore did provide a sacristy, and the arms of Innocent which it bears, inside and out, presumably indicate that that pope finished it. Its purpose was not quite the usual one, for all except minor robing was regularly a ceremony performed in the pope's apartment, before the procession down to the chapel, and most liturgical hangings were stored elsewhere in the palace; but it provided space for relics, for liturgical books, plate, and furnishings, and it served as lodging for the papal sacristan. The present door is to the right of the altar, but it bears the arms of the Borgia pope, Alexander VI (1492–1503); the original door of Sixtus was to the left of the altar. The first sacristy door, like the present one, would have been on the raised level at the west of the chapel, an area properly called the presbytery, which supported not only the altar but also, on an extension on the left, the papal throne; there would properly be a baldacchino over the altar, and another over the throne. The steps leading up to this level now number four; originally there were three, and the reason for the increase (c. 1550–60) was not to change the level but the superficial area, to provide more space for seating. The expansion of the bureaucracy – for a number of curial officials had the right to sit on these steps – also forced an expansion of the area for the whole corporate Chapel by the movement of the containing screen eastwards at about the same time. The original position of the screen is quite clearly marked on the floor (in fact just above a single symbolic step which remains) and on the choir-gallery which it adjoined; its precise position was nearly halfway down the chapel, but a little over a metre nearer the entrance.

The most radical modification of Sixtus's chapel was, however, the destruction in 1534–35 of the membering of the altar wall to make way for Michelangelo's *Last Judgement*. In order to provide an uninterrupted surface from the vault almost to the floor, all three cornices were removed, two windows exactly like those of the side-walls were bricked up, and the stone frame around the frescoed altarpiece was, in the end, removed too (Michelangelo at first tried to preserve it). The size and shape of the lost altarpiece can be documented rather pre-

Another feature of Cosmatesque work was its vivid colour, of which the dense grouping of the smaller pieces increased the effect, and its preciousness. This is a detail of the pavement outside the choir, showing the circles down the centre of the floor; they are not independent, but blend into one another, creating a forward movement down the Chapel. In this case the mosaic pieces were probably re-used from some other building.

31

This is the opening in the elegant choir-screen through which one passes to the most sacred part of the Chapel. The choir-screen is in many respects just like an iconostasis, of the kind that in Early Christian churches had separated off the presbyterium from the quadratum populi. It consists of a low wall, decorated on the outer side with marble slabs, on which a series of small pilasters support an architrave, on which sacred images (icons) in the form of paintings or statues were placed. Or, as in this case, the architrave bears candlesticks, here eight in number. Between the pilasters is a light grill, originally of gilded iron but now of wood. Originally the

candlesticks were also gilded, and were seven in number, recalling the seven candelabra of the Apocalypse, but when the screen was moved the space previously occupied by the singing gallery was filled by an eighth. The panels display putti *bearing the coat of arms of Sixtus IV, or foliage patterns. The craftsmen involved in this exquisite work are not known; it is not even certain whether they were trained in northern Italy or in Tuscany or the Marches.*

cisely, and the original altar wall can be reconstructed as on p. 29; above the first cornice the pattern of repeating bays, each like those on the side-walls, was continued with only one change, the support of the single pendentive not on a pseudo-capital but at a higher level on a large bracket. The presence of this bracket seems to indicate that there was no central pilaster in this case between the windows, and it has been suggested that the clear space so provided would accommodate a uniquely axial figure of Christ between the first pair from the series of the popes. In the next zone below were the first frescoes in the cycles of the Old and New Covenants. Repositioning the altar-frame and the screen as they were originally yields once more a nice detail of planning: that the altarpiece would have been exactly framed by the door in the screen when seen from the entrance of the Chapel.

The structure of the vault described above is of great strength at almost all points, for its complex curvature is intrinsically rigid; the exception is the length down the centre where a thin shell has minimal curvature on one axis only. Here it proved to be vulnerable to the slightest outward movement of the side-walls. From the machicolated exterior passage that circles the building, approximately at the level of the crown of the vault, one may see that the long north wall of the chapel has remained dead straight while that to the south has bowed outward. This visible movement was probably the cause of an alarming fault that developed in the Spring of 1504 and rendered the chapel unusable for half a year. In the diaries of the Masters of Ceremonies one of them describes the chapel as 'ruinous, and all shattered', the other as 'split down the middle,' and from them we learn too that Julius II had the chapel 'repaired with chains above the main vault and in the vaults below.'[5] In August the chapel is even described as being 'under construction', and it was first back in use on 18 October. The 'chains' placed by Julius below the chapel are invisible now, but those above can still be seen; they are twelve great rods running laterally, anchored in the side-walls at such a level that they also transfix the convex curve of the vault like skewers through a roast. This repair could not have been achieved without the destruction of the floor and of the internal walls of the apartments on the uppermost level, and indeed not without extensive excavation into the stonework of the vault itself; and this consideration, together with the evident seriousness of the initial rupture, suggests that any previous painting of the vault would have been severely damaged. The current restoration of the ceiling frescoes has revealed that the long crack in the vault running out of the north-west corner, a crack that continued to move, had been repaired with inset bricks before Michelangelo painted over it the *Judith* spandrel. That repair was presumably made in the summer of 1504, and presumably, too, it was only a tributary of the greater break down the centre of the vault, where the plaster-surface is indeed remarkably irregular. Within two years of the repair, at the latest by May 1506, Pope Julius was planning a new vault decoration by Michelangelo – and in fact a remark made by Bramante on that occasion implies that discussions had started much earlier.[6] Michelangelo recorded that he began work on 10 May 1508, and towards the end of the same month workmen were 'on the high cornices', presumably erecting his scaffold.

The origin of Michelangelo's commission, then, lies in a structural problem, the first of many in the chapel which have, probably, a single cause. The previous Great Chapel had been demolished, in part at least, because its walls were leaning, and Aurelio Brandolini had attributed its decay to its site. Just to the south, in fact, the north nave wall of Old St Peter's was leaning alarmingly too. The area between, which is one of the lowest points of the Vatican site as a whole, drained a large catchment area on the Vatican Hill, and its soil was sandy. Nicholas V had intended a new courtyard here specifically to drain the whole palace site. So the problem in the Sistina in 1504 was not to do with the roof, but to do with its foundations.

A particular area of weakness in the foundations showed up a little later under the eastern party-wall with the Sala Regia. At Christmas in 1522 the lintel of the entrance door split, and a part of it killed a Swiss guard alongside Pope Adrian VI, at that moment entering the chapel. At the conclave in October 1523 the cardinals assembled in the chapel were so frightened by cracks opening up that Antonio da Sangallo was called in to check its stability. In 1538 the east wall needed repair again, and new foundations. On one of these occasions damage was caused to the two narrative frescoes which closed the two Sistine cycles, damage that led to their eventual replacement somewhat later in the century. In 1569 the architect Vignola was paid for advising on how to prevent the chapel's threatened collapse, but by this date the problem mainly concerned the north wall; at about the same time Pirro Ligorio was also consulted, and he supervised reinforcement of the northern foundations and buttressing. There is massive subsequent buttressing on this side.

To return to the problem of the vault. The necessary destruction of the apartments above was followed, but at uncertain dates, by remodelling of the whole upper part in two stages. The pitched roof was raised and extended over the machicolated passage, and then it was raised again to provide a second floor above the vault, apparently to make a barracks. The first stage may be connected with a payment in the first year (1513) of Leo X's pontificate for about 40 square metres of new roof over part of the chapel, and the second stage was already complete by the early 1530s for it is recorded in Heemskerck's drawing of that date. The remarkable construction over the sacristy, with large arched openings like a loggia or *altana*, was added a year or two later, for it is clearly seen in an engraving made before 1536. It was probably built, therefore, by Clement VII (1523–34); and since it would curtail severely the light entering the windows in the altar wall its construction has something to do with Michelangelo's closure of these windows to make room for the *Last Judgement*, initially a project of Clement's. But this pope's decision to redecorate the altar wall may also have been prompted by damage there following an accident during the mass in April 1525, when the altar-curtains went up in flames. We do not know how much damage was done; and it seems more obvious, perhaps, that Pope Clement's symmetrical commission to Michelangelo, never taken further – to paint the *Fall of the Rebel Angels* on the entrance wall – was a reaction to the very serious damage there to the 15th-century frescoes.

This chapter of accidents may fittingly close with one which mercifully did not happen. Paul IV Carafa (1555–59) intended the destruction of the *Last Judgement*, and the removal of the altar wall altogether, to allow an extension of the chapel into the sacristy. That project was probably related to the expansion of the corporate Papal Chapel, and the problem was solved, it seems, by moving the screen in the other direction.

The cantoria or singing gallery of the Sistine Chapel is about five metres long and two metres wide, and was placed on the right wall (looking towards the altar), borne on brackets springing from the level of the top of the wall of the choir-screen. It has a richly decorated coffered ceiling and, towards the Chapel, a splendidly decorated and gilded balustrade, the work of the same school of craftsmen as the choir-screen.

The present altar of the Sistine Chapel, free-standing and of marble, is 18th-century; the original was of stone and grouted into the wall. The crucifix is standard altar furniture. The original altar also had an altarpiece, by Perugino, representing the Assumption of the Virgin, *but this, and the entire original decoration of the altar wall, was removed with the insertion of Michelangelo's* Last Judgement.

FUNCTIONAL DESIGN AND SYMBOLISM

The Sistina was built, as we have seen, to a purpose – to a specific and unique purpose. Accumulated experience with the Great Chapel, and perhaps with the chapels at Avignon as well, must have helped with the functional planning of this one. The reading of this functional design is to be made on the basis of the books from the library of the Masters of Ceremonies, who were accommodated in the chapel and surely consulted on its construction. There is some evidence that there was a ceremonial drawn up under Sixtus; we have to use the next to survive, produced for Innocent VIII in 1488, and the copious diaries and ceremonial commentaries of two immediately subsequent Masters of Ceremonies, Johannes Burchard and Paris de Grassis. Their testimony remains relevant because change in these matters was extremely slow, and in principle to be avoided.

The mosaic marble floor of the chapel drew the attention of Sixtus's panegyrists and historians, and with good reason, for it is the most splendid of a group of Renaissance floors in Rome in which the conventions of medieval design – Constantinian, it was believed – were revived. This floor, like the medieval and Byzantine ones, was related in a straightforward and practical way to its furnishings, and established certain reference-points and patterns which ensured tidy and symmetrical movements in the liturgy.

The space between the steps up to the presbytery, that is the altar-area, and the screen was largely taken up by the *quadratura*, which is seating for the cardinals arranged symmetrically around three sides of a square, the fourth side towards the altar being left open. The original *quadratura* was a wooden bench with a high back covered with tapestry and formed round a square of dimensions that would fit exactly, it seems, over the frame of the 'carpet' in the centre of this space. The long lateral space between the *quadratura* and the triple steps, called the *vestibulum*, was seating-area reserved for junior members of the papal household, who sat on the floor in rows at right angles to the steps, facing the pope enthroned on the left; this area is provided with a series of rectangles which would help to impose some order on this arrangement. The wide frame of the 'carpet' on this side, not covered by the cardinals' benches, contains small rectangular and triangular patterns which regulate the positions of the pope's prayer stool and of the paschal candlestick. The patterns within the *quadratura* and above the steps, before the altar, are chosen from a wide repertory of traditional forms, but chosen, it would seem, to encourage orderly movement; the pattern inside the bigger square, for example, would locate the fourfold censing performed in this space, that is of each of the three benches of cardinals and then of the altar, and regularize the central circle formed by the cardinals themselves at four points in the mass, during the Kyrie, the Gloria, the Credo and the Agnus Dei. The three smaller patterns immediately in front of the altar relate to three positions of the celebrant.

Outside the screen the floor-pattern, on a slightly lower level, is appropriately of very different design, dominated by the path from the entrance door. This path was a processional route, and was lined by the papal bodyguard, who kept it clear of those outside the screen who were not entitled to join the corporate chapel within. It was used, in this liturgy, four times during a mass for the ceremony of

Drawing by an unknown artist in the Albertina, Vienna, representing the Assumption of the Virgin *by Perugino, originally painted on the wall over the altar of the Sistine Chapel but destroyed to make way for Michelangelo's* Last Judgement. *The composition is traditional, showing the Madonna surrounded first by seraphim, then by a tier of winged angels making music. The apostles are disposed in two groups, separated by the kneeling St John, beneath. Kneeling beside St John is the donor, Sixtus IV, with his tiara beside him on the ground.*

Pontifical Entrance and Exit – four times because the procession reforms during the mass to collect the reserved Sacrament from the Chapel of St Nicholas across the Sala Regia. The path is decorated with a continuous double spiral which encloses six circles, the largest, nearest the entrance, being of porphyry; this is strictly a *rota porphyretica* such as is found at this point in the floors of many of the major Roman churches, including Old and New St Peter's, and it marks the spot at which a pope, a celebrant, or a pilgrim will pause on entrance, and kneel. The entrance to the path, however, is the point from which the "istorie" on Michelangelo's ceiling should first be seen, and from this viewpoint there seems a conscious reflection of the proportions (just under 6:1) of the long rectangle on the floor in those of the long painted frame around the histories. And it may be added here that according to the greatest of ceremonial authorities, Innocent III (1198–1216), the long succession of the *Ancestors* of Christ at the opening of the New Testament, the subject of Michelangelo's garland of lunettes and spandrels, is symbolized in the acts of Pontifical Entrance and Exit.

The broad division of the chapel as a whole is an adaptation to papal requirements of a standard medieval arrangement: the liturgical origin of the area enclosed by the screen is to be traced to the *chorus,* or *schola cantorum,* raised on one step, with a further three steps to the *presbyterium* within, as is still to be found in a basilica such as San Clemente. We do not know the arrangement of steps in the earlier Great Chapel of the Vatican, but it is fair to note the step at the screen in the palatine chapel of the Lateran, the Sancta Sanctorum, and in the Clementina at Avignon. The rather curious, even awkward, way in which Sixtus's screen formerly abutted onto the choir-gallery, interrupting at one-third of its length, is undoubtedly derived from the position of a medieval pulpit, or *ambo,* overhanging the areas inside and outside the screen; but there is also a strong possibility that it follows the arrangement introduced in the Great Chapel by Martin V in 1420–21, since his provision of a choir-gallery is listed in the same group of payments as a modification of the screen. Sixtus's gallery, in any case, was called a *pulpitum,* and it seems that the symbolism of the pulpit, defined once more by Innocent III in the same text, *De sacro altaris mysterio,* so often cited by Renaissance Masters of Ceremonies, was not forgotten; for Innocent said that it signified the eminence from which the divine message or prophecies were delivered, specifically in the Sermon on the Mount, which is the subject of the fresco placed immediately above it in the Sistine history cycle.

The screen in its revised position supports eight large candelabra; originally it supported seven, the eighth position being then blocked by the choir-gallery. But the number was not accidental. On the 14th-century screen of the Great Chapel it seems that there were regularly six, as on the screen of Old St Peter's, and Martin V appears to have added one more. Now Paris de Grassis had a lot to say about the seven he knew in the Sistina. The number was proper to the pope alone, and they had, he said, their origin in the seven carried processionally before the pontiff in the early liturgy, and then placed during the service around him or in a line across the church; and he traced that custom to Roman imperial processions, whence they came to the pope through the Donation of Constantine. Sixtus's candelabra are in fact as Constantinian in design as they could reasonably be, given their variety, for their models are the great marble candelabra now in

The lower storey, so to speak, of the pictorial decoration of the Sistine Chapel consists of a fictive wall-hanging extending all round the space. The hangings are divided by real, architectural pilasters, which extend up into the storeys above, providing a strong and definite rhythm or scansion for the whole Chapel.

the Vatican from Santa Costanza, where they had flanked the porphyry sarcophagus of Constantina, the position to which Sixtus indeed restored them. So, the candelabra must have signified the papal *imperium* in the same way for Sixtus as for Paris de Grassis; but they were also, if we follow Innocent III and Renaissance sources, spiritual symbols too, for their seven lights signify the Seven Gifts of the Holy Spirit (Isaiah 2, 2).

The seven candelabra have ecclesiological and spiritual significance appropriate to their imposing scale and position. But at this level of the chapel the decoration provided by Sixtus was dominated by the gold and silver frescoed tapestries, richly 'woven' with the pope's

This is another view of St Peter's in construction by Maarten van Heemskerck (see page 25) (Florence, Uffizi, Gabinetto dei disegni e delle stampe). On the left, slightly off a side view, is the Sistine Chapel, somewhat simplified.

(Right) Ideal reconstruction of the original appearance of the Sistine Chapel.

(Opposite page) The Sistine Chapel seen from the northwest, or from the back, in other words from the opposite end from the entrance from the Sala Regia and the Cappella Paolina. This end is unencumbered in the view taken by Heemskerck (above); it has since been cluttered by various small buildings. But the Chapel still retains its fortress air, accentuated by the fortified gangway, originally unroofed, that circles the upper part of the building.

emblems. There is no question that he also endowed, or intended to endow, the Chapel with real hangings, but we know almost nothing about them. Changeable tapestries, however, should conform to the five colours symbolic of the feasts and seasons of the calendar, white, green, red, purple and black. Gold and silver tapestries, the intended permanent or non-seasonal decoration of the lowest zone, have nothing to do with the calendar but were symbolic of Papal Majesty.

THE FRESCO DECORATION OF SIXTUS IV

The portal leading into the Sistine Chapel from the Sala Regia.
This is the proper entrance into the Chapel, opening into its eastern part, at the opposite end to the altar (the Chapel is oriented to the west). The usual entrance today, however, is through the Porta Borgia beside the altar wall and Michelangelo's Last Judgement, *to the right as one looks towards the altar. Entering through this door (which the public are unable to do), one sees the whole Chapel laid out before one at a glance.*

The Sistine Chapel is sometimes thought to be an unsophisticated building, almost a building without an architect. But a careful study of its style would show that while it is indeed restrained it is not ingenuous. We have seen, for example, that the upper cornice marks not only the spring of the window-arch but also the spring of the 'pendentive', at which point it provides a pseudo-capital by breaking forward over the pilaster. This pseudo-capital is a rare antique form and its revival by 1477 is precocious. However the restraint is sophisticated too, for it provides the frame of a premeditated pictorial decoration; as conceived, and as in fact executed, architecture and painting were united in one continuous idea, continuous to a degree altogether exceptional in the 15th century and requiring, one might think, collaboration between a receptive architect and a great architectural decorator, such as Melozzo da Forlì.

The perfection of the chapel of Sixtus must be recovered by an effort of the imagination, for it has been severely compromised by the additions of later popes. The more creative changes, affecting the vertical or layered balance of the decoration, were those of Julius II – creative and complementary, as should be expected of the nephew of the founder. The sense of continuity in the project for the new ceiling decoration is well expressed in the account submitted in May 1508 by the mason collaborating with Michelangelo, Piero Rosselli, "for a part of cleaning up the vault of Pope Sixtus in the Chapel, and plastering and doing what is necessary to get it finished by Pope Julius." Nevertheless the figural and symbolic balance of the decoration was clearly disturbed by Julius, and even when that top-heavy situation was restored by Leo X, by the addition of Raphael's equally heroic figural tapestries in the lowest zone, the resulting equilibrium was achieved at the expense of the Sistine band of histories, to some extent by their eclipse.

The destruction of the horizontal integrity of the Sistine scheme came later and was more brutal; it came about by drastic changes to the end walls. Disastrous structural damage to the entrance wall, which has been described in the previous chapter, led to the substitution of two of the histories in a discordant style, and to the replacement of the shattered inner frame of the ceremonial entrance-door by a curiously informal and misshapen embrasure. At the other end one's admiration for Michelangelo's *Last Judgement,* even for his very sensitivity to the containing structure, cannot be unmixed with regret for the loss of continuity of window-rhythms and cornices, of the meeting of the history cycles over the altar, of the altarpiece framed to reflect the entrance-door – in a word, of symmetry. The result of all this is a false sense that the chapel is tunnel-like, its original decoration arranged in two flat, opposed files. Initially a closed decorative system, inwardly-turned, had been conceived in a natural, seemingly inevitable, harmony with the whole building, as continuous and integral as the shape and support of the tremendous vault.

A consideration of the vault in relation to the space of the Chapel clarifies the way in which the number three becomes intrinsic to the decoration. The proportions of the plan, approximately three-to-one, coexist with a wall-system that produces six bays on a long wall, two on a short wall, and yields six windows and two, and eventually twelve 'pendentives'. An early project for Julius's 'finishing' of Sixtus's vault featured twelve *Apostles* as naturally as the more complex definitive one yielded twelve *Prophets* or *Sibyls* and nine histories. And

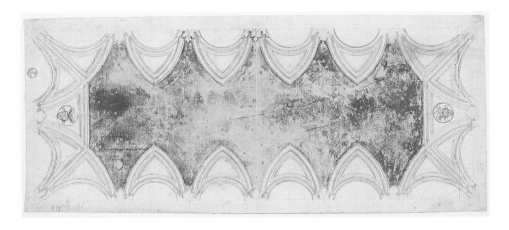

Pier Matteo d'Amelia: Design for the vault of the Sistine Chapel, late 15th century (Florence, Uffizi, Gabinetto dei disegni e delle stampe).
Pier Matteo's drawing reflects a traditional design for the ceilings of chapels, found for instance in Giotto's Scrovegni Chapel in the Arena at Padua. It was in place of a design like this, in full accord with the rest of the 15th-century decoration of the Chapel, that Michelangelo painted his High Renaissance ceiling.

Michelangelo's first idea for the Sistine Chapel ceiling (reconstruction by E. la Roche).
Michelangelo's earliest ideas for the ceiling adhered more closely to the design of the previous painted ceiling, and were more traditional notably in their insistent subdivision into squares, circles and lozenges. These tend to create an overloaded and static effect; Michelangelo's subsequent solution was both more dynamic and more unified.

in the same way there were inherent in the chapel's structure a sixfold division of the history cycle on the long walls, and the natural division of these bands, by the division of the space by the screen, into four groups of three. The importance of the number three in the decoration, the imposition of dominant triple rhythms upon thematic structure as well as design, is derived in the first instance from the 'fit' of the decoration to the structure, and is not plausibly endowed with meaning, as for instance of the Trinity.

The decorative scheme is also controlled by venerable traditions and by practical considerations. In very general terms the idea of parallel history cycles devoted to the Old and New Covenants, both unfold-

40

ing from the altar towards the entrance, is rooted in basilical decoration, notably in Rome. But it would have been impossible within the conventions of the period that these cycles should have been placed at floor-level. Entirely practical thinking about damage and visibility, and perhaps a no less important habit of not thinking illusionistically, almost invariably raised figural decoration of this kind well above head-level, and the resultant lowest tier might be filled, just as in domestic decoration, with real tapestry; a fiction of tapestry was common too, as in the late 13th-century decoration of San Francesco at Assisi or the palatine chapel of Nicholas III at the Lateran. Sixtus's scheme, as we saw in the previous section, provided both for the reality and the fiction, and in the former, at least, he followed the tradition of the earlier Great Chapels in the Vatican and at Avignon. The history cycle and the tapestry zone below are separated by a restrained entablature but together surmounted by an extremely prominent one. Below the principal entablature the two orders of pilasters, dividing histories and tapestries, exist only in paint, and they are decorated with *all'antica* candelabra designs. But above the main cornice, where the wall is a little set back to make a passage, a set of real pilasters effects both a continuation of the façade-system and a transformation to the structurally more complex zones of windows and vault. The pictorial structure becomes more complex at the same point, in two dimensions and in three. A triple rhythm is set up by the arches of niches flanking the larger arch of the window, the niches painted as if seen from below in the same way as the window embrasures. The series of the *Popes* set in these niches, for the sake of their legibility, are not seen as if illusionistically from below, yet they cast, it seems, realistic shadows into their shell-headed concavities. All

Left-hand wall of the Sistine Chapel (facing the altar):
(Left) Domenico Ghirlandaio and workshop: The Crossing of the Red Sea *("Congregatio populi a Moyse legem scriptam accepturi" – "The gathering of the people to receive the law of Scripture from Moses")*

(Centre) Sandro Botticelli and workshop: The youth of Moses *("Tentatio Moysi legis scripte latoris" – "The temptation of Moses, the bearer of the law of Scripture").*
(Right) Pietro Perugino and workshop (including Pinturicchio): The circumcision of the son of Moses *("Observatio antique regenerationis a Moyse per circoncisionem" – "The performance by Moses of the old rite of regeneration, through circumcision").*

these shadows describe a pictorial light which has its source in the windows, now lost, over the altar; and in fact it is the stream of this fictional but surely symbolic light that is respected and described throughout the decoration of the Chapel, including the histories and the tapestries. It is a powerful force working, if only subliminally, upon the spectator's perception of unity, between fresco and fresco, and between all frescoes and the building. In the lunettes above the *Popes* the Sixtine decoration once continued, according to Vasari; but he does not tell us how.

THE VAULT

The remark made by the mason preparing the Chapel for Michelangelo, that Julius was finishing what Sixtus had begun, might be taken to mean that the vault had not previously been painted; but in the context of structural restoration in which the remark must be read it might mean nothing of the kind. And it is hard to believe that Sixtus left a bare vault when every other surface was decorated. As it happens there survives in Florence a drawing which is a model for the decoration of Sixtus's vault; it is a drawing made with extreme care and painted with the purest lapis lazuli – a drawing, in fact, of the kind made for a patron's approval and not a working drawing. On it is an inscription in the hand of the architect and collector Antonio da Sangallo which informs us, first, that it was made for the Sistina, secondly, that it was made by Pier Matteo d'Amelia (a well-known decorative specialist), and, thirdly, that it was not carried through in this form: Michelangelo did in 'with figures'.

The sequence should be read from right to left, and originally began with the *Finding of Moses* on the altar wall, destroyed to make way for Michelangelo's *Last Judgement*. Each scene aligned with a corresponding scene in the *Life of Christ* on the opposite side of the Chapel; the carefully worked out correspondences were spelled out in the inscriptions (thus Moses giving the law was an Old Testament precedent for Christ giving the law, the temptation of Moses anticipated the Temptation of Christ, circumcision was regarded as the Old Testament equivalent of Baptism, and was ranged opposite the *Baptism of Christ*).

Sangallo's observation that the vault was not painted in this way may mean little, of course, if he simply did not realize that Michelangelo's painting was preceded by another – but that is hard to believe of a man in Antonio's position. An alternative to be considered is that the eye of an architect spotted that the vault drawn by Pier Matteo was, to begin with, structurally different from the one painted by Michelangelo, which is unconventional in the corners. The more usual form is represented by the Piccolomini Library in Siena, where in each corner the concavities of adjacent spandrels meet in an emphatic diagonal groin; Pier Matteo designs the framing in his corners to accommodate just such a groin. But in the corners of the Sistina we see the two spandrels combined in one field, and the groin suppressed. We may draw one of two conclusions: either Michelangelo cut back the tufa of the vault so as to eliminate the groin (as Raphael did in the Stanza della Segnatura); or, alternatively, the vault was initially built in this unusual way, in which case the drawing precedes the actual construction of the vault. The manner of the repair of the *Judith* corner seems to favour the second conclusion, but not conclusively. In any case it is to be remembered that to a great extent the painted decoration was worked out with the architecture. And it is particularly credible that an understanding should have been sought early in the case of the decoration of the vault, for the most economical way for the latter to be effected would be for the painters to work from the same scaffolding as the masons and plasterers, that is, in 1479–80.

The project by Pier Matteo was different in one other respect from any that was executed: he intended to separate the 'pendentives' at

Proceeding from the altar wall, these scenes from the New Testament were parallelled by the scenes from the *Life of Moses* in the Old Testament opposite. Parallelling the *Finding of Moses* had been the *Nativity of Christ,* which was also destroyed to make way for Michelangelo's *Last Judgement.* It is notable that each workshop was given two parallel scenes, in order that their compositions should also harmonize, though Ghirlandaio seems to have gone for contrast between the violence of the *Crossing of the Red Sea* and the peace of the *Calling of the Apostles.*

each end of the chapel from the starry blue Vault of Heaven, and to place upon them the arms of Sixtus. In the event the arms over the door were sculpted massively in stone at the base of the 'pendentive', and given gilded metal ribbons – matching, in fact, the form painted illusionistically on alternate pilasters in the window-zone. There is reason to believe that something similar was placed at the base of the 'pendentive' over the altar and then removed to make way for the *Last Judgement.* The drawing also shows the bottom of each 'pendentive' masked by very large acanthus leaves which seem to spring from the capitals, a feature also to be found in the Camera degli Sposi, painted by Mantegna in the 1460s. If the principal field was indeed painted as it was foreseen in the drawing it may be visualized looking something like the intense blue barrel-vault of the Arena Chapel in Padua; and such a similarity was perhaps not casual, since Sixtus had completed his education and begun his teaching career in the University of Padua. At the same time it must be remembered that blue and gold were the heraldic colours of the Della Rovere popes.

THE SIDE-WALLS: CHRONOLOGY AND DIVISION OF LABOUR

We have seen that the pictorial decoration, specifically the history series, was described by Sixtus's secretary Andreas of Trebizond as an addition after the cessation of the Florentine War late in 1480. Fragmentary documentation indicates

Right-hand wall of the Sistine Chapel (facing the altar):
(Left) Pietro Perugino and workshop (including Pinturicchio): The Baptism of Christ *("Institutio nove regenerationis a Christo in baptismo" – "The institution by Christ of the new rite of regeneration, in baptism").*

that there were three phases in the decoration of the walls. The third and longest campaign was the subject of a contract, dated 27 October 1481, between the supervisor of the Vatican Palace (also, probably, the architect of the Sistina), Giovannino de' Dolci, and four master-painters, Cosimo Rosselli, Botticelli, Domenico Ghirlandaio, and Perugino; it provides for the painting of ten bays – that is, the last ten bays – with histories and tapestries beneath, by 15 March 1482. The painters are to be remunerated at the same rate as that agreed for four bays already done by the same artists, and that clause refers back to

(Centre) Sandro Botticelli: The Purification of the Leper *("Tentatio Iesu Christi latoris evangelice legis" – "The Temptation of Jesus Christ the bearer of the law of the Gospels").*
(Right) Domenico Ghirlandaio and workshop: The Calling of the Apostles *("Congregatio populi legem evangelicam recepturi" – "The gathering of the people to receive the law of the Gospels").*

45

Detail of Domenico Ghirlandaio's Crossing of the Red Sea. *The dramatic scene called for violent contortions and expressions in the figures. The rider of the horse is evidently Pharaoh, whose hard heart was the cause of so much anguish, and the unleashing of divine anger against those who failed to submit to God's chosen representative.*

the second campaign; but the price for the 'first four stories' by these artists was not in fact agreed until 17 January 1482. This team-work, accounting for 14 bays in all, was distinct from the first campaign, the decoration of the altar wall, for which Perugino alone was responsible; and as that campaign included an altarpiece it naturally did not provide a precedent to be mentioned in later agreements. The second campaign – the four bays, one allotted to each of the team – accounted for the first four (reading from the altar downwards) either to the left or to the right – more probably the right, where Botticelli's fresco, the *Purification of the Leper,* seems less mature in style than his *Youth of Moses* in the group opposite. The period for completion provided in the contract of October 1481 – about five months for ten bays – was no doubt optimistic, but it could not have been absurdly out of line with progress by the same painters on the second phase; and the team may therefore be assumed to have begun work in the summer of 1481 (Ghirlandaio was still in Florence on 19 July). Perugino's work on the altar wall, lesser in extent, required proportionally and perhaps absolutely more time, because of planning decisions and the making of cartoons for decorative parts that could be reused later, but this first campaign might all have been accomplished, nevertheless, in the Spring of 1481; and as we have seen the diarist Jacopo da Volterra referred to construction work proceeding in March 1481, and to painting in December. In fact he is not likely to be strictly accurate in his second report, as one must expect the painters to suspend work in the winter months, and that delay was no doubt a reason, or an excuse, for the four painters not to meet their deadline in March 1482. They seem, however, to have missed it by some considerable margin.

The third campaign was to yield ten bays, including all six (probably) on the left wall, the two nearest the entrance on the right, and the two on the entrance wall itself (now replaced). In order to understand the planned division of labour it is necessary to study the last of the Moses cycle to survive, the *Testament of Moses,* now usually attributed solely to Signorelli, who was not one of the contracting parties. But it is evident that this fresco was begun by Perugino, whose style of drawing is clearly to be seen towards the left. At a certain point Perugino abandoned his work, and Signorelli perhaps took over because he had already been Perugino's assistant in the *Giving of the Keys* (fifth from the altar on the right). Signorelli subsequently painted the lost fresco on the entrance wall, the *Conflict over the Body of Moses.* It is not easy to understand Perugino's withdrawal. All we know for certain is that he, Botticelli, and Ghirlandaio undertook a major fresco project in Florence early in October 1482: Botticelli and Ghirlandaio are said to have been already back in Florence by 31 August 1482, and Rosselli by November.

To return to the division of the work. In the first campaign Perugino was the only master-painter concerned. That was natural enough, for in 1478 he had painted for Sixtus the apse of the Pope's other large chapel, the Cappella del Coro in Old St Peter's, which was also his mausoleum. In the second campaign, on whichever side the four painters began, Perugino and his workshop were responsible for the bay nearest the altar wall, Botticelli the second, Ghirlandaio the third, and Rosselli the fourth. In the third campaign they began the ten bays in question by repeating their order of appearance in the first four bays from the altar, probably on the left. At that point a new pattern had to be agreed for the remaining six bays, and it was decided to give the fifth bays, which as we shall see are of special importance, to Botticelli (left) and Perugino (right). Perugino also got (originally) the sixth on the left (the *Testament of Moses*), Rosselli the sixth on the right (the *Last Supper*), and Ghirlandaio one on the entrance-wall (the *Resurrection*). We cannot guess to which of the four the last of the Moses cycle on the entrance-wall was originally allocated. An inequality between the team was inevitable, and Botticelli and Perugino did the most important work; but it must be remembered that an inequality of planned labour, which would be against the spirit of the contract, could be avoided by the careful allocation of the *Popes* in the window-zone, and the lost lunettes, to the four workshops.

Perugino was familiar to Sixtus, but the employment of the rest was not so natural. To the three Florentine artists who joined the team in the summer of 1481 we must add four more Tuscan artists whom we know to have been engaged in minor capacities: Piero di Cosimo, Fra Diamante, Bartolomeo della Gatta, and Signorelli – the latter eventually rising to a major position. The overwhelmingly Tuscan character of the decoration of the walls in the second and third campaigns is to be interpreted in relation to Andreas's observation that the painting of the walls followed the Truce. For even admitting the propensity of artists to ignore individually their governments' quarrels, the scale of Sixtus's dependence upon a Tuscan team could scarcely have been accomplished without the cooling of Lorenzo de' Medici's anger, and it even looks as if the making of the team might have been a gesture in the settlement. There are other well-attested examples of Lorenzo using the reputation of Tuscan artists in diplomacy.

Detail of Sandro Botticelli's Youth of Moses. *During his sojourn with Jethro, Moses went up on the mountain, where he received from God the order to remove his sandals before setting foot on the ground by the Burning Bush.*

THE SIDE-WALLS: DESIGN AND STYLE

To look along the two opposed files, each of six histories, that survive is to be struck by the acceptance, by all the artists concerned, of a common style, to the extent at least of accepting the discipline of common figure scale, horizon, colour range, landscape convention, and overall rhythmic plan. Yet they were, one may assume, in reality the characteristics of a style established by Perugino in the first campaign here, the lost work on the altar wall. The same assumption may help us to visualize the two lost histories, the *Finding of Moses* on the left and the *Adoration of the Shepherds* on the right, each subject offering opportunities for broad landscapes. There is no other hint to help us with the first of the Moses set, but Perugino's treatment on several other occasions of the *Adoration of the Shepherds* produced a centralized composition, with the shepherds dispersed in prayer outside an open hut. The two frescoes, in any case, were divided and joined by a central pilaster, like those of the side-walls, and the space available would yield fresco-fields of the same proportion as the rest of the histories. Below the central junction of the history cycles was the altarpiece, which was again in fresco, about 2.7×2 metres; its stone frame is recorded in ceremonial documents. The subject was the *Assumption,* and its representation of the Virgin's triumph refers to the Chapel's dedication to her. A highly finished

Detail of Pietro Perugino's Circumcision of the son of Moses. *The woman in the foreground is Moses's wife Zipporah, leading her second-born by the hand, while the first-born looks with pious reverence on the angel who has met them on their way. The angel orders them to institute the rite of circumcision, which is performed, to the right of the fresco, on Moses's second son.*

47

drawing survives in Vienna, either a presentation drawing for the patron's approval or copy after the painting: Sts Peter and Paul, twin founders of the Roman Church, are foremost among the apostles, and St Peter on our left, the first Pope, introduces the kneeling Sixtus to the Virgin by touching him on the shoulder with one of the Keys. The altarpiece was therefore both votive offering and memorial of the man who built the Chapel; it is the only explicitly personal contribution he made to the figural decoration, and reasonably it was small in relation to the histories. The character of the repeated parts of the chapel's decoration, however, was also established by Perugino on the altar wall in fictive tapestries on either side of the altarpiece (but interrupted by a door to the sacristy on the left), and in the niches of the window-zone and the mysterious lunettes above.

The surviving part of the series of the *Popes,* which is based upon the papal history written by Sixtus's librarian, Platina, begins now on the side-walls with Clement I (left) and Anacletus (right). Initiating the sequence by projecting Platina's list backwards necessarily places

Left-hand wall of the Sistine Chapel, continued:
(Left) Luca Signorelli: The Testament of Moses *("Replicatio legis scripte a Moyse" – "The codification of the law of Scripture by Moses").*

(Centre) Sandro Botticelli and workshop: The Punishment of the Sons of Corah *("Conturbatio Moysi legis scripte latoris" – "Opposition to Moses, the bearer of the law of Scripture").*
(Right) Cosimo Rosselli and workshop: The Descent from Mt Sinai *("Promulgatio legis scripte per Moysen" – "The promulgation by Moses of the law of Scripture").*

the first two after Peter, Linus and Cletus, in the extreme left and right niches at the top of the altar wall. The real problem concerns the area between the windows, where St Peter, the first of the popes, must have been represented. Continuation of the system of the side-walls at this point would have produced two more niches divided by a pilaster; and it has been suggested that these niches would have been occupied by Christ and his Vicar. But it seems inconceivable that Christ could have been displaced from the centre, and there is much to be said for an alternative hypothesis. At this point in the chapel the unique high bracket that supports the pendentive (if it is original, and not a substitution to make more space for the *Last Judgement*) indicates that the field between the windows was clear of any architectural pilaster, leaving room for a composition with a centralized Christ flanked by Peter and Paul, the twin founders with whom Platina in fact began his history. It would then remain to imagine an architectural fiction of niches which would accommodate the three figures; there is room only for three equal niches.

The most striking revelation of the recent cleaning of the wall-frescoes is the quantity of gold on them. This gilding is not applied in the manner common in 15th-century painting, to ornaments such as hems of robes, but it is to be found in the landscape too, on trees and buildings; and it does not merely decorate, it picks out highlights and accentuates relief and detail. And further the gold in the figural frescoes is to be seen in relation to the extensive gilding of architectural members throughout the Chapel, whether fictional or real: that is, the quite elaborate gilding of frames, cornices, screen,

Continuing in a direction away from the altar, the sequence has to be read from right to left. The *Descent from Mt Sinai* by Cosimo Rosselli, the weakest of the artists employed in the Chapel, represents the dispensation of the Ten Commandments, and is parallelled in the New Testament by the Sermon on the Mount. The *Punishment of the Sons of Corah* in Botticelli's picture shows what happens to those who disobey God's representative: the disobedient sons of Corah are swallowed up into the ground on the left of the fresco. The Arch of Constantine behind is provided with a modern inscription driving home the message. The *Testament of Moses* was painted by Signorelli, though he was not among the artists originally contracted for the walls; he probably took the place of Perugino, who returned to Florence. Representing the handing over of leadership to Joshua and the death of Moses, this scene parallels the *Last Supper* on the opposite wall. Not only the first two 15th-century frescoes but also the last two, painted on the entrance wall of the Chapel, were lost in the 16th century: one represented an apocryphal scene after Moses's death, the other Christ's *Resurrection*.

candelabra, and choir-gallery. Seen in this way the primary function of the gold is to unify, as the painted light does, the decoration and the structure; and indeed the gilding does not interrupt the painted light but reinforces it, making painted forms seem to respond to light in the same way as real ones do. But the exceptional quantity of surface gold must be understood in two other ways, arising from the peculiar functions of the chapel. Several of the occasions prescribed for the Great Chapel were vespers, and when evening ceremonies were conducted in artificial light the reflection of candlelight from the gold must have brought not only a great magnificence to the whole chapel but also clarification to the reading of the histories. The idea of using so much gold, however, is most probably to be traced to the tradition of specifically palatine chapels to which, artistically, the Sistina belongs. For we must think not only of the great basilical cycles of Rome, some in mosaic, but also of the Chapel of Nicholas V in the Vatican itself, painted by Fra Angelico (1447–49), and then of the still more sumptuous chapel of Nicholas's friend, Cosimo de' Medici, by Michelozzo and Benozzo Gozzoli (*c.* 1459) in Palazzo Medici in Florence. The surface richness of Cosimo's chapel has much to do with its illumination, which was almost entirely artificial. But the example of Benozzo's frescoes was followed in the Sistina not only in this matter of their gilding, but also in other aspects of their sumptuousness, for example the delights of landscape – distant prospects, varieties of foliage, the flight of birds – or the veristic complexities of costumes and portraits.

The *Sermon on the Mount* by Cosimo Rosselli matched very neatly the dispensation of the Ten Commandments on the opposite wall, but the *Giving of the Keys to St Peter* does not seem to fit with Moses's *Punishment of the Sons of Corah.* Instead the direct parallel to the opposition to Moses of Corah's sons is set in the right-hand background of Perugino's picture, where an attempt by the Pharisees to stone Christ is represented. The *Giving of the Keys* is given prominence because of its importance as the justification of papal authority, and is parallelled not so much by the punishment the sons of Corah receive as by Moses's investiture with power, which is also part of the story. Cosimo Rosselli's *Last Supper* (with further scenes from Christ's Passion seen in the background) parallels the death of Moses on the opposite wall. Further 15th-century frescoes, subsequently repainted after their deterioration, finished the cycle on the entrance wall, representing on this side the *Resurrection of Christ* and on the other the *Conflict over the Body of Moses.*

THE SIDE-WALLS: ICONOGRAPHY

Pope Sixtus's secretary, Andreas of Trebizond, very succinctly described the Chapel's pictorial decoration: "You have added painting of both [systems of] law," that is, the Old and New Covenants. He must have known what we have learnt only recently – another important result of the restoration – that there was to be a set of bold inscriptions, in the frieze above the history-cycle, which act as captions *(tituli)* to each. By good luck some lacunae in the recovered texts could be restored from a list published in 1513; but by bad luck that list did not include those on the end-walls, which we have lost. The twelve texts that we have are not unusual in the 15th century in providing commentary on painted histories. What is exceptional is the way in which they make instantly visible a thematic structure in the cycle as a whole. It is a strictly typological structure, that is, it presents episodes in pairs as anticipation and fulfilment, and it contrasts explicitly the two systems of law: the Written Law of Moses, and the Evangelical Law of Christ. Andreas was exactly the sort of person who would be called upon to compose such a set.

Although the inscriptions of the altar wall are missing the system clearly began there. In the *Finding of Moses* and the *Adoration of the Shepherds* the rôle of Moses as antetype of Christ would have been established, with a particular meaning; for the second was conventionally interpreted as Christ's appearance to the Jews, the first as a prefi-

Right-hand wall of the Sistine Chapel, continued:
(Left) Cosimo Rosselli: The Sermon on the Mount *("Promulgatio evangelice legis per Christum" – "The promulgation of the law of the Gospels by Christ").*

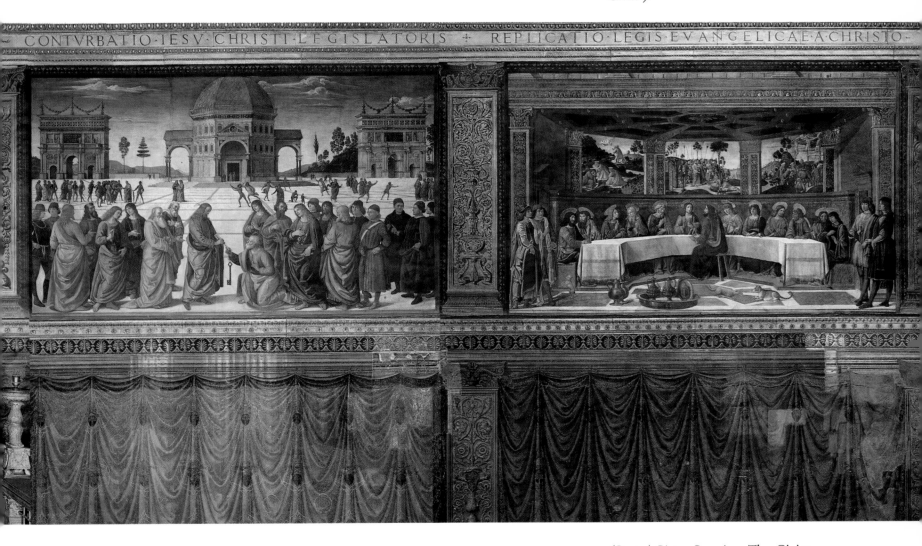

guration in the Old Testament of his appearance to the Gentiles. The choice of subjects respected the tradition of devoting altar-walls to the Epiphany (a tradition respected again in the substitution of the *Last Judgement,* the Second Coming), and it was related precisely to the symbolism of the altar itself, where the Crucifix between two candles stood for Christ the Cornerstone, between and joining the two peoples, Jew and Gentile. To this symbolic knot were later tied both Michelangelo's ceiling and Raphael's tapestries.

(Centre) Pietro Perugino: The Giving of the Keys to St Peter *("Conturbatio Iesu Christi legis evangelice latoris" – "Opposition to Jesus Christ, the bearer of the law of the Gospels").*
(Right) Cosimo Rosselli: The Last Supper *("Replicatio legis evangelice a Christo" – "The codification of the law of the Gospels by Christ").*

The two sets of inscriptions are as follows, numbered from the altar-wall:

LEFT

1. OBSERVATIO ANTIQUE REGENERATIONIS A MOYSE PER CIRCUMCISIONEM.
2. TENTATIO MOYSI LEGIS SCRIPTE LATORIS.
3. CONGREGATIO POPULI A MOYSE LEGEM SCRIPTAM ACCEPTURI.
4. PROMULGATIO LEGIS SCRIPTE PER MOYSEN.
5. CONTURBATIO MOYSI LEGIS SCRIPTE LATORIS.
6. REPLICATIO LEGIS SCRIPTE A MOYSE.

RIGHT

1. INSTITUTIO NOVE REGENERATIONIS A CHRISTO IN BAPTISMO.
2. TENTATIO IESU CHRISTI LATORIS EVANGELICE LEGIS.
3. CONGREGATIO POPULI LEGEM EVANGELICAM RECEPTURI.
4. PROMULGATIO EVANGELICE LEGIS PER CHRISTUM.
5. CONTURBATIO IESU CHRISTI LEGISLATORIS.
6. REPLICATIO LEGIS EVANGELICE A CHRISTO.

The precisely and consistently typological nature of these texts is obvious from this list (as it would have been to the spectator of the Chapel), and needs no elaborate commentary. 1 right, over Perugino's *Baptism of Christ*, refers in an unexceptionable way to the initiation of the new life through Baptism, the *regeneratio* alluding specifically to the Fall of Man. Left, over Perugino's *Circumcision*, indicates the antetypal initiation that confirmed the Old Covenant with Jehovah; it is certain that the presentation of the story from Exodus is modified by a reading of the *Historia scholastica* of Petrus Comestor, who in fact directly compares the purificatory effects of Circumcision and Baptism, in the latter case the water being qualified by the adjective *regenerativa*. In another familiar exegetical handbook, the *Glossa ordinaria*, circumcision is interpreted as a figure of the healing, purifying power of the Holy Spirit – like the Dove that descends on Christ in the *Baptism*.

The pairs continue in this way. For the moment we may leave aside the second and fifth on each side. 3 left and 3 right present the *Congregatio*, that is the Preparation of the People, Synagogue and Church, for the reception of the Covenants, of the Written Law of Moses in the *Crossing of the Red Sea*, of the Gospel of Christ in the *Calling of the Apostles*, both painted by Ghirlandaio. 4 left and 4 right present the *Promulgatio*, the Announcement or Delivery of the Covenant, from a height, by Moses in the *Descent from Mt Sinai* and by Christ in the *Sermon on the Mount* (over the *pulpitum*, the choir-gallery). 6 left and 6 right present the *Replicatio*, the Affirmation of the Covenant, by Moses in the declaration of his *Testament*, by Christ in the *Last Supper*. The rigorous parallellism in successive phases of the establishment of the two Covenants between God and Man is in fact achieved by reversing the biblical sequence between 1 left and 2 left; typology takes precedence over strict history. No literate spectator can miss the point, for it is expressed in the formal composition of the texts themselves, with minimal change of words: *Replicatio Legis Evangelice a Christo*, and *Replicatio Legis Scripte a Moyse*.

But the same formal approach to the texts reveals a special relationship between the second and fifth in each set, that is to say between the central *tituli* of groups of three. This longitudinal correlation is a clear signal for a reading more complex than the typological alone,

Detail of Cosimo Rosselli's Sermon on the Mount: *the group standing in the foreground towards the left. As in most other frescoes in the cycle, the by-standers are portraits of members of the papal court, though they cannot now be identified. The bearded figure wears the chain of the Order of Malta.*

Detail of Pietro Perugino's Giving of the Keys: *the group in the foreground on the left of the apostles immediately flanking Christ. The two figures on the far left, as their different stance and different, contemporary costume show, are again portraits. The scene in the background again involves St Peter: it represents the* Tribute Money, *the story represented most famously by Masaccio in the Brancacci Chapel in the Carmine in Florence.*

52

and it is to be applied to the special treatment of these central bays by the artists. The length of the chapel, it will be remembered, was originally divided approximately at the centre by the screen into two three-bay spaces. This physical reality is acknowledged and accentuated by the rhythm of colour change in the fictive tapestries: gold-silver-gold, gold-silver-gold. And the hierarchy in the three-bay system is acknowledged, too, in the allocation of the four central histories to the two most important artists, Botticelli and Perugino, and it is then again accentuated by the imposition by both of them of strongly centralized and tripartite design. In the case where one artist, Botticelli, was responsible for two central bays on one wall, 2 left (the *Youth of Moses*) and 5 left (the *Punishment of the Sons of Corah*), the thematic association between them is marked by a balance of individually asymmetrical vertical strips of wall, which frame them symmetrically as a pair.

The four bays thus isolated are curious in another way. Their *tituli* refer to marginal episodes in the histories – to Proof of, and Opposition to, Moses and Christ – and carry the twin burdens of continuous historical sequence in each file and typological pairing between files. The four principal subjects are set free, as it were, to establish a separate system: a system of four metaphorical representations of the Institution of the Papacy.

Tentatio Moysi begins the text over Botticelli's *Youth of Moses,* 2 left: the Proof (or Test) of Moses. In the peripheral scenes Moses is certainly, as explained in the *Glossa ordinaria, figura Christi;* when he kills the Egyptian in the desert he is specifically a prefiguration of Christ defeating the Devil, obviously referring across to Christ's temptation in the desert in the scene opposite, the *Purification of the Leper.* But in the central episode, where Moses waters the flocks of the daughters of Jethro, he is on the one hand a figure of the Good Shepherd, and on the other the emergent leader of the Chosen People. The represented sequence from Exodus 2-3, as a whole, illustrates God's appointment of Moses as Prince and Judge. It is significant at this point that the papal throne is placed under the strip of architecture down the right edge of this fresco; in fact the lower right corner is exceptionally left empty to accommodate from time to time a canopy over the throne.

In another subsidiary episode, from Exodus 2,1–14, when Moses sought to mediate between two quarrelling Hebrews, he is challenged: 'Who made thee a prince and a judge over us?' The same challenge occurs in the story, from Numbers 16, upon which Botticelli's *Punishment of the Sons of Corah* is based. The two frescoes together, 2 left and 5 left, illustrate the division of the three God-given powers in the Old Covenant, of Prince and Judge in Moses and of Priest in Aaron. The challenge, the *Conturbatio* in the inscription, is illustrated in the *Punishment of the Sons of Corah* by the scene on the right where the congregation of Israel gathers against Moses; in the fresco they in fact prepare to stone him, an action not specified in the text but introduced to point up the typological parallel to the stoning of Christ before the Temple in the margin of the fresco opposite, the *Conturbatio Iesu Christi.* But just as the Jews challenge the authority of Moses, that God-given authority which must be proved by the earth's swallowing of the dissident sons of Corah, so Moses in turn challenges their aspirations to the Priesthood. And it is the central episode in the fresco, in fact two superimposed or layered episodes, which affirm the

Detail of Cosimo Rosselli's Last Supper: *head of St Peter. St Peter, on Christ's right, looks not towards the Saviour but, with perplexity, towards Judas, seated (in the usual scheme before Leonardo's* Last Supper *in Santa Maria della Grazia in Milan) in front of the table.*

THE CIRCUMCISION
OF THE SON OF MOSES

Details of Perugino's Circumcision of
the Son of Moses: *(right) the angel halts
Moses on his way after leaving Jethro;
(below) a scene of country life in the
background, of no particular relevance
to the story but of a certain charm. The
confrontation of Moses and the angel,*

*who halts him so dramatically, is the
centre of the picture, and serves to lend
compositional unity to the series of
events represented (among them, in the
background, Moses saying goodbye to
Jethro). The message that the angel bears
is that Moses should circumcise his
second son, which takes place on the
right.*

separate powers of Moses and Aaron, to whom and to whose descendants, alone, the Priesthood is given. The inscription within the fresco, on the attic of the triumphal arch over the altar, "Let no man take this honour unto himself, but only he that is called of God, as was Aaron" (Hebrews 5, 4), is a commentary both upon the authority of the Priesthood in the Old Covenant and upon the God-given (not assumed) Priesthood of Christ in the New. It should be noted that Aaron the High Priest pointedly wears blue and gold, the Della Rovere colours, and a papal tiara – that cannot be a careless

anachronism, but reminds us that the three crowns are sometimes held to symbolize the powers of Prince, Judge, and Priest.

It is a commonplace of Renaissance commentaries to compare the pope with Moses *and* Aaron. The divided powers of the Written Law devolve first upon Christ, then upon His Vicar, and finally upon his successors the popes. That, essentially, is the point of the *tradition* illustrated in the niche series in the Sistina. But the devolution itself is illustrated in the central episode of the fresco opposite the *Punish-*

Detail of Perugino's Circumcision of the son of Moses: *the circumcision. The circumcision is performed by Moses's wife Zipporah, according to a rather obscure passage in the Bible, Exodus 4, 24–26: "... Then Zipporah took a sharp stone, and cut off the foreskin of her son, and cast it at his feet (Moses's), and said, 'Surely a bloody husband art thou to me'."*

55

THE BAPTISM OF CHRIST

Then cometh Jesus from Galilee to Jordan unto
John, to be baptized of him. But John forbad him,
saying, I have need to be baptized of thee, and
comest thou to me? And Jesus answering said unto
him, Suffer it to be so now: for thus it becometh us
to fulfil all righteousness. Then he suffered him.
And Jesus, when he was baptized, went up
straightway out of the water: and, lo, the heavens
were opened unto him, and he saw the Spirit of
God descending like a dove, and lighting upon him:
And lo a voice from heaven, saying, This is my
beloved Son, in whom I am well pleased.

MATTHEW 3, 13 – 17

*Perugino and workshop (including Pin-
turicchio):* The Baptism of Christ, *with
a detail (below) of God the Father giving
his blessing from Heaven. Perugino had
no shortage of precedents to draw on for
his representation of one of the most
important images of Christian iconography. He follows tradition in repre-*

*senting the scene with strict centrality,
building the picture round the axis of
God the Father, the Holy Spirit, and the
Son. But he has emphasized this centrality in his own way, by creating strong
triangles (the outlines of the hills, contrasting against the sky; the files of by-
standers) that converge on the sacred
moment.*

The tondo *in which the figure of the Almighty, surrounded by cherubim, appears is a Renaissance version of the medieval almond-shaped* mandorla. *The
tradition was rather more dramatically
modernized by Michelangelo in his
Creation of Adam for the Sistine
ceiling.*

ment, that is, Perugino's *Giving of the Keys,* 5 right. This episode
(Matthew 16) illustrates the transmission of plenary authority, now,
through Peter to the Roman Church, and the divine selection in the
presence of the other apostles of Peter as its Head. It is perhaps the
most familiar proof of the primacy of the Pope. And the full meaning
of the pairing of these two frescoes might be found in the formulation
of Saint Cyprian's commentary on Matthew 16 (in his *Letters,* of
which there was a printed edition in 1471): the enemies of the One
Church under the One Head are exactly the equals in sacrilege of
Corah and his family and will suffer the same fate. That formulation
was the origin of the threat of the same punishment, in bulls against
schismatics promulgated by both Della Rovere popes.

It is clear that this scene was allotted to Perugino, but probable that most of the execution was devolved on the workshop, and in particular on Perugino's leading assistant, Pinturicchio. Among the by-standers, marked by their different, contemporary costumes, there again appear portaits of interested parties, unfortunately not now identifiable.

The subject of the principal episode of the remaining 'central' fresco, Botticelli's *Purification of the Leper*, 2 right, has troubled historians. It is an illustration, which can be followed verse by verse, of the ceremony of the purification of the leper prescribed in Leviticus 14. It has nothing directly to do with the *Tentatio Iesu Christi*, which is represented again in marginal episodes. Its meaning, however, as metaphor is one which would be familiar to most of those who sat by right within the screen, before it. The subjects of the Christ cycle are all taken from the Gospel of St Matthew, with the exception of this and of the Stoning of Christ, 5 right (John 10, 22–31). In the most authoritative commentary on Matthew, which is St Jerome's, lies the origin of the *Purification of the Leper* as metaphor, and precisely in his

THE GROSSING OF THE RED SEA

Details from Ghirlandaio's Crossing of the Red Sea: (right) the splendid figure of the woman kneeling to Moses's right, in the grip of a divine rapture as she plays her cithara. The reference is to the passage in the Bible, Exodus, 15, 1f, when "Then sang Moses and the children of Israel this song unto the Lord, and spake, saying, 'I will sing unto the Lord, for he hath triumphed gloriously: the horse and his rider hath he thrown into the sea'."

The engulfment of the army of Pharaoh by the waters (Exodus, 14, 23 f) might have been handled more dramatically by an artist better suited than Ghirlandaio to such scenes; however, it was decided to make the centrepiece of the fresco this famous and rousing episode rather than to feature large the sequel, shown over on the left, to which the inscription refers: the promulgation of the law of Scripture to the people on the mountain. The somewhat odd column corresponds to the biblical passage, Exodus 14, 24: "And it came to pass, that in the morning watch the Lord looked unto the host of the Egyptians through the pillar of fire and of the cloud, and troubled the host of the Egyptians, and took off their chariot wheels, that they drave them heavily: so that the Egyptians said, Let us flee from the face of Israel; for the Lord fighteth for them against the Egyptians."

Moses himself (above) is still in the grip of the Lord's command that he should stretch forth his hand over the sea, as a result of which the people of Israel passed through dry-shod, while the Egyptians were overthrown by the waters.

THE CALLING OF THE
FIRST APOSTLES

Details of Ghirlandaio's Calling of the Apostles: *(above) Christ calling in one group of disciples, from the left-hand background; (below) Christ calling in James and John, the sons of Zebedee, from their boat. Christ also appears in the central foreground. The convention, known as continuous narration, whereby a single protagonist can appear*

several times or several episodes can be represented in a single space, is used throughout the Sistine Chapel: indeed it was indispensable.

explication of Matthew 16, the promise of the Giving of the Keys. He compares and contrasts the Power of the Keys, to distinguish between sinners and innocent (in later scholastic terms, the *Potestas ordinis*), with the power of the priests of the Old Covenant to distinguish between the leprous and the clean. It is a comparison which rests upon the interpretation of leprosy as a metaphor of sin, which is a constant of Christian exegesis and of the social history of leprosy.

The *Purification of the Leper* stands, then, as a metaphor of the root of

the power of the Priesthood of the New Covenant, given symbolically through the Keys, and as a clarification of a distinction: for the
new High Priest has the power not only to recognize the cleansing
performed by God, but himself to perform the act of justice, to loose
and to bind. Saint Jerome's metaphorical conjunction of Leviticus 14
and Matthew 16 found its way into the standard exegetical hand-
books, the *Sententiae* of Petrus Lombardus, the *Catena Aurea* of
Thomas Aquinas, and the *Glossa ordinaria;* it was followed in the

*Looking on at the central scene, in
which Christ calls Simon, soon to be
named Peter, are once again by-standers
in contemporary dress. Despite the pleas-
ant qualities of the landscape, with its
hilltop fortress ringed by curtain walls
and its passing flight of birds, the interest of artist was evidently directed towards the figures.*

61

commentaries most widely read in the 15th century, those of Nicolaus de Lyra and Torquemada; and it was the very foundation of 15th-century understanding of the doctrine of the Keys. As it was invoked in Gratian's *Decretum* it found its way into innumerable medieval texts on canon law and discussions of the sacrament of Penance; and it was invoked again in the papal address to newly invested cardinals. It should have been well within the interpretative grasp of the *Capella papalis*.

In the *Purification of the Leper* the High Priest wears blue and gold again, but not quite a tiara. The most prominent witness, to the right of centre, is Sixtus's most prominent nephew, in a sense his heir, the Cardinal Giuliano Della Rovere, later Julius II; behind him stand two

Details from Rosselli's Descent from Mt Sinai: *(above) Moses receives the Ten Commandments from God the Father, cloaked by a cloud of angels. The exquisite sleeping figure is probably the young Joshua, Moses's successor, who is mentioned as being with him (Exodus 24, 13), though the Bible does not say that he slept.*

oak trees, one pruned to the pattern adopted in the family's coat of arms. Therein lie the clues for the reading of another metaphor concretized by Botticelli, the representation of the Temple of Jerusalem by Sixtus's largest architectural enterprise, the rebuilt Hospital of Santo Spirito, of which Cardinal Giuliano was Protector. The building stands as a symbol of Sixtus's charity, and should be seen as a reflection, as it were, of the canopy of trees shading the well in the fresco opposite, the Youth of Moses, where the Good Shepherd waters the flock. But it has been pointed out that it should also be compared with the Temple in the *Giving of the Keys*, in that fresco inscriptions contrast the greater opulence of Solomon and the greater spiritual riches of Sixtus, a contrast which seems symbolized in the styles and materials of the two painted buildings. And the circulation of ideas between the four 'central' frescoes is illustrated again by the stoning of Christ in the *Giving of the Keys*, the *Conturbatio Iesu Christi*

Moses (below), seeing the people devoted to the worship of the Golden Calf (right), broke into pieces the tablets he had just received from God at the top of the mountain (opposite page). His anger is the central focus of the fresco, devoted to the promulgation of the law.

The 'nymph' (far right) has no particular role in the scenes shown, but is typical of the kind of filling that these crowd scenes required. She may be compared with similar 'nymphs' by Rosselli's fellow artists, notably Botticelli's wood carrier in his Purification of the Leper.

63

THE SERMON
ON THE MOUNT

Blessed are the poor in spirit,
for theirs is the kingdom of heaven.
Blessed are they that mourn:
for they shall be comforted.
Blessed are the meek:
for they shall inherit the earth.
Blessed are they which do hunger
and thirst after righteousness:
for they shall be filled.
Blessed are the merciful:
for they shall obtain mercy.
Blessed are the pure in heart:

for they shall see God.
Blessed are the peacemakers:
for they shall be called
the children of God.
Blessed are they which are
persecuted for righteousness' sake:
for theirs is the kingdom of the
earth.
MATTHEW 5, 3 – 10

Cosimo Rosselli: The Sermon on the
Mount, *with a detail (above) of two of
the audience, who seem to be looking at
one another with that kindness and
meekness that the Sermon stressed. They
are set into what is evidently a group of
contemporary portraits, but their identity has not been convincingly demonstrated.*

of the inscription, which took place before Solomon's Temple on the
feast of the Dedication, and interrupted the parable of the Good
Shepherd, and the prophecy of the One Flock and of those other
sheep "which are not of this fold", to be united under the One
Shepherd: the prophecy, that is, of the mission of Christ to unify Jew
and Gentile which devolves upon Peter and the papacy. And the two
figures on the right are architects, one of them presumably Giovannino de' Dolci, responsible not only for the Sistina but also, probably,

for Santo Spirito as well; they stand there as witnesses of Christ's promise to Peter: "On this Rock I will build my Church."

By a natural focus, then, upon the central bays in the two halves of the Chapel there is introduced into the typological sequences of foundation and affirmation of the Old and New Covenants between God and Man a second theme appropriate to the place, the nature and origin of the God-given powers descended upon and exemplified by the papacy. There are undoubtedly other complexities. It has been

On the right of Cosimo's painting, the subsequent episode of Christ's healing of a leper is recounted. The disease of leprosy was often understood as a metaphor for a moral or religious ill. Quite possibly Cosimo Rosselli's pupil Piero di Cosimo had a hand in this fresco, though there is no consensus about which parts he may have painted.

65

THE TESTAMENT OF MOSES

Details from Signorelli's Testament of Moses: *at the top of the fresco (above), the moving scene of Moses in his old age being shown by an angel the Holy Land that he will never reach.*

And the Lord spake unto Moses that selfsame day, saying, Get thee up into this mountain Abarim, unto mount Nebo, which is in the land of Moab, that is over against Jericho: and behold the land of Canaan, which I give unto the children of Israel for a possession: and die in the mount whither thou goest up, and be gathered unto thy people ... Yet thou shalt see the land before thee; but thou shalt not go thither unto the land which I give the children of Israel. DEUTERONOMY 32, 48–52

There follows (central) the death of the prophet, set to the left of the fresco beneath the preceding scene and further into the distance. The artist has followed the usual scheme for the death of a saint, showing Moses extended full length while mourners express their grief in various ways around him.

This detail (right) from the lower zone of the fresco is one of the finest groups within it. Moses is a magnificent figure, delineated with great solidity and force. Turning, he consigns his staff to the kneeling Joshua, who is also a noble figure. The by-standers are also finely modelled, notably a youth with his head to one side wearing a gold chain.

This scene is the focus of the fresco, though it is set somewhat to the right of the composition. The old prophet reads out the law to the people, shown in all their variety of age and sex listening, with his head almost in silhouette against the glowing light of the Promised Land. It is perhaps Aaron who leans on his staff in the foreground. The basis for the fresco is the text of Deuteronomy, presented as a speech of Moses to the people, in which he rehearses the vicissitudes through which he was brought them and the laws he has given them, both the Ten Commandments and others.

believed that some subjects refer to contemporary ecclesiological events. The potentiality of the *Punishment of the Sons of Corah* as a commentary upon the fate of schismatics has been mentioned. The difficulty with these further 'meanings' is sometimes that inception of the scheme precedes the event, sometimes that an association may be fortuitous. Such uncertainties arise in the case of the *Crossing of the Red Sea*, 3 left; in a Crusade Bull of 1480 Sixtus exhorted Christians to

Cosimo Rosselli: The Last Supper. *The subsequent scenes of Christ's Passion, the Agony in the Garden, the Kiss of Judas and the Crucifixion, are set in panels over the scene, ambiguous between scenes seen through windows and pictures on the wall.*

As usual, Judas is placed on the forward side of the table, in isolation. On his shoulder sits a little devil, a somewhat old-fashioned touch. The confrontation between Christ and Judas (and also Peter) is unusually direct; it seems to be echoed, rather incongruously, by the confrontation of dog and cat on the floor behind Judas.

trust themselves to God, Who had drowned Pharaoh's hosts, and the fresco had still not been painted when, in September 1481, the papal fleet recovered Otranto from the Turks. Was the subject, however, already chosen? Or was a new subject chosen, an improvisation which may explain a less-than-perfect 'fit' between history and *titulus, Congregatio Populi*? It is the nature of great and complex works of art that they may sustain both a plurality and an accretion of meanings.

Details from Botticelli's Youth of Moses: *(above) Moses kneeling before the Burning Bush, from which he received the first intimation of his mission to liberate the Israelites from their servitude to Pharaoh; (central) the scene, wonderfully conceived by Botticelli, in which Moses meets the daughters of Jethro by the well, which was made the centrepiece of the fresco. The two women especially are witness to Botticelli's rhythmic line and the vitreous brilliance of his colouring.*

… Now when Pharaoh heard this thing, he sought to slay Moses. But Moses fled from the face of Pharaoh, and dwelt in the land of Midian: and sat down by a well. Now the priest of Midian had seven daughters: and they came and drew water, and filled the troughs to water their father's flock. And the shepherds came and drove them away: but Moses stood up and helped them, and watered their flock. And when they came to Reuel their

Contrasting to the calm of the central zone the scene on the right represents Moses's first of several acts of righteous anger. He kills an Egyptian who had struck a fellow Hebrew, the incident that set in train his eventual liberation of his people. Behind, just to the right of the well, he drives off the shepherds who had been a nuisance to the daughters of Jethro, and enables them to bring their flock to drink. He subsequently marries one of the daugthers of Jethro, Zipporah, and on the left is shown, it seems, departing from Jethro's land on his way back to Egypt.

father, he said, How is it that you are come so soon to day? And they said, An Egyptian delivered us out of the hand of the shepherds, and also drew water enough for us, and watered the flock. And he said unto his daughters, And where is he? why is it that ye have left the man? call him, that he may eat bread. And Moses was content to dwell with the man: and he gave Moses Zipporah his daughter.   Exodus 2, 15–21

71

THE PUNISHMENT
OF THE SONS OF CORAH

Details from Botticelli's Punishment of the Sons of Corah. *The parallel between the challenge to Moses's authority and opposition to the papacy hardly needed to be stressed in the inscription; nor did the parallel between the hellbound engulfment of the challengers and the papal threat of excommunication. It was made clear enough by the pairing of this scene with the* Giving of the Keys to St Peter.

And Moses said unto Corah, Be thou and all thy company before the Lord, thou, and they, and Aaron, to morrow; And take every man his censer, and put incense in them and bring ye before the Lord every man his censer, two hundred and fifty censers; thou also, and Aaron, each man his censer.
And they took every man his censer, and put fire in them, and laid incense thereon, and stood in the door of the tabernacle of the congregation with Moses and Aaron.   NUMBERS 16, 16–17

(Below) The story of the Punishment of the Sons of Corah is in the Book of Numbers, 16. This scene on the left-hand side of the fresco is the end of the story: "And the earth opened her mouth, and swallowed them up, and their houses, and all the men that appertained unto Corah, and all their goods."

In the central scene (left) Moses and Aaron behind him (detail above) call upon the rebels to present themselves with their censers and incense for burning at the altar, to see the judgement of the Lord. At Moses's invocation, the rebels are duly confounded.

The scene on the right of the fresco (detail below) shows the rebels gathering in threatening mood round the figure of Moses, accusing him "Ye take too much upon you". Botticelli brilliantly demonstrates his command of dramatic gesture and expression.

THE HEALING
OF THE LEPER

The more familiar events in this fresco are those in the background, where Christ is shown three times undergoing the Devil's temptation: on the left, in the wilderness (detail below), in the centre, at the top of the Temple of Solomon in Jerusalem (right) and on the right (far right) in the wilderness once more,

where Christ finally casts the Devil off the cliff. The devil appears as a friar, until in the last scene he is revealed as the monster he is beneath his habit. Christ returns to Galilee: there he shortly healed a leper, whom he commanded (Matthew 8) to "go thy way, shew thyself to the priest, and offer the gift that Moses commanded". This is almost certainly the scene shown in the foreground, with the leper over on the right of the altar with a man checking he has been cured and preparations for the purification according to Moses's command, given in Leviticus 14, proceeding in front of the altar. Two birds, the gift Christ meant, were required for the rite: they are brought by the woman bearing a basket on her head on the left. One of the birds was "killed in an earthen vessel over running water" and is evidently being brought to the High Priest by an acolyte in the foreground. The moral to be drawn from the story, of course, is that even Christ's work required the sanction of the priesthood, the leader of whom was now the Pope. The Temple in the centre reflects the architecture of Sixtus IV's own hostel or hospital in the Vatican city, a symbol perhaps of the pope's role as intermediary between the pilgrim and the presence of God.

74

Then was Jesus led up of the spirit into the wilderness to be tempted of the devil, and when he had fasted forty days and forty nights, he was afterward an hungred. And when the tempter came to him, he said, If thou be the Son of God, command that these stones be made bread. But he answered and said, It is written, Man shall not live by bread alone, but by every word that proceedeth out of the mouth of God.

Then the devil taketh him up into the holy city, and setteth him on a pinnacle of the temple. And said unto him, If thou be the Son of God, cast thyself down: for it is written. He shall give his angels charge concerning thee: and in their hands they shall bear thee up, lest at any time thou dash thy foot against a stone. Jesus said unto him, It is written again, Thou shalt not tempt the Lord thy God.

Again the devil taketh him up into an exceeding high mountain, and sheweth him all the kingdoms of the world, and the glory of them; And said unto him, All these things will I give thee, if thou wilt fall down and worship me. Then saith Jesus unto him, Get thee hence, Satan: for it is written, Thou shalt worship the Lord thy God, and him only shalt thou serve.

MATTHEW 4, 1–10

(Following page) Pietro Perugino: The Giving of the Keys to St Peter. *Perugino's limpid clarity and characteristic compositional simplicity are seen at their best in this very important scene of the Sistine Chapel decoration; it is justly a famous example of the ideal perspective explored so passionately in the 15th century.*

75

S. STEPHANUS ·
ROMANUS

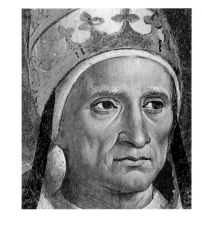

URBANUS ·
ROMANUS

S. CORNELIUS ·
ROMANUS

S. ANTHERUS · GRECUS

S. DIONISIUS ·
ROMANUS

S. ZEPHERINUS · ROMANUS

Left-hand wall of the Sistine Chapel (facing the altar):

The effigies of the popes flanking the first three windows from the altar: From right to left: Zephyrinus, Urban I, Anterus, Cornelius, Stephen I, Dionysius, *respectively 15th, 17th, 19th, 21st, 23rd and 25th supreme pontiffs.*

The figures are arranged in pairs between each window (or, in the entrance wall, fictive window), and disposed on either side of the pilasters rising through from the level below; the original decoration of the lunettes above them, before they were painted by Michelangelo, is not known.

The sequence of popes runs along both long walls and across the entrance wall; originally, it also ran across the altar wall, but the first popes, located there, were swept away by Michelangelo's Last Judgement. *Probably Christ was represented in the very centre, flanked by Peter and probably Paul, then Linus and Cletus, second and third popes. The chronological sequence is not followed down the wall, but alternates from side to side; so opposite these are the 16th, 18th, 20th, 22nd, 24th and 26th popes.*

A brief historical note on those represented here: St Zephyrinus (199–217) was accused by Hippolytus and Tertullian of being too tolerant towards the heresy that God the Father and God the Son were One Person. Urban I (222 – 230) was a Roman, governing the Church in the time of the Emperor Alexander Severus. Anterus was pontiff only one year, 235–236. Cornelius (251 – 252) had to face the bitter persecution of Decius and to decide how to treat those who renounced the Faith because of it. Stephen I (254–257) argued the case for the baptism of those who had renounced against St Cyprian of Carthage. The monk Dionysius (259–268) seems to have been occupied mostly with theological controversies emanating from that hotbed of them, the eastern Mediterranean.

S. SIXTUS · ROMANUS

S. ANICETUS · SIRUS

S. ELEUTE[RIUS]

S. EVARISTUS ·
GRECUS

IGINUS ·
GRECUS · EX ATHENIS

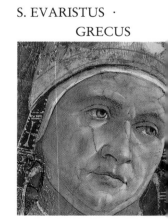

S. SIXTUS · ROMANUS

The left-hand wall of the Sistine Chapel, continued:

From right to left: Clement I, Evaristus, Sixtus I, Hyginus, Anicetus *and* Eleutherius, *respectively fourth, fifth, seventh, ninth, eleventh and thirteenth popes (though an alternative tradition would have them fifth, sixth, eighth, etc.).*

Apart from the Acts of the Apostles, the oldest surviving document of the early popes is a late 2nd-century catalogue of their names and dates: ending with Eleutherius, it contains 12 popes, and runs from the year 65 to 189. Quite possibly the humanist biographer of the popes and director of the Vatican Library, Plátina (his appointment was recorded in a fresco by Melozzo da Forlì, see page 11) was involved in the preparation of the Sistine Chapel list; perhaps Platina also provided the Latin inscriptions on the sill of the niche in which each stands, for example "Iginus grecus ex Athenis"; this is followed by the length of their pontificate in years and months, a record of their martyrdom where appropriate, and the dates of their pontificates.

Some historical notes: Clement I (89 – 97) is known for a letter to the Corinthians, taking them to task for disobeying their priests, and for a large body of other work popularly ascribed to him; according to the Liber Pontificialis, *he was martyred under Trajan. Evaristus, a Jew of Bethlehem, was pontiff 98–105. Sixtus I, a Roman, governed the Church from 116 to 125; several letters relating to the doctrine of the Trinity are attributed to him. Hyginus (137–140) was a Greek from Athens, and therefore inevitably regarded as a philosopher. The name of Anicetus, a Syrian (156–166), is linked to the rise of a dispute over the date of Easter. Pope Eleutherius (175–179), a Greek, was called upon to fight the heresy of Montanus, and was accused by Tertullian, as were others, of weakness and sloth in so doing.*

S. ANACLETUS ·
GRECUS ·
EX ATHENIS

THELESPHORUS ·
GRECUS

S. ALEXANDER ·
ROMANUS

S. PIUS · ITALUS

S. VICTOR · AFER

S. SOTHER ·
ITALUS · EX FUNDIS

The right-hand wall of the Sistine Chapel (looking towards the altar): The effigies of the popes flanking the first three windows from the altar. From left to right: Anacletus I, Alexander I, Telesphorus, Pius I, Soter and Victor I, respectively third (bis), sixth, eighth, tenth, twelfth and fourteenth popes. There was some confusion in the sources about the third pope, whether he was Cletus or Anacletus, or whether Cletus and Anacletus were the same pope or not. Here, to make sure, both Cletus and Anacletus were included: Cletus was originally on the altar wall. The series of popes was particularly appropriate to the overall scheme of the decoration of the Chapel, in which the correspondences between Old and New Testament were presented not simply for their own sake but also to emphasize the sanctity and sacred mission of the priesthood, led by and symbolized by the Pope. Many of these popes had in exemplary fashion fought heresy or the temporal enemies of the Church; many had been martyred. The Sistine Chapel was in many respects the equivalent of a secular ruler's palatine chapel, and it served in addition as the hall of conclave for the election of a new pope. The series of painted popes embodied the continuity of the office, the rich tradition of papal example, and the immutability of papal power and aims.

Some historical notes on these popes: Anacletus (77–88), as we have seen, was a phantom of Cletus. Alexander I (106–115), a Roman, is not distinguished. Telesphorus (126–136) is no more distinguished, despite his powerful presence in effigy, with his penetrating gaze and the urgency of the message from his book. Pius I was pontiff from 141 to 155. Soter (167–174) is remembered for the ardency of his charity towards the poor. Victor I (189–190) is known for his energetic part in the debate over the date of Easter, which he fixed on the Sunday following the 13th day after the March full moon.

S. CALISTUS ·
ROMANUS

S. PONTIANUS ·
PONTANUS

S. FABIANUS

84

The right-hand wall of the Sistine Chapel, continued:
From left to right: Calixtus I, Pontian, Fabian, Lucius I, Sixtus II and Felix I, respectively 16th, 18th, 20th, 22nd, 24th and 26th supreme pontiffs. (Lucius is incorrectly inscribed as a non-existent "Voius".) Each pope is as it were imprisoned in his niche with its scallop shell back, shown in marked foreshortening to compensate for the view from below. The succession of standing figures, dressed in similar long, ceremonial, dignified gowns, was hardly an opportunity for the artist to show off his skill. Nevertheless there was a determined attempt to vary as much as possible the poses of the individual popes, and to impart life into their features (quite arbitrarily conceived, of course). Particularly admired is the figure of Sixtus II, attributed to Botticelli. Most of these popes were done by the workshops, it seems, of Botticelli and Ghirlandaio. Obviously they never had as much importance as the scenes from the Lives of Christ and Moses below, and they were then almost entirely overshadowed by the lunettes painted by Michelangelo above them in colours quite dazzling by comparison.

Some historical notes on these popes: Calixtus I (212–222), a Roman, had a turbulent pontificate, full of theological controversy, notably with Hippolytus, the critic of Pope Zephyrinus (see page 79), over the definition of the Trinity. His tomb, located by persistent tradition in the Trastevere district of Rome, seems to have been one of the first to have been honoured by the construction of a basilica, the present Santa Maria di Trastevere. Pontian (230–235) was apparently martyred in the mines of Sardinia. Fabian, pontiff from 236 to 250, was also martyred, in the Decian persecution. Lucius I was pontiff from 235 to 254. Sixtus II (257–258) was martyred almost immediately after becoming Pope, together with St Lawrence, in the persecution of Valerian. Felix I (269–274) is known for his proclamation of the Divinity of Jesus Christ, an issue which took on great importance in the Council of Ephesus in 431.

. VOIUS · ROMANUS

S. SIXTUS ·
SECUNDUS · GRECUS

S. FELIX · ROMANUS

85

THE LATE FRESCOES
ON THE ENTRANCE WALL

The entrance wall of the Sistine Chapel: the effigies of the popes and (below) the *Resurrection of Christ* and the *Conflict over the Body of Moses*. The two scenes (below) constituted the conclusion of the *Lives of Christ and Moses*, with the *Conflict over the Body of Moses*, an apocryphal and very obscure story, being brought in

S. [CAIUS ·] DALMATA

S. MARCELLINUS ·
ROMANUS

obviously in order to match the *Resurrection of Christ*, the only appropriate ending to His cycle. Involved in the legend of the conflict over Moses's body by angels and devils was the fear that it might be made an object of idolatry, though the precise correspondence between this scene and the neighbouring one might have been Christ's harrowing of the devils in Hell. The 15th-century frescoes quite rapidly deteriorated, and were replaced in the later 16th century by frescoes of indifferent quality that have themselves deteriorated.

86

The artists concerned were Henri van den Broeck, known as Arrigo Fiammingo, who died in Rome in 1597, and Matteo da Leccio. They may well have preserved the basic composition of the 15th-century frescoes, but their late Mannerist style is dominated by the influence of Michelangelo, and in particular by that of his *Last Judgement* opposite. The Christ of the *Resurrection* is a weak repetition of the Christ of the opposite wall, and the devils in the *Conflict over the Body of Moses* derive from the nudes of the Damned there.

The 15th-century effigies of the popes, concluding the series, have, however, survived. From left to right, they are Caius, Marcellinus, Eutychian and Marcellus, respectively 28th, 29th, 27th and 30th popes. Caius, whose inscription reveals him to be Dalmatian (Slav), was pontiff from 283 to 296 and was supposedly related to the Emperor Diocletian. Marcellinus (296–304) had to face the horrendous persecution this Emperor instituted; according to a tradition ac-

S. MARCELLUS · ROMANUS

S. EUTICHIANUS

cepted by St Augustine, he lacked the strength himself to stand up to it, but later was redeemed by his penitent reassertion of the Faith and was duly martyred. Eutychian was pontiff from 275 to 283. Marcellus (307–309) is the last of these popes, and the last but one of the pre-Constantinian popes (he was followed by Eusebius, 309–310).

JOHN SHEARMAN

RAPHAEL'S TAPESTRIES FOR THE SISTINE CHAPEL

Julius II was succeeded by a pope of very different temper, character, and education; for Leo X had been Giovanni de' Medici, son of Lorenzo, and the contrasting experiences of his life had left him a man of patience as well as culture. With Julius he shared one priority, the assertion of the Papal Majesty, but he had a greater respect for convention, and for mostly positive reasons would probably not have been the man to tear down Old St Peter's and begin a new basilica. However, that great and apparently interminable enterprise was one of the problems with which he had to deal, and with it the consequence that still more of the major ceremonies of the calendar were performed in the Sistine Chapel. We have seen that Sixtus always intended his chapel, like its predecessors, to be hung with tapestries on great occasions, and it seems that he in fact supplied some. But Leo was the first to order a tapestry set which was intended, first, to make a precise 'fit' with the architectural realities of the place and, secondly, to be figural, and indeed to complement in one further degree the historical and symbolic content of the Sistina's decoration. It would certainly have appealed to Leo's sense of history and of propriety that such a commission was a recreation of the great endowments of the Roman basilicas of the Carolingian Popes Leo III

The tapestries representing the Lives of Sts Peter and Paul *to designs by Raphael were commissioned by Leo X and were intended to be hung along the lower 'storey' of the Chapel, as they are seen here. The tapestries were stolen in the Sack of Rome and it was some time before they were recovered. On the occasion of Raphael Year, 1983, they were rehung in the positions for which they were intended, as shown.*

and Leo IV; but nobody could have been unaware that such tapestries, even as recently as Nicholas V's gift to St Peter's, had been proper only to basilicas, and that this set expressed the new status of the chapel. The commission may also have been a criticism of the vertical imbalance resulting from the intervention of Julius and Michelangelo; what is certain is that the effect was to restore the balance.

The commission was given to Raphael in 1515, and within two years he had designed and painted ten large cartoons – full-sized coloured drawings in gouache – which were despatched to Brussels for weaving (seven cartoons survive in London). The project was one of the highest priority to the artist, not only for the supreme importance of the place but also because it tested him in direct confrontation with Michelangelo. He made here a contribution to the tradition of history painting in some respects of more significance – to artists such as Rubens and Poussin – than that of the Stanze frescoes. The Brussels workshop of Pieter van Aelst represented the highest quality available in tapestry, and it could work with the finest dyes, and gold and silver thread; but the technique then in use entailed the reversal of design in weaving. Raphael therefore had to think, with that peculiar clarity which so distinguished him, of the precise visual relationships to the existing decoration which would best create a new unity. The results were visible at least in part before his death in 1520, for seven tapestries were delivered and hung in the Chapel late in 1519; all ten had been delivered before Leo's death in 1521.

The tapestries were certainly planned for specific positions, for their dimensions and proportions vary greatly; and it is obvious that their vertical borders replace the painted pilasters separating fictive tapestries in the lowest zone painted for Sixtus. Using dimensions,

The Lives of Sts Peter and Paul, *figured on the tapestries, were chosen and illustrated in full and careful accord with the pictorial decoration of the Chapel. After the Old Testament on the ceiling and on one wall, and the New Testament on the other wall, the Acts of the Apostles on the 'ground floor' were entirely appropriate. The individual scenes were also harmonized:* St Paul preaching at Athens, *for example, was placed under the* Descent from Mt Sinai *(with the* Ten Commandments*);* St Peter healing the lame man *beneath the* Purification of the Leper.

(Above) the Miraculous Draught of Fish. *These tapestries were woven in the Netherlands to designs prepared by Raphael in Rome, seven of which have survived and are in the Victoria and Albert Museum in London. The Netherlandish tapestry-weavers were acknowledged throughout Europe as the finest of the craft.*

direction of lighting, historical sequence, and relevant pictorial conventions, a reconstruction may be made and tested; in fact in 1983, in one of the most memorable events of the Raphael Anniversary Year, the reconstruction was even tested by a rehanging. But a full rehanging has been impossible since 1527, when the tapestries were stolen, for by the time they were returned Michelangelo's *Last Judgement* had removed the spaces for tapestries either side of the altar (the *Miraculous Draught of Fishes* on the right, the *Stoning of St Stephen* on the left). There were some unexpected results of the rehanging in 1983. Most spectators felt that the Chapel had never looked so beautiful in living memory. And no doubt this was partly because the colours of the tapestries, faded and altered as they are in part, appeared harmonious with and structurally related to those of the frescoes above in a quite unforeseen degree; for example, the dark red frame immediately around the 'picture' of each tapestry was seen very clearly to imitate the illusionistic 'porphyry' frames round the Sixtine histories.

The Leonine tapestries are made up of two groups, four from the life of St Peter, six from the life of St Paul. They extend and complement the existing histories (ending hitherto with the *Resurrection of Christ*) by presenting a sequence, beginning with four pairs, of critically significant examples of the rôles of the two founders of the Roman Church, examples which also illustrate their missions separately to the Jews and the Gentiles respectively. The Petrine set is naturally placed beneath the Christ cycle (Peter is Christ's Vicar, and prince of the apostles), while the Pauline set as appropriately falls beneath that of Moses (the *doctor gentium* beneath the *doctor populi*); this arrangement also places Peter on the Epistle side of the altar, Paul on the Gospel side, relating their missions to the destinations of the two parts of the New Testament. That it also places Paul, apparently, in the position of honour on the (proper) right of the altar may seem strange now, but it was well known, and in fact demonstrated in 1515, that the best established tradition placed the twin Founders in this way.

The pairing of the tapestries, inspired by the typological structure of the Sistine history cycles, begins with the selection of the fisherman Peter and the sinner Paul (in the *Stoning of Stephen*), and continues with the appointment of the two founders, the consignment of the Keys to Peter in the *Feed my Sheep* on the right, and the revelation to the 'chosen vessel' in the *Conversion of Saul* on the left. These opposed appointments are placed below the Institution of the Written and Evangelical Law in the frescoes above, and it is clear that vertical thematic relationships are being made. So, again, in the next pair – which as a pair illustrate the first miracles of Peter and Paul – the *Healing of the Lame Man at the Beautiful Gate* is placed beneath Botticelli's *Purification of the Leper*; to the superficial thematic correspondence of healing there is to be added, partly because leprosy is a metaphor of sin, a deeper doctrinal point, for the fresco above clarifies the Power of the Keys in the New Covenant which is exercised in the tapestry where Peter admits the Lame Man to the Heavenly Temple. These pairings and vertical relationships continue. But an odd feature of the commission is that it ends with one tapestry in the Pauline set which was placed outside the screen, not opposite a Petrine tapestry but opposite the choir-gallery, the *pulpitum*. This tapestry, *Paul Preaching at Athens*, where the Apostle speaks to the Gentile philosophers, was to be below the fresco (the *Promulgatio*) where Moses descends from Mount Sinai with the tablets of the Law and confronts idolatry. When the tapestry was hung the Prince of Preachers would seem to bring his message out to those beyond the screen, excluded from the corporate Papal Chapel, and the tapestry (initially the cartoon, in reverse) was so designed that Paul's audience would seem, to some extent illusionistically, to be continued and completed by the modern crowd.

Detail of Raphael's tapestry, St Paul preaching at Athens. *The vigorous figure of St Paul has a monumental quality that Raphael had not yet achieved in his earlier frescoes in the Stanze, and that was in part a response to Michelangelo.*

The design of the tapestries, indeed, is no less brilliantly responsive to their situation than are their themes. The *Healing of the Lame Man* may stand as an example, where gesture and the performance of ritual, the superimposition of temple pediments, colour (Peter in yellow and blue under the High Priest), and tripartite design all accord with Botticelli's *Purification of the Leper*. But further, Raphael built into his opposed triads of tapestries within the screen an overall

Raphael's tapestry of St Peter healing the Lame Man. *The composition is divided and dominated by its luxuriant twisting columns, typical of the increasingly loaded decorativeness of the later Raphael and his workshop.*

centralized and triple rhythm which is harmonious with the larger thematic and visual design of the Sistine histories. There is much to be said for the view that the contribution made by Leo and Raphael to the Sistina was the most sympathetic and concordant, in some ways the most intelligent, addition ever made there; and certainly the character of that intelligence expresses the conciliatory instinct of this pope as accurately as it does the extraordinary sensitivity of his artist.

The vividness of the depiction of the lame and crippled invites comparison with the depiction of the same subject by Masaccio and Masolino in the Brancacci Chapel in the Carmine in Florence nearly 100 years earlier.

91

Between 1508 and 1512 Michelangelo laboured on the Sistine Ceiling. He undertook the task at the behest of Pope Julius II with great reluctance, for he considered himself primarily a sculptor rather than a painter, and was also averse to postponing an earlier commission he had received from Julius, the construction of the Pope's tomb in St Peter's basilica. He was about 33 years old when he began. Although in the early stages he employed some assistants, he soon went about painting the immense surface practically single-handed. When he was finished, he had created one of the greatest art monuments of all time – a fact recognized by his contemporaries and confirmed by the appreciation of connoisseurs and art historians in the centuries that have intervened to this day. Through the ages Michelangelo's painting style has not appealed to everyone's taste, but nobody had dared deny how breathtaking was his achievement. "There is no other work to compare with this for excellence, nor could there be," said Michelangelo's contemporary, the artist Giorgio Vasari in his *Lives of the Artists*. "It is scarcely possible even to imitate

JOHN O'MALLEY, S.J.

THE THEOLOGY BEHIND MICHELANGELO'S CEILING

The monumental architectural structure of illusion created by Michelangelo on the vault of the Chapel culminated in the nine rectangles, alternatively of larger and smaller size, forming the 'lid' of a heavy framework of arches and ribs. Perched or otherwise supported on the basement of the structure are 20 nude figures, male youths of an extraordinary beauty, that some say are genii or angels. It is fairly clear, however, that their metaphysical status is the same as that of the architecture they adorn, a novel version of the classical Atlas figure or caryatid. At least Ascanio Condivi, Michelangelo's biographer, says as much: "But not less admirable than all this is the part that does not belong to the story. I mean certain nudes (ignudi)..."

what Michelangelo accomplished."[1] Vasari and others like him were impressed by Michelangelo's technical skills and by the revolution in style that his work expressed and presaged. Vasari was awed by the sheer physical discomfort the task entailed – "having to work with his face turned upwards" – but that was in the long run only a minor factor to be taken into account in assessing the Ceiling.[2] Much more important were the skills in depiction, the mastery of foreshortening, the grace and effective arrangement of the figures, the convincing architectural framework, the sheer extent of the surface to be painted, the sublime beauty of the whole. "Indeed," continued Vasari enthusiastically,[3] "painters no longer need to seek new inventions, novel attitudes, clothed figures, fresh ways of expression, different arrangements, or sublime subjects, for this work contains every perfection possible under those headings." The history of art has subsequently shown that Vasari here rather badly overstated his case, but there is no doubt that that fateful day in 1512 when the Ceiling was unveiled to the public marked a great watershed. Painting would never again be the same.

Since Vasari's day art critics and historians have continued to analyse

Like caryatids or Atlas figures, the function of the ignudi is to support something, in this case the bronze medallions that do "belong to the story". They are also related to putti who hold coats of arms, for the oak leaves and acorns by them refer to Sixtus IV and Julius II's family coat of arms, their family being Della Rovere, "of the oak".

Since the ignudi had no narrative or symbolic meaning, but were only decorative, Michelangelo could give free rein to his imagination in their depiction. They might be called expression for expression's sake. Though they are highly expressive, what they express is something visual, and can only approximately be put into words.

These ignudi were obviously close to

The Persian Sibyl (below), the prophet Daniel (above). In the centre, the Separation of the sky and water. Opinion is divided among experts on the exact interpretation of the Creation scenes, and Michelangelo's reticence in giving pictorial clues, while increasing the mystery and solemnity of the grand happenings, has made absolute certainty difficult to obtain.

Between the families of the Ancestors in the window coves, the Creation of the sun and moon. The Almighty is engaged in a twofold action, giving the artist the opportunity of a daring perspective interplay in the extraordinary duplication of God's figure.

Between the thoughtful prophet Jeremiah (below) and the superb Libyan Sibyl (above) is the first scene of the Creation surrounded by a nebulous void. It will be observed that the order of events, from the entrance to the altar wall, is reversed from the historical sequence. It proceeds logically, however, from divinity and purity, as displayed on the altar wall, towards the weaknesses and failings of humanity throughout history.

Below, the punishment of Haman, an episode in the story of Esther and Ahasuerus. Above, the episode in which God inflicts punishment on the Jews by a plague of snakes, but also sends forgiveness and salvation through the healing powers of the Brazen Serpent made by Moses. In the centre the figure of the prophet Jonah, recoils half blinded by the light that the other prophets and Sibyls seem dimly to perceive. This image of revelation concludes the wall cycle and is both its perspective and moral focus.

The insertion of the *Last Judgement* into the harmonious, indeed serene, decorative scheme of the Sistine Chapel was an extremely bold and disruptive undertaking.

The disruption is some measure of the changed nature of the times, even if the original stimulus to the commission had been the deterioration of the frescoes that were there. It need not be stressed that between the completion of the Ceiling in 1512 and the painting of the *Judgement* in the 1540s there had supervened the traumatic Sack of Rome and the unresolved crisis of the Reformation.

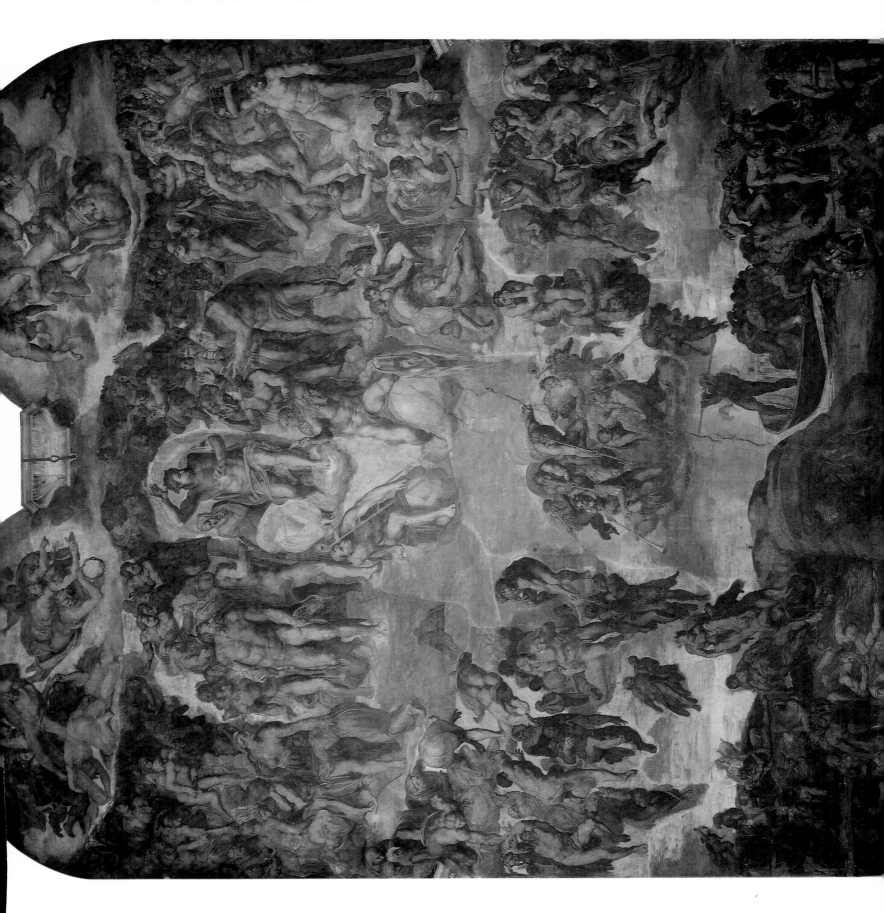

MICHELANGELO'S GREAT MASTERPIECE: THE SISTINE CHAPEL CEILING

Michelangelo invented an illusionistic architectural structure, transforming the Chapel into a kind of barrel-vaulted cathedral, rising from its massive base towards an open sky. The base is constituted by the monumental thrones on which the *Sibyls* and *Prophets* majestically sit, with their *genii* beside on the throne-backs and *putti* of fictive marble on the arms. Separating these thrones are the hollows or coves (over the windows) in which the *Ancestors of Christ* are painted, and above them, in the remaining space, nudes of fictive bronze. The four corner fields, the so called 'spandrels', are the largest single fields for painting, given over to dramatic biblical subjects. On the entablature that surmounts the thrones, which runs all the way round the four walls, are seated, in five separate groups, the famous *"ignudi"*, arranged in contrasting pairs, in diverse attitudes – in extraordinarily diverse attitudes. Between them the pairs hold by ribands a fictive bronze medallion with a further biblical scene on it. Finally, in the very centre of the ceiling, like veils spread across arches, are nine scenes from Genesis, in alternating sizes, corresponding to the presence or absence in the bay of *ignudi*.

large painting depicting the Story of the Flood, exalting the mission of Noah. For this reason it is placed in the middle of the Noah sequence; chronologically it should have come after the following scene, Noah's Sacrifice.

Between the Erythraean Sibyl and the impressive prophet Isaiah, there is the scene which most scholars describe as showing Noah's sacrifice. The Sistine Chapel ceiling as a whole represents the first acts of man after the expulsion from Paradise: the new sin of man and the new covenant with God.

In the centre, the scene of the Fall: the first Man and Woman reach out to touch the Tree of Knowledge, around which coils a snake, the upper part of whose body and head is that of a woman — an odd relapse into an earlier symbolism. Beyond the Tree, Adam and Eve are expelled from Paradise by an avenging angel.

Between the prophet Ezechiel (below) and the Cumaean Sibyl (above) is the scene of the Creation of Eve who is plucked forth from Adam's fifth rib. Noteworthy are the splendidly composed nudes, in a variety of spontaneous poses, surrounding the biblical scenes.

At the centre of the vault the place of honour is reserved for the most famous of the Sistine Chapel paintings — the Creation of Man. Here the central theme of Genesis is depicted in one of the most dynamic expressions of imagery known to Western art. The tension and flow of cosmic creation are concentrated in the vibrant touch of God's finger.

O man, take account
of how splendidly God has made you;
your bodily form
exceeds all others ...

PIETRO MARSI, SERMON PREACHED IN THE SISTINE CHAPEL, ABOUT 1480

He designed each ignudo separately; by contrast, the fictive bronze nudes in the coves are mirror images of one another, done in reverse directions from the same cartoon.

Michelangelo's heart, and are certainly related to the Slaves he carved for Julius II's tomb, which were again architectural figures essentially like caryatids or Atlas figures.

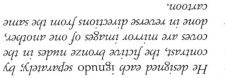

The Ceiling has caught the attention of art historians especially in the 20th Century.

Though they serve chiefly perhaps as elements of the illusionistic architecture of the vault, the fictive bronze medallions borne by the ten pairs of ignudi *all have stories to tell, complementing the smaller of the stories taken from Genesis on the central part of the Ceiling. In a decorative and a more general sense they constitute clusters offsetting the larger scenes of the centre of the Ceiling, and so are a significant element in its overall rhythm. The stories the medallions tell, which no contemporary record identifies, are taken from the Book of Kings and from other parts of the Old Testament, and seem all to serve as ex-*empla, *as moral tales illustrating the consequences or catastrophes following on obedience or disobedience to divine law. They are painted in a bronze monochrome, enlivened by highlights in gold; there was a large place for precious materials in the Renaissance vision of ideal classical architecture.*

Michelangelo's skills and techniques. The restorations now under way provide them with an unprecedented opportunity to further their study and to examine close-up just how the Ceiling was painted and to see almost with Michelangelo's own eyes the problems that had to be overcome. Several of the contributions to this volume are the first fruits of this experience and give promise of a new appreciation for Michelangelo's technique, including his use of colour. We shall be the beneficiaries of studies of the Sistine ceiling as it has never been studied before, even by Michelangelo's contemporaries, who saw it before it was damaged by water leaking from the roof and covered by the grime of centuries.

There is, however, another aspect of the Ceiling that has engaged the attention of art historians, especially in the 20th century. As they have studied that complex surface, they have asked what it signifies and what plan underlies the choice of subjects. Is some philosophical, anthropological, or theological message – or series of messages – intended to be conveyed? In more technical terms, what is the programme that inspires all the paintings of the Ceiling – by whom was it conceived, and what does it mean?[4]

Ascanio Condivi, a contemporary of Michelangelo and one of his first biographers, states quite simply that the Ceiling depicts "almost all of the Old Testament."[5] As a generic statement Condivi's description hits the mark fairly well. When we begin to survey the Ceiling, we see the cycle of seven Prophets and five Sibyls of heroic proportion framing the Ceiling in their niches running along the four sides. Down the centre stretch the nine panels with scenes from the opening chapters of Genesis, and in the medallions placed on the sides of the smaller panels are scenes taken from some of the historical books of the Old Testament. In the four corners are other historical episodes, like David's slaying of Goliath. In the lunettes along the walls, over the windows, and in the triangular spaces above them are figures from the Old Testament representing the ancestors of Christ. Although the so-called "wisdom literature", like the Psalms and Proverbs, is not explicitly presented, the prophetic and historical books are as comprehensibly in evidence as anyone could desire. Moses is notably absent, of course, for his story was fully told below in the frescoes painted for Sixtus IV.

Close observers have noted, however, the inadequacy of Condivi's description and the many iconographical and iconological problems it fails to take into account. Why were *these* Prophets and *these* Sibyls chosen, why *these* scenes from Genesis – why Genesis at all? Students of the Ceiling have rejected out of hand that it might be an altogether haphazard conglomeration, for that thesis fits neither with what we know about Michelangelo nor with what we know about the highly sophisticated Renaissance culture that produced him.

The problem is immensely complicated. A solution requires, in the first place, a correct identification of the scenes and figures, and even Michelangelo's contemporaries have sometimes failed us in this regard. The scene now generally identified as the *Sacrifice of Noah,* placed between the *Deluge* and the *Fall,* was thought by both Vasari and Condivi to be the *Sacrifice of Cain and Abel.* Vasari stated that the medallions represented scenes from the books of Kings and Samuel, yet it now seems certain that this description is only partially accurate. The fact that the medallions do not follow a strictly historical sequence from one part of the Bible raises in pointed fashion the

PROPHETS AND SIBYLS

question of why episodes were interspersed, for instance, from the book of Maccabees and why they were placed where they were. The diligent research of the past few decades has notably advanced the identification of the subjects of the paintings, but the cleaning of the Ceiling will surely enable historians further to confirm and, if necessary, correct their findings.

There is a related problem. How much of the Ceiling is purely decorative, and how much of those seemingly decorative parts have a meaning not generally recognized? Do the nude young men, for instance, so prominent on the four corners of each of the nine episodes from the opening chapters of Genesis, represent anything beyond human beauty and serve merely an architectonic function, or are they angels intimately related to the iconology of the Ceiling, as has been proposed recently by several art historians?[6] The garlands of oak leaves and acorns that some of these *ignudi* hold surely refer to the oak and acorns of Pope Julius II's coat of arms, but do they signify anything further?[7] Questions like these abound.

But, even with all the subjects correctly identified, the central problem still remains, and is even intensified. What is the overall plan, and what vision underlies it? Is the vision Michelangelo's, or did he give expression to a programme articulated by others? These are the questions that have challenged art historians and given rise to an immense literature on the subject.

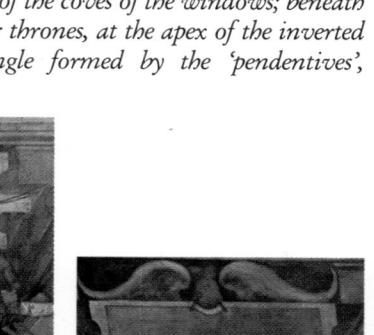

The putti *bearing the tablets with the names of the Prophets and Sibyls constitute a series of "ignudi" in themselves. Each* Prophet *and* Sibyl *is set on one of the 'pendentives' that descend on either side of the coves of the windows; beneath their thrones, at the apex of the inverted triangle formed by the 'pendentives',*

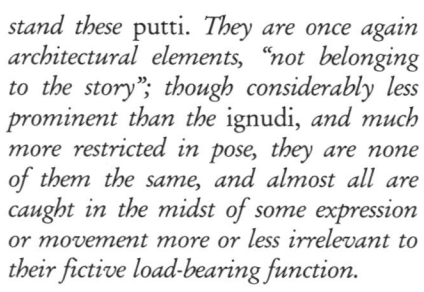

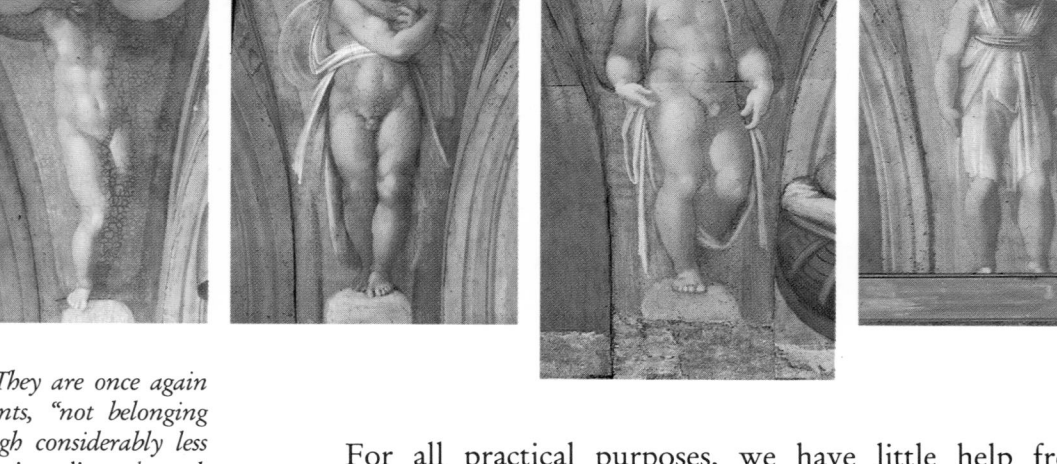

stand these putti. *They are once again architectural elements, "not belonging to the story"; though considerably less prominent than the* ignudi, *and much more restricted in pose, they are none of them the same, and almost all are caught in the midst of some expression or movement more or less irrelevant to their fictive load-bearing function.*

For all practical purposes, we have little help from documents contemporary with the painting. We know that Julius II first gave Michelangelo the commission to paint the twelve *Apostles* in the positions now occupied by the *Prophets* and *Sibyls* and that he wanted the rest of the area covered simply with decorations. This was to replace the blue sky filled with gold stars painted for his uncle, Sixtus IV. Michelangelo, in a letter of 1523 addressed to his friend Gianfrancesco Fattucci, informs us that he soon convinced the Pope that the original commission would be a "poor thing" and the Pope then gave him a free hand to do whatever he wanted – "quello che io volevo."[8] From that statement, which is the only direct comment we have from Michelangelo or anybody else on the origins of the Ceiling, we could easily infer that the resulting programme was Michelangelo's and Michelangelo's alone.

Some art historians take Michelangelo more or less at his word. To do so almost necessarily implies a relatively simple and straightforward programme, for no one maintains that Michelangelo had a scholar's knowledge of philosophy or theology. I say "relatively", for it is now clear that the Ceiling poses problems that do not admit simplistic explanations. Michelangelo was, after all, a devout reader of the Bible and of commentaries on it, and he admired during his early years in Florence the great religious reformer Savonarola. During those same years he at least to some extent associated with the humanists and Neoplatonic philosophers connected with the Medici household. He loved Dante, was himself a poet, and happened to be a genius as well. He cannot, therefore, be excluded as the originator of the programme, and, even if there were another source for it, some contribution by Michelangelo would seem likely. As in every work of art, moreover, the translation of idea into image was altogether the artist's creation. The revival of Neoplatonic philosophy in Renaissance Florence led some scholars, notably Charles de Tolnay, to an interpretation of the Ceiling along those lines.[9] The generic and casual quality of whatever seeming Neoplatonism we find in Michelangelo's sonnets, however, has made critics doubtful that such an interpretation is altogether adequate.[10] Edmund Leach's "structuralist" interpretation, of the type

The Prophets *and* Sibyls *are probably the most prominent figures on the entire Ceiling, and certainly the largest – offering the greatest opportunity for Michelangelo's powers of bold, monumental design. They are also marvellously expressive, seemingly filled with the divine wisdom by which they are possessed, sometimes vehement, sometimes tormented; there is no precedent for them in the history of art except perhaps the very different, but also highly expressive,* Prophets *carved by*

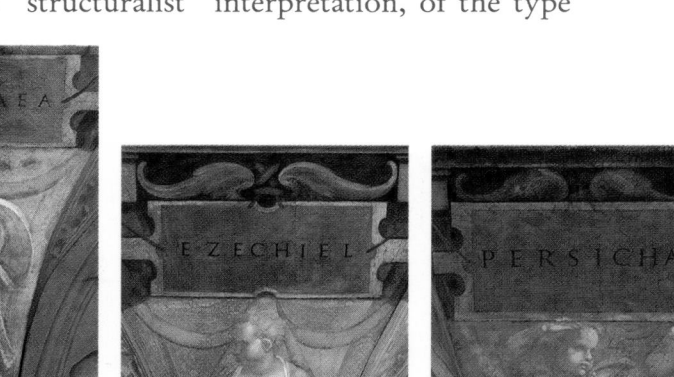

made famous by Claude Lévi-Strauss, while intriguing, does not touch the historical question of the origins of the programme.[11]

The weight of scholarly opinion today favours the hypothesis that some "learned theologian" or group of theologians planned what Michelangelo executed, or at least that he had some theologian as a fairly regular consultant. The more complicated – yet unified and coherent – the programme is seen to be, the more necessary these hypothetical theologians. But who were they, or who was he? Where do we look to find them or him? By what criteria do we judge the plausibility of a candidacy?

"Plausibility" is – and seems destined to remain – the operative word. The search for candidates has been extraordinarily diligent;

Donatello for the campanile *of Florence Cathedral. Here, however, the series of Prophets is conjoined with a series of Sibyls, unmistakably extending the message of Salvation beyond Judaeism and into the classical world – a reflection of the instincts and enthusiastic classicism of the Renaissance in general and of Rome and the papal court in particular. The Sibyls owe their place here to the tradition that they prophesied the Coming of Christ before the writing of the Gospels, bringing Revelation to the Gentiles independently of biblical testimony.*

THE PROPHET ZECHARIAH

All this was done, that it might be fulfilled
which was spoken by the prophet saying,
Tell ye the daughter of Sion,
Behold, thy King cometh unto thee,
meek, and sitting upon an ass,
and a colt the foal of an ass
MATTHEW 21,4–5; ZECHARIAH 9,9

archives have been combed and theological treatises devoured. Yet, for all that, no word has been unearthed that indisputably ties a given theologian or school of theologians to the programme of the Ceiling. One cannot predict the future, but given the high quality of the research of the past 50 years, it is unlikely that the kind of explicit and conclusive evidence I am talking about will ever come to light. We must content ourselves, it seems, with likelihood and speculation.

Older theological works like St Augustine's *City of God* and St Bonaventure's *Tree of Life* have been proposed as full or partial keys to the programme, with contemporaries of Michelangelo like Egidio da Viterbo and Marco Vigerio as more immediate transmitters of the visions underlying these works.[12] Michelangelo's known esteem for Savonarola has led to the suggestion that Sante Pagnini, one of Savonarola's disciples, was directly or indirectly the contemporary source.[13] Each of these proposals, as well as others like them, has its merits, but also its problems, which critics have been quick to point out. The arrangement and liturgical functions of the Chapel have in almost every case also been adduced as influencing the choice and location of scenes and figures, and that is a proposal that, at least in the abstract, has indubitable merits.

An extremely important assumption underlies all theological interpretations that demand some other source for the programme than Michelangelo himself. That assumption is that the figures and scenes have more than one meaning. Besides standing for what is actually depicted, they have a further and deeper sense. The prophet Jonah, for instance, stands not only for himself but is also a "type" or "sign" of Christ, who according to Matthew's and Luke's Gospels (12, 38 – 41; 16, 4; Luke 11, 29) spent three days like Jonah in the belly of the whale, i.e., in the tomb after His death and before His resurrection.

The basis for such multiple meanings is incontrovertibly sound. As the relationship between Jonah and Christ illustrates, it finds some justification in the New Testament itself. Almost from the beginning of Christianity such a "figurative" or "allegorical", as distinct from a "literal" or "historical", interpretation of Scripture enjoyed favour with almost all exegetes. In certain circles during the Italian Renaissance, this allegorical mode of interpretation was intensely employed. Some art historians have gone so far as to speak of a "cult of the enigmatic" by Michelangelo and his generation.[14] Indeed, this penchant for the esoteric would seem to be according to them a hallmark of the "Renaissance theology" that inspired the Ceiling. This means in practice that not only must "allegory" be invoked from time to time to help explain the Ceiling, but that it is an interlocking and all-pervasive system that descends to the minutest details. As the system has been applied, it practically eliminates purely decorative elements in the Ceiling and is able to discover in most instances a single, not easily accessible, theme that links together all the parts and the hundreds of figures. The Ceiling that results is therefore understood by them to be dominated, for instance, by an underlying programme about the Church, about the Eucharist, or about Pentecost.

This brings us to the problem of the "Renaissance theology" of which the Ceiling is supposedly an expression. The lamentable fact is that the Renaissance has been an era singularly neglected by historians of theology – a result of deep prejudices springing from the Protestant Reformation and the Catholic Counter-Reformation alike. Despite some recent studies that have begun to remedy the situation, our

The prophet Zechariah occupies the pendentive descending to the entrance wall of the Chapel: he is seated in profile, with his legs turned out towards the viewer, at the desk at which he composed. Beside him are two genii embodying his heavenly inspiration.
Zechariah is one of the most important of the minor prophets; his book is studded with apocalyptic visions. One of his notable prophecies was the entrance of Christ into Jerusalem, and he has much to say of the Temple there. It is difficult, however, not to say hazardous, to attempt to read into the physiognomy given him by Michelangelo either this or that passage in the book or his general character as a prophet.

The Delphic Sibyl *is placed on the first pendentive from the entrance wall on the left-hand side of the Chapel facing the altar. With her* genii *who consult a book, and her own scroll, she is conceived very much in the manner of a prophet, rather than with any reference to the procedure of the oracle of Apollo at Delphi that was closed down by the Christian Emperor Theodosius in the 4th century. In Michelangelo's brilliant invention, she turns great rolling eyes and parts her lips as if she were under the actual seizure of her prophecy.*

Dies irae, dies illa
Solvet saeclum in favilla
Teste David cum Sibylla

The day of anger, that day
Will undo the age in fire
As David said and the Sibyl
FROM THE REQUIEM

knowledge remains piecemeal and unsystematic. One conclusion has, however, emerged: Renaissance theology is a richer and more complex phenomenon than had previously been assumed.[15]

The thesis could be defended, in fact, that in the decades immediately preceding the Reformation it was in Rome that the most varied, original and creative theological work was being done in all Europe. Whereas north of the Alps theology laboured until Luther almost exclusively within the problems and methods of scholasticism as found in its late-medieval exponents, Rome anticipated the revival of the study of the Fathers of the Church and of St Thomas Aquinas that we associate with later generations.[16] It similarly anticipated critical study of the text of the Bible and of the Hebrew language.[17] Even more striking perhaps was a new kind of interpenetration between Christianity and the study of the pagan classics, which we automatically consider typical of the Renaissance.

Nothing is perhaps more characteristic of classical culture than its concern with rhetoric – that is, its "pursuit of eloquence", its cultivation of the art of public speaking or oratory. At the papal court by the time of Julius II a new "rhetorical" way of preaching had been devised that was a result of this particular conjunction of the classical tradition of oratory with the Christian preoccupation with preaching or "proclamation of the Word."[18] Since the sermons at the court normally dealt with passages from the Bible, the new "sacred rhetoric" had implications for exegesis.

This rhetoric was for the most part a revival of the art of panegyric, i.e. a revival of speeches that recounted and praised the deeds of a

hero. Since it dealt with the life and actions of a great person or even a deity, this kind of oratory fixed on supposedly historical facts in an historical setting. Thus, alongside a tradition in the Renaissance of heavy allegorizing, there developed as well a more straightforward approach when the principles of panegyric were applied to the Old and New Testaments. Moreover, since panegyric has praise as its usual purpose, it forced certain themes to emerge with great prominence. Important among these would be celebration of the goodness and "dignity" of God, Christ, the saints, or the created universe – to present them as worthy objects of praise.

THE PROPHET JOEL

These reflections on certain aspects of theology in Renaissance Rome do not automatically invalidate the highly allegorical interpretations of the Ceiling that some art historians have proposed, for Michelangelo's "theological expert," if he had one, could still very well have been somebody whose interest in hidden meanings was as pronounced, say, as Egidio da Viterbo's. What these reflections do provide, however, is another way of "reading" the Ceiling and helping us see it with different eyes.[19] We thereby try to enter the minds of some of those who first saw the results, especially preachers at the court.

While preachers and theologians of the Italian Renaissance would have seen the events and personages depicted on the Ceiling in their

And it shall come to pass afterward, that I will pour out my spirit upon all flesh; and your sons and your daughters shall prophesy, and your old men shall dream dreams, your young men shall see visions ... And I will shew wonders in the heavens and in the earth, blood, and fire, and pillars of smoke ... JOEL 2, 28 – 32

The prophet Joel *occupies the pendentive opposite the* Delphic Sibyl, *the first from the entrance wall on the right-hand side of the Chapel facing the altar. He reads his message urgently from the scroll he has extended before him. Joel's book in the Old Testament is entirely taken up with the theme of the triumph of the Jewish people and the punishment to be wrought upon their enemies by the advent of Jehovah.*

historical immediacy, they never meant to challenge the old assumption that the function of the Old Testament was to point to the New and that it in many particulars foreshadowed it, which the correlation between the Moses cycle and the Christ cycle on the lower walls demonstrates beyond a doubt (cf. Luke 24,27). Nonetheless, it must be stated at the outset that the most secure and best known of the allegorical meanings of the Old Testament were those clearly grounded on texts from the liturgy or the New Testament, as in the case of Jonah. These meanings would have been accessible to most persons who had entrance to the Chapel. They are relatively few in number but of great importance, and I will point them out as we move along.

To help us appreciate the Ceiling as it was appreciated by contemporaries of Michelangelo, I propose to utilize in this essay both the findings and hypotheses of art historians, who have so enriched our understanding of the Ceiling, and the results of my own researches

110

THE PROPHET ISAIAH

The prophet Isaiah *is placed beside the* Delphic Sibyl *on the second pendentive of the left-hand wall of the Chapel facing the altar. He is interrupted from thought by the inspiration brought to him by the putto at his shoulder. Isaiah's prophecies are some of the most important of the Old Testament, and also its first, and largest, book of prophecies. It is full of Messianic references, and dominated by a vision of the providential unfolding of history; it is perhaps best known for Isaiah's strictures on Babylon, reflecting the fall of the city and the liberation of Israel from its empire.*

into the sermons preached in the Sistine Chapel itself during the Renaissance. Once the Ceiling is fully restored, art historians will then again be willing to address the subject with the skills of their discipline. Until that time, all that somebody like myself, an historian of religious culture, not an art historian, can do is present their earlier findings in a partial way and relate them to my own specialization.

Let us turn to the Ceiling itself. Because of their central position, the nine panels from Genesis perhaps first strike our eyes. But the *Prophets* and *Sibyls* cover a similarly large space, the space that Pope Julius was especially concerned to have painted. In fact, they are equally, or more, dominant than the central panels. At once we catch a deceptive flaw in Condivi's description, for the *Sibyls* are pagan priestesses and never appear in the Old Testament. Why then are they here, and here so emphatically?

To spectators of the Ceiling during the Renaissance, the Sibyls would represent one of their deepest convictions. Whereas God spoke most authoritatively through the Prophets of the Hebrew tradition, elements of his revelation were communicated in various ways "to the Gentiles." This supposed fact helped explain how the Roman Empire was "prepared" for the Gospel when it was finally proclaimed by Jesus. It also allowed the men and women of the Renaissance to embrace more wholeheartedly what they found good in the classical tradition. Fiercely negative though preachers and theologians at the papal court might be towards heretics and schismatics – categories in which they would sometimes include the Muslim Turks who were then threatening Europe – they adopted a much gentler attitude towards the "good pagans". As one of the preachers in the Chapel said during the pontificate of Sixtus IV in 1482: "Anaxagoras, Zeno, Socrates, Plato and Aristotle, as well as other upright philosophers who worshipped one God and led lives of virtue – these I would never judge damned to eternal fires".[20] In understated terms this sentiment anticipated Erasmus's famous and startling invocation some decades later, "St Socrates, pray for us!"[21]

This phenomenon represents simply another phase of the tradition of reconciliation between classical culture and Christianity that, while it had serious opponents, also had serious advocates, like Thomas Aquinas. During the Renaissance this impulse gained peculiar strength and special emphasis, due to the recovery of large bodies of ancient literature and to the respect that literature evoked. While attempting to assert the uniqueness of Judeo-Christian revelation, men and women of the Renaissance saw God as too benign to exclude from His love persons who through no fault of their own fell outside that tradition. Both the Reformation and the Counter-Reformation tended to propound more cautious views on this matter. But the God Renaissance rhetoric praised and celebrated was not grudging; He was munificent and magnanimous in His gifts to all who sincerely sought Him.

That fact surely accounts to a large extent for the revived interest in the Sibyls during the Italian Renaissance. In the classical tradition Sibyls were those mantic priestesses who dwelt in shrines and uttered enigmatic judgements and prophecies. A body of their supposed oracles, much of which had been authored by Jews and Christians over the course of several centuries, was known to the Fathers of the Church and quoted by them. Messianic in character as many of these pseudo-oracles were, they were evidently designed to help gain the

... and there was given to him the book of the prophet Isaiah.
He opened the book and found the place where it was written,
"The Spirit of the Lord is upon me, because he has anointed me to preach
good news to the poor. He has sent me to proclaim release to the captives and recovering of sight to the blind,
to set at liberty those who are oppressed ..."
LUKE 4, 17–19, 21

THE ERYTHRAEAN SIBYL

As snow melts in the sun,
so in the wind the oracle of the Sibyl
was lost in fluttering leaves
DANTE, PARADISO XXXIII, 64–66

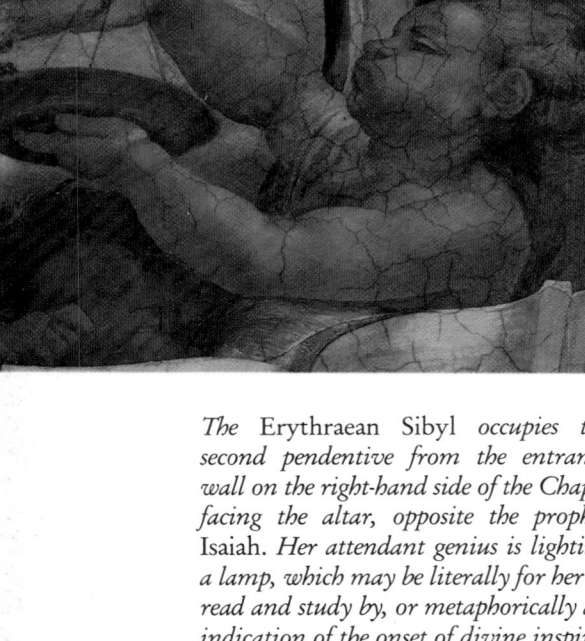

The Erythraean Sibyl *occupies the second pendentive from the entrance wall on the right-hand side of the Chapel facing the altar, opposite the prophet Isaiah.* Her attendant genius is lighting a lamp, which may be literally for her to read and study by, or metaphorically an indication of the onset of divine inspiration. Erythraea, or the particular city of that name from which the Sibyl came, was a city of Ionia; there has been speculation that Michelangelo's choice of five of a total availability of ten classical Sibyls was governed by geographical considerations, the Delphic Sibyl representing Europe, the Erythraean Asia, but of course the Phrygian Sibyl, whom he did not include, could have represented Asia just as well.

THE CUMAEAN SIBYL

The Cumaean Sibyl *occupies the third or middle pendentive on the left-hand side of the Chapel facing the altar. The Cumaean Sibyl was the most famous of the Sibyls: she it was who led Aeneas into the Underworld, and who, rather more importantly for the Sistine Chapel, prophesied the birth of a Saviour in Virgil's* Eclogue IV, *which until the Renaissance was universally regarded as referring to Christ. She bears a book so prominently perhaps because she has also been identified with the Sibyl who visited King Tarquin and offered him the Sibylline books in which the future of Rome was written; eventually he bought the last one, which was stored in the Capitol until it was destroyed by fire in the 1st century BC.*

pagan world to Jewish or Christian beliefs. The messianic preoccupations of the Sibyls were seen to be confirmed by the promise made by the Cumaean Sibyl in Virgil's fourth *Eclogue,* of a "new progeny from heaven" that would initiate a "return of the Golden Age". Men and women of the Renaissance enthusiastically endorsed the venerable opinion that this utterance foretold in veiled terms the birth of Christ during the reign of the Emperor Augustus, when Virgil wrote.

Michelangelo was by no means the first to attempt representation of the Sibyls in the art of the Renaissance, but no one did it more monumentally than he.[22] For the first time, in the Sistina, he thereby expressly joined Greco-Roman culture with the Hebrew world. The very fact that he painted the Sibyls for the pope's own chapel shows how orthodox and broadly acceptable they had become. But why he chose the five he did, out of a pool of ten or twelve, is still by no means clear, and speculation on the subject is wide-ranging. Given her prominence in Virgil's *Eclogue,* and thereby her conjoining of Rome and the Church, the Cumaean Sibyl could hardly be bypassed, and Michelangelo places her prominently in the centre of the Chapel. The Delphic, Erythraean, Persian and Libyan Sibyls stem from Greece, Ionia, Asia, and Africa respectively, and perhaps are meant to suggest the geographical extent of prophecies to the Gentiles. They would thus intimate the universal mission of evangelization of the Church and possess an ecclesiological significance.

If this inference is correct, the Sibyls would evoke further response from those who saw them. We must remember that we are dealing with the age of Columbus and other great explorers and also with the age when western Europe felt beseiged and threatened by Turkish expansion from the east. Often the warning was heard at the court, even before the great Turkish campaigns launched in the 1520s, that Christianity had been reduced to a mere "corner" of the world. The discovery of the new lands and the new peoples awakened hopes that this process was being counterbalanced, and that the "Christian Empire" would now finally fulfil its prophesied destiny to reach to "the ends of the earth" (Psalms 18 [19], 5), where it would proclaim its message of salvation to all peoples.[23]

This universal proclamation of the Gospel was often interpreted in Christian literature as a sign that "the end is nigh". Although frequently invested with threats of destruction and cataclysmic upheaval, the "last times" were also seen as of indeterminate duration and marked by a return to the "Golden Age" that had prevailed "in the beginning". Such optimism, usually expressed with caution, was prevalent at the court during the Renaissance.

There is no doubt, in any case, that the preachers and theologians there were eager to extol the happy condition that the advent of Christianity had brought to the world. Christianity was considered in this perspective as the last of the three great stages in human history: before the Law (of Moses), under the Law, under Grace – *ante legem, sub lege, sub gratia,* as the ancient formula had it (cf. Romans, 5 – 8). In the last age, God more fully manifested His goodness, and in the Incarnation of Christ, the Messiah, He fully realized the human dignity that was first manifested in the creation of Adam. Preachers gloried in such eschatological motifs and in the linking of "beginning" and "end".

The members of the papal court during the Renaissance were well schooled in the idea that all antiquity was "preparation for the Gospel". They believed this was true of pagan antiquity, as the

The last age, sung of by the Cumaean Sibyl, is coming;
the great cycle of ages is beginning again from the beginning.
The Virgin (Astraea) is returning, the age of Saturn is coming back;
a new generation has come down from the high heaven.
But you, Lucina, be kind to the boy being born …
VIRGIL, ECLOGUE IV, 4–8

presence of the Sibyls in the Chapel testifies, but they believed it pre-eminently true of the Old Testament, which accounts for most of the Ceiling. There is no doubt therefore that Michelangelo's programme, especially with its inclusion of the "ancestors of Christ", is Messianic in its import.

Today biblical scholars see the prophets of the Old Testament as "spokesmen for God" in the historical context of their times. The older tradition saw them particularly as visionaries of the future who predicted the Messiah and the "Golden Age" he would initiate. This was certainly the understanding the Renaissance had of them and indicates how one must interpret Michelangelo's figures.

This Sibyl, by contrast to the two we have seen, is represented as an old woman. According to classical legend, she was loved by Apollo, who offered her as many years of life as she held grains of sand in her hand; but did not grant that she should retain her youth through the hundreds of years involved.

THE PROPHET EZECHIEL

The word of the Lord also came unto me, saying,
Son of man, thou dwellest in the midst of a rebellious house,
which have eyes to see, and see not;
they have ears to hear, and hear not:
for they are a rebellious house.

EZECHIEL 12, 1–2

The prophet Ezechiel *is placed on the middle or third pendentive of the right-hand wall of the Chapel facing the altar, opposite the* Cumaean Sibyl.

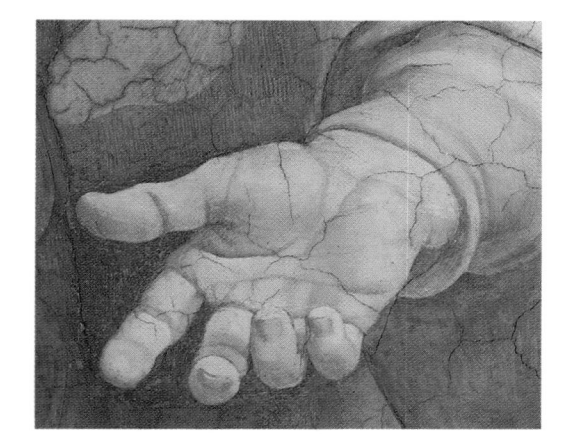

As one entered the Sistine Chapel from the ceremonial door at the rear, the first *Prophet* to meet one's vision would be *Jonah* at the far end. He was among the last painted by Michelangelo and palpably demonstrates the artist's matured mastery of foreshortening and other skills. Condivi states: "But most remarkable of all [the Prophets and Sibyls] is the prophet Jonah, situated at the head of the vault, because, contrary to the curve of the vault and by means of the play of light and shadow, the torso which is foreshortened backward is in the part nearest the eye, and the legs which project forward are in the part which is farthest. A stupendous work, and one that proclaims the magnitude of this man's knowledge, in his handling of lines, in foreshortening, and in perspective."[24] The most dramatic of the Sistine *Prophets* in his stance, *Jonah* is also the most dramatically placed – right over the altar.

At this point the relationship between the Ceiling and the liturgical functions of the Chapel must enter into consideration. During the Renaissance, unlike today, the Chapel built by Sixtus IV was the normal location for religious services in the Vatican, even for the

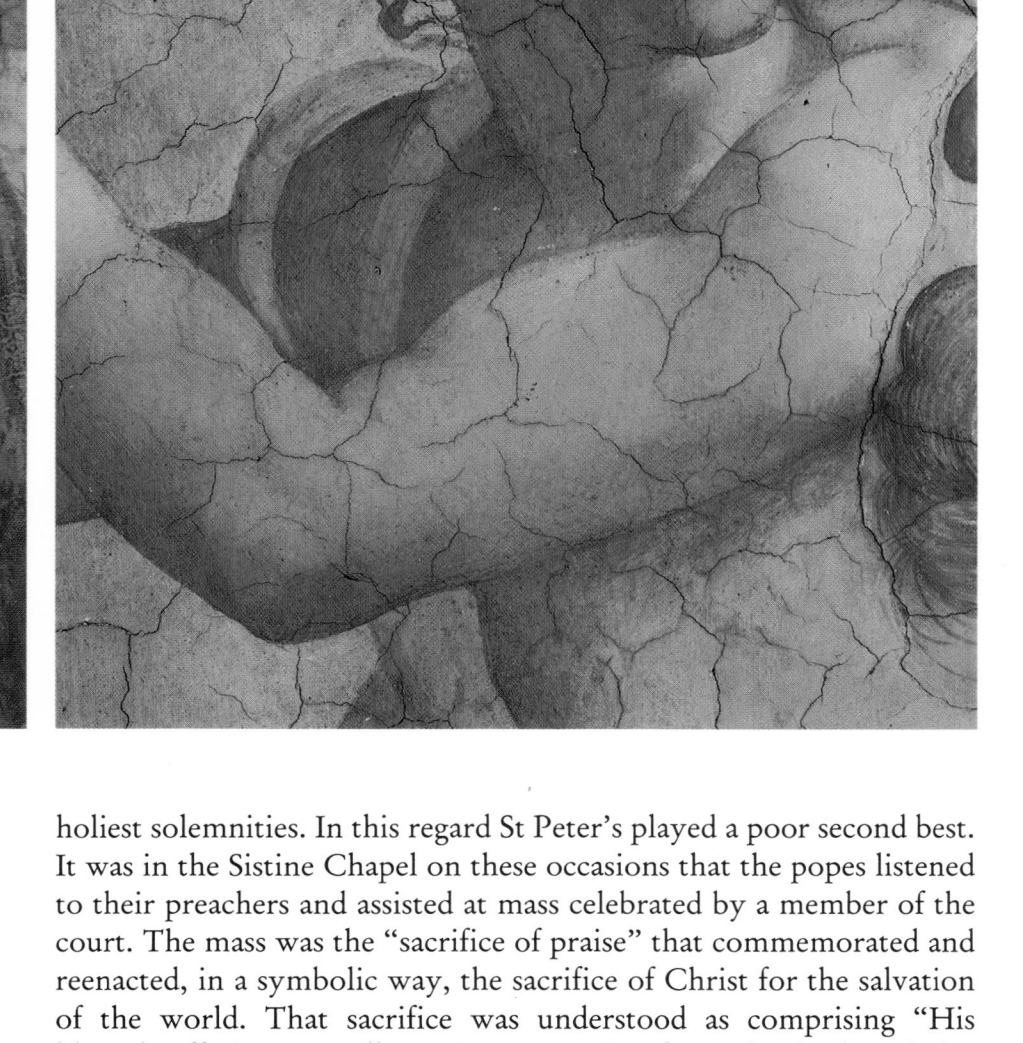

The prophet is represented in impetuous movement, a movement that some have related to a reaction to the Erythraean Sibyl beside him, but which surely has to do with his inspiration and with the angelically beautiful genius with whom he is in almost eye-to-eye contact, and who is himself in corresponding movement. The almost frantic energy of the head of this prophet is particularly outstanding.

The book of Ezechiel is rich in visions: particularly famous, and a theme of Renaissance art as well, is what is often known simply as "the vision of Ezechiel", that of the tetramorph with whom the Evangelists were identified and from which they derive their symbols. The prophet stressed his investiture by God to proclaim His glory and discomfort His enemies, and attacked particularly idolaters. There are also many references to the Babylonian captivity and to the punishment and vindication of Israel, and a detailed description of the new Temple of Jerusalem.

holiest solemnities. In this regard St Peter's played a poor second best. It was in the Sistine Chapel on these occasions that the popes listened to their preachers and assisted at mass celebrated by a member of the court. The mass was the "sacrifice of praise" that commemorated and reenacted, in a symbolic way, the sacrifice of Christ for the salvation of the world. That sacrifice was understood as comprising "His blessed suffering, as well as His resurrection from the dead, and also His glorious ascension into heaven", as the text read at every mass succinctly stated.[25] With Jesus Himself making the connection in the Gospels between Jonah and His own death and resurrection, art historians correctly point out the appropriateness of Michelangelo's location of that prophet and the whale over the altar.

Art historians see a further, equally valid, relationship. The Sistine Chapel was dedicated to the Assumption of the Blessed Virgin Mary, and, before Michelangelo painted the *Last Judgement* on the altar wall, Perugino's fresco of that event adorned it, along with paintings of the *Finding of Moses* and the *Nativity of Christ*. The Assumption of the Virgin indicates and is the first fruit of the final perfection of the salva-

THE PROPHET DANIEL

The prophet Daniel *occupies the fourth pendentive from the entrance and the second from the altar on the left-hand side of the Chapel facing the altar. Alone among his peers, he is shown writing, turned in an elegant spiral such as will become the hallmark of Michelangelo's art. In his book Daniel narrates events in the first person; some of these events have enjoyed particular fame, such as the Feast of Belshazzar, the three young men in the fiery furnace, and Daniel himself in the lion's den. Daniel's also is the expression "feet of clay", which comes from his allegory of a statue representing four kingdoms in four different materials. He was interpreter of dreams at the courts of Nebuchadnezzar and Belshazzar.*

tion wrought by Christ, for it reflects the Lord's own resurrection and ascension and foreshadows the happy destiny of all the saved, the Resurrection of the Body. In Jonah we see, therefore, one of the clearest correlations between the functions of the Chapel, its dedication to the *Assumption,* the frescoes that antedated Michelangelo's Ceiling, and the Ceiling itself. Art historians have postulated other, similar relationships, most of which we will not have the space to discuss, but this is among the most persuasive. If Michelangelo's so-called *Last Judgement* now covering the entire altar wall is better understood as testifying to the Christian hope in the Resurrection of the Body – a recent interpretation that has a basis in the original commission and in the subjects depicted – the artist continued the correlation in that later painting.[26]

Jonah has a still further significance that merits him his emphatic place in the Ceiling. He is the only one of the seven prophets to have been spokesman to the Gentiles, preaching as he did to the people of Nineveh. He thus somehow unites in himself the function of both Prophet and Sibyl and suggests the essential identity of their Messianic visions.

The choice and placement of the other six *Prophets* do not admit of easy explanation. All seven of them, indeed, have been interpreted as representing the seven gifts of the Holy Spirit (Isaiah 11, 1–2).[27] Other historians have mounted intelligent arguments deriving from the

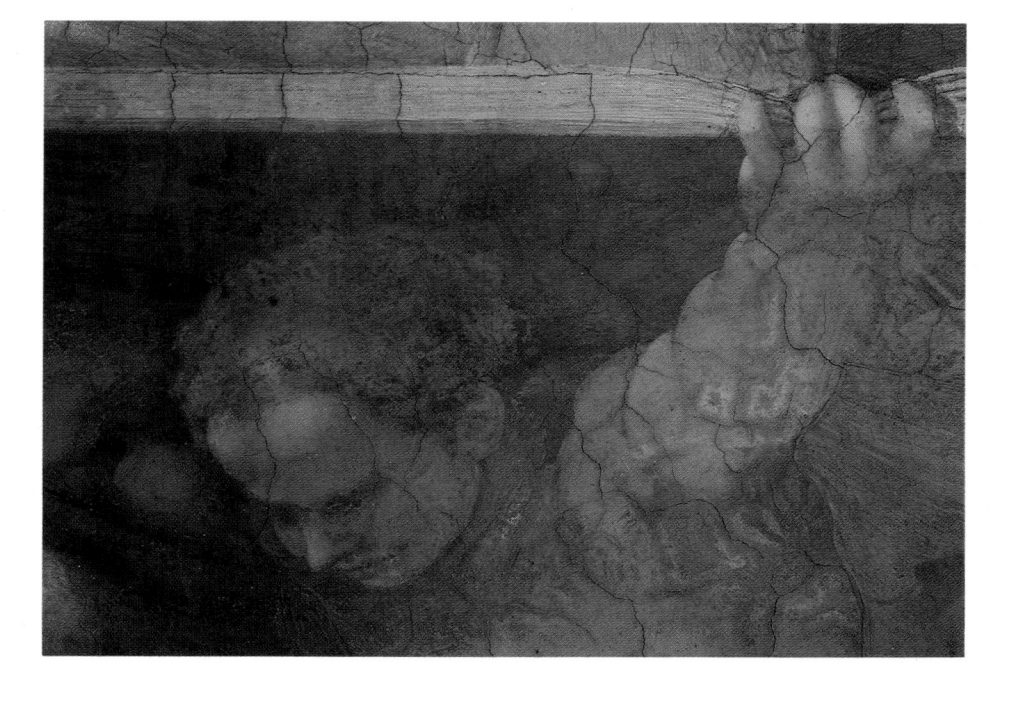

mystical significance of their names to relate them to a nearby panel from Genesis or to a neighbouring Sibyl.[28] They have also adduced some of the prophets' more characteristic utterances for the same purposes, as well as to relate them to the liturgies of the Chapel.

Zechariah, for instance, was the first *Prophet* painted by Michelangelo, and he sits over the ceremonial door, at the other end from *Jonah.* Zechariah's name was interpreted to mean "mindful of the Lord" or "memory of the Lord" – a fitting sentiment to be inculcated, surely, as one left the Chapel. Moreover, he was the prophet quoted by Jesus (Matthew 21, 5) as predicting his entrance into Jerusalem on Palm Sunday, the beginning of the week in which He suffered and died, when He accomplished humankind's salvation commemorated at the

THE PERSIAN SIBYL

The Persian Sibyl *is placed on the fourth pendentive from the entrance and the second from the altar on the right-hand side of the Chapel facing the altar, opposite the prophet* Daniel. *She is even older than the* Cumaean Sibyl,

and turned away from the spectator in gnarled introspection. Her figure is somewhat exaggerated: she sits on her throne with enormous haunches, and in the emphasis on the turn of her shoulders Michelangelo has made her into a hunchback.

altar. Through the great door the pope and his entourage entered the Chapel with great liturgical solemnity each year in commemoration of the first Palm Sunday. But relationships like these are subtle and tenuous, and we have little indication that they would have been easily accessible in a coherent pattern even to well-educated spectators during the Renaissance, though they probably would have delighted them if they discovered them or had them pointed out by some "learned theologian". Along with straightforward history and narrative, theologians of the Renaissance continued to take pleasure in the "mysteriously meant".

Whatever mysterious or allegorical meaning might have been intended for the first five panels from Genesis, they narrated events that played an especially prominent role in the preaching at the court and would have struck an extraordinarily rich chord in the minds and hearts of those who saw them – the Creation of the world and the Creation of man and woman. In fact, God's creative "deeds", done "in the beginning", were one of the two favourite themes in that preaching, the other being the Incarnation of Christ. Since the frescoes painted earlier on the lower wall narrated the total history of Christ's Incarnation from His birth to His resurrection, Michelangelo surely did not want to repeat it and would, understandably, look to the Old Testament. No surprise, therefore, that he might choose as a subject the famous opening chapters of the first book of the Bible. Nonetheless, the stories depicted in the first five panels were remarkably in accord with the tastes and interests of "Renaissance theology".

Why the Christian mystery of Creation emerged so prominently at this time was largely due to the rhetoric of panegyric that preachers and theologians applied to God. As they searched out the "deeds" of their divine hero for the purpose of praise, the first to strike them was that out of the void He had created the splendour of the physical universe. Focusing on this fact allowed the preachers to utilize all the rhetorical skills of their profession as they described to the congregation with vivid detail the beauty of the sun and the moon, the bounty of the earth, the variety of its flora and fauna. When God constructed the universe, said a typical preacher from the court in 1497, He constructed a magnificent temple and then decorated it with such skill that all who gaze upon it admire its beauty and wonder at its magnitude.[29]

Again typically, the preacher turned next to the most extraordinary part of God's Creation found in that temple – man. Of all the sections of the Ceiling, none is better known or more frequently reproduced than the *Creation of Adam*. None would have impressed men of the Renaissance more forcefully, for it captured one of the most pervasive themes of their rhetoric – the "dignity of man", created as he was "in the image and likeness" of God.

Like the preacher just mentioned, a number of others in the Sistine Chapel quoted or paraphrased in this regard the famous *Oration on the Dignity of Man* by the Renaissance thinker, Giovanni Pico della Mirandola. Scholars have long tried to associate the *Oration* with the painting, but only recently have they been able to establish this secure contextualization. Although Pico clashed with Pope Innocent VIII over the *Oration* in 1487 and was forced to recant part of it, he was rehabilitated by the next Pope, Alexander VI. From that time onwards we find passages from the *Oration* interwoven into sermons at the court – done in such a way as to suggest that the listeners were familiar with them and would have recognized them.[30]

THE LIBYAN SIBYL

Although the theologians and humanists associated with the papal court expended special effort in praising man's spiritual qualities, they by no means neglected the beauty and harmony they saw in the human body. Indeed, that is the point where their panegyrics often began, as they invited their contemporaries to admire the attractiveness of its contours, the artful disposition of its members, the order of the whole. The panegyrics used considerations like these both to argue the existence of God and to discover His nature. When Vasari in his *Lives* described the *Creation* scenes on the Ceiling as a revelation of "the greatness of God" and of His "love and creative power," he echoed what persons in the Renaissance would have seen there.[31] He

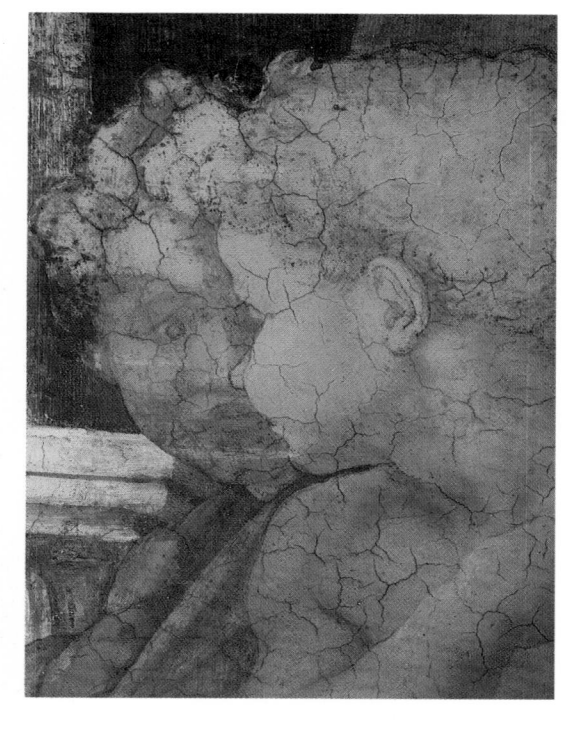

The Libyan Sibyl *occupies the first pendentive from the altar on the left-hand side of the Chapel facing the altar. She is justly one of the most famous figures of the Sistine Ceiling, both for the extraordinary elegance of her movement and for her ethereal beauty. She is in many ways a fully Mannerist figure; she steps with an exaggerated daintiness on the sill of the base of her throne, and all the brilliant design of her movement has become a little divorced from her functional role, even from the expression of Sibylline inner life. It is also a typically Mannerist trait that it is difficult to decide whether she is opening or closing, picking up or putting down her enormous book.*

goes on to describe Adam as "a figure whose beauty, pose and contours are such that it seems to have been fashioned that very moment by the first and supreme Creator rather than by the drawing and brush of mortal man."[32] Vasari's description, Michelangelo's painting, and the theology of the court here all coincide.

For once, at least, we have help from a sonnet by Michelangelo himself. In it the "image and likeness" theme recurs, and can almost be taken as a commentary on the painting:

> *né Dio sua grazia mi si mostra altrove*
> *più che 'n alcun leggiadro e mortal velo;*
> *e quel sol amo perch' in lui si specchia*
> God, in His grace, shows Himself nowhere more
> To me, than through some veil, mortal and lovely,
> Which I will only love for being His mirror.[33]

Whatever other significance even the *ignudi* might hold, they, along

THE PROPHET JEREMIAH

The prophet Jeremiah is placed on the pendentive nearest the altar on the right-hand side of the Chapel looking towards the altar, opposite the Libyan Sibyl. In his thoughtful, not to say gloomy pose it is probably legitimate to see a reference to his historical character, for Jeremiah was known above all for his lament for the destruction of Jerusalem, even if today there is doubt about his authorship of it. The scale of the figure is even larger than that of his predecessors; the brushwork is freer and bolder.

Behold, the days come, saith
the Lord, that I will make
a new covenant with the house
of Israel, and with the house
of Judah:
Not according to the covenant
that I made with their fathers
in the day that I took them
by the hand to bring them out
of the land of Egypt …
I will put my law in their
inward parts, and write it in
their hearts; and will be
their God, and they shall be
my people.

JEREMIAH 31, 31–33

with the figure of the reclining Adam, must be seen as manifestations of human dignity reflecting the divine.

Problems there are, of course, even with the scenes from the biblical story of Creation. What is the significance, for instance, of the double image of God in the large second panel? Are the first three panels, in their very triplicity, meant serially to suggest the Trinity? And, as always, how much is "doubly meant"? Art historians have found in the *Creation of Adam* an allegory of the Incarnation of Christ, who is the "second Adam" according to St Paul.[34] Because of its clear and well recognized grounding in the New Testament, this interpretation must be taken seriously. It fits with the Messianic foreshadowing the Renaissance would have seen in the Ceiling as a whole. Persons in Rome were, besides, familiar with ancient Greek Fathers like Basil of Caesarea and Gregory of Nyssa, who invested the Creation of Adam with a strongly Christological interpretation and saw the Incarnation as its perfect fulfillment, intended even "in the beginning".[35]

Some scholars interpret the *Creation of Eve* as an allegory on the founding of the Church, for Eve is the type of Mary, and in Christian theology Mary is a symbol of the Church. They argue that the proximity of the panel to the portentous Cumaean Sibyl, its central location in the series of nine, and its place right over the spot where the marble screen originally divided the *presbyterium* from the rest of the Chapel demand some deeper significance than the mere "history" itself. The *presbyterium*, containing the altar and sometimes referred to as "the Holy of Holies" (*Sancta sanctorum*), was generally reserved for the cardinals and certain other dignitaries, lay and clerical,

attached to the court. One fact is certain and has often been pointed out, though what it means is variously interpreted: God appears in every scene over the portion of the Chapel nearer the altar, whereas He never appears in the four panels in the rear.

Those last four panels were the first Michelangelo painted, working as he did from the rear of the Chapel towards the altar. The figures in this part of the Chapel, including the Prophets and Sibyls, are smaller than the rest and the narrative scenes more crowded. Critics convincingly maintain that Michelangelo realized, once the scaffolding had been taken down from the rear of the Chapel in the summer of 1510,

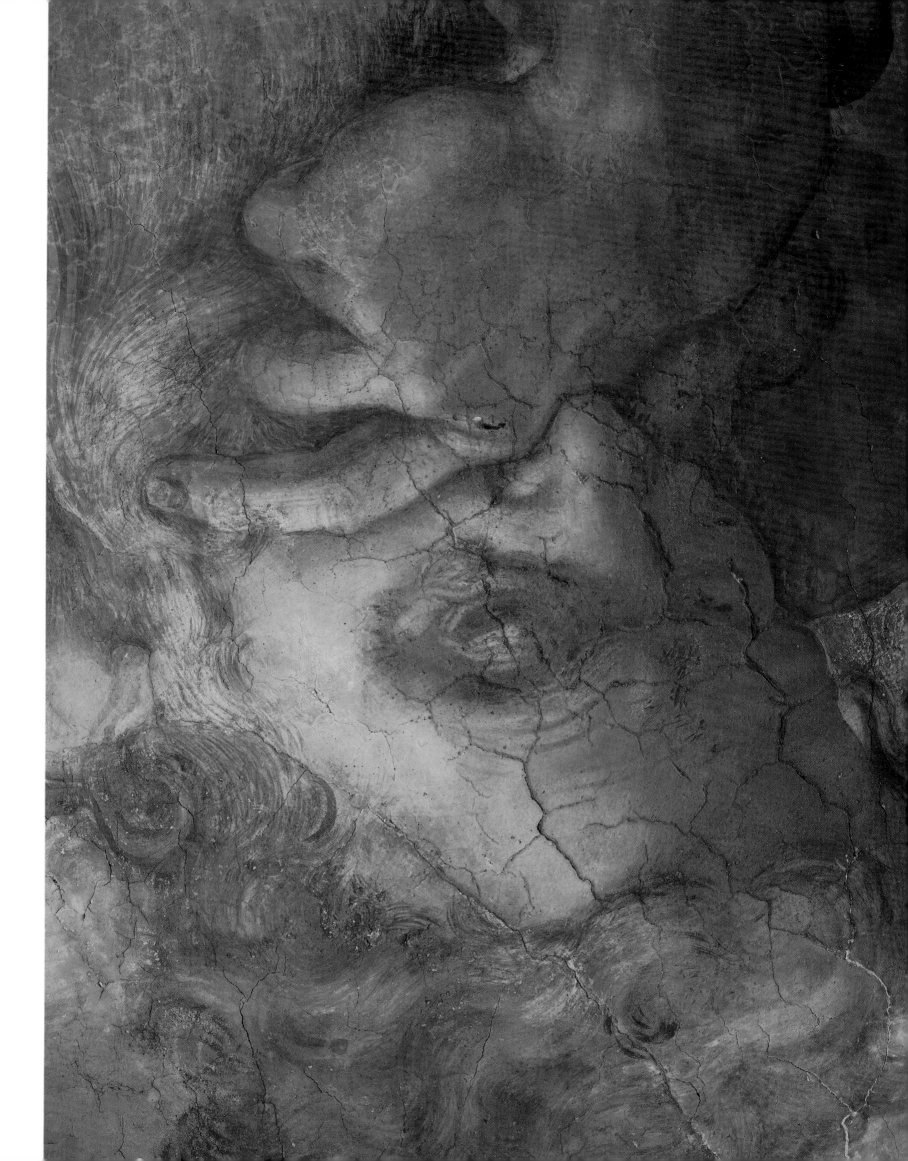

The prophet Jonah *is set on the pendentive descending over the altar, opposite
Zechariah* on the entrance wall of the
Chapel. There is a considerable contrast
between the first and the last of the
series. It may be that Jonah rather than
another prophet was set over the altar
because his three days in the belly of the
whale were regarded as a type of the
Resurrection – especially since Jonah
appears with his whale, and not with the
book or scroll that the other prophets
bear. It is not clear how his violent
movement should be understood: it does
not seem to be the onset of inspiration. It
almost recalls the recoil with which the
soldiers guarding the tomb of the resur-
recting Christ were represented.

that he needed to simplify and enlarge the figures of paintings
removed some 20 metres from the floor below. About six months
elapsed before he took up his work again. Many of the figures, especially some of the *ignudi,* are now more animated, even contorted, in
their poses.

If the first five panels depict the goodness of God and the excellence of
His Creation, the last four suggest different, less happy, themes, especially the *Fall of Man* and the *Deluge.* Too neat, probably, would be
the division of the scenes into divinity for the first half, and humanity
for the second, but it does some justice to what we find. It would be
unthinkable in a series like this, of course, not to include the Fall.
There were, moreover, important precedents in Renaissance art for
this scene, most notably Masaccio's fresco in Santa Maria del Carmine
in Florence, which surely influenced Michelangelo's depiction of
Adam and Eve being driven from paradise.

In the Christian story, the Fall is almost as fundamental as the

THE PROPHET JONAH

In the Renaissance the prophet Jonah was probably the most admired of the series: this is Condivi on the figure: "But the most admirable of all is the prophet Jonah, placed at the head of the vault, for, in contradiction to the physical nature of the site, by the use of light and shade, the torso foreshortened inwards is painted on the part that is actually nearest the eye, and the legs which stretch outwards on the part actually furthest away. Quite stupendous, and demonstrating the degree of understanding this man has in the art of lines, contours, foreshortening and perspective."

The detail (below) of the two hands of the prophet repeats in little the 'difficulty' of the foreshortening: they are foreshortened in completely opposite directions, in contrasting "use of light and shade".

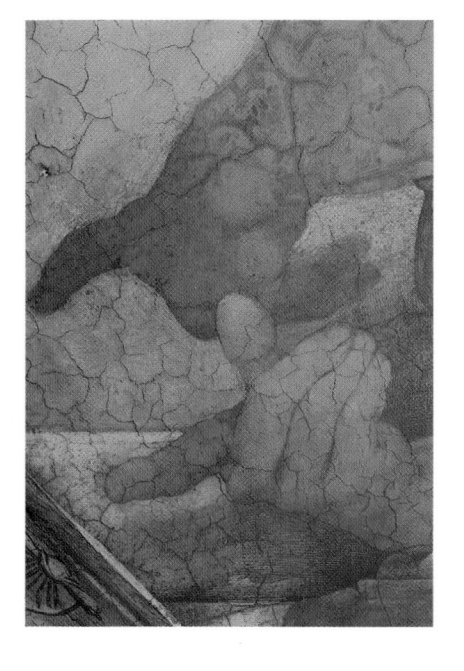

Creation and Incarnation, and, in the opinion of most theologians, it was the event that made the Incarnation necessary. This connection is important, for it allowed the Christian Church to take a surprisingly benign view of the catastrophe through which, according to St Paul, "sin entered the world". The Fall was a catastrophic sin, true, but it was also celebrated in an important liturgical hymn as *felix culpa* – "happy fault, which required so special and so great a Saviour!" Preachers at the court quoted that hymn, the so-called *Exultet*, again and again with surprising insistence, and it would anyway have been well-known because of its dramatic place in the liturgy of Holy Saturday.[36] I mention it because it both emphasizes and mitigates the distraught sadness of Adam and Eve as Michelangelo depicted them leaving Paradise, and ties the Fall of the human race to the Salvation to be effected by Christ. Just as the Renaissance interpreted the whole of the Old Testament as looking forward to the Incarnation, it particularly invested the Fall with Christological overtones.

THE SEPARATION OF LIGHT AND DARKNESS

The central scenes of the Ceiling: nine episodes from Genesis.

The central scenes of the Ceiling: nine episodes from Genesis.
The Separation of Light and Darkness is the first of the scenes, placed at the altar end of the Ceiling. Though this means that a spectator entering from the ceremonial door of the Chapel would be presented with the episodes in reverse chronological order, there was a certain logic in placing the acts of creation, featuring God the Father himself, nearest the altar. The moment illustrated by Michelangelo is that after the creation of light itself,

"And God saw the light, that it was good; and God divided the light from the darkness."

This figure seems to be the one praised particularly by Paolo Giovio, who said that "Among his outstanding male figures there is to be seen in the middle of the Ceiling the image of an old man flying to heaven, depicted with such symmetria *that, though one might gaze at him from different parts of the Chapel, he always seems to turn and to persuade one's deceived eyes that he is moving".*

Michelangelo bypassed, so it now seems, the story of Cain and Abel and moved to the longer history of Noah, which begins in Genesis, 6. Next to the Expulsion of Adam and Eve from paradise, the Deluge was the most famous punishment for sin in the Old Testament, touching the whole human race. Its inclusion in the programme causes, therefore, no surprise. But unlike the Fall of Adam and Eve, the Deluge is also explicitly a story of the salvation of the just, as Noah's ark floating like a temple in the central background of Michelangelo's fresco reminds us.

Inside the ark, salvation. Christian theologians and preachers consistently interpreted the ark as a "type", a foreshadowing image, of the Christian Church. That image was such a commonplace, not in the least esoteric, that practically everyone would immediately have recognized it, and seen it as introducing an ecclesiological element into the Ceiling. "Under Grace" salvation was effected in and through the Church. All this must not obscure, however, the "historical" sense of the original act of God's salvation of Noah and his family.

The two panels on either side of the *Deluge* pose greater problems, not least because the *Sacrifice of Noah* is out of historical sequence: the sacrifice occurred after the Flood, not before it. We must note, in any case, that according to legend, the Erythraean Sibyl married a son of Noah, which surely explains why she sits adjacent to this panel in the Ceiling; she probably reappears in the panel itself as the priestess who stands at Noah's right.[37] The presence of the *Sacrifice of Noah* was appropriate, surely, in a chapel intended for the celebration of the sacrifice of the mass, of which it was a "type".

The iconography of the final panel, the *Drunkenness of Noah*, admits several plausible interpretations. One tradition of exegesis would see in this derision of a parent a type of the mocking of Christ by the Roman soldiers and others during the last hours of His earthly life. More faithful to the literal sense of the story and more in accord with a recurring theme in the Chapel is the tradition that interprets the event as the original separation of the Gentiles from the Chosen People – a separation that Christ would heal by his "New Covenant", celebrated at the altar. Interpreted in this sense, the "Drunkenness" is a fitting conclusion to the Genesis cycle and leads easily to the significance of the double series of *Prophets* and *Sibyls*, which concludes over the opposite altar wall with *Jonah*, Hebrew Prophet to the Gentiles.

Whatever might be the iconography of the scenes in these last two panels, Michelangelo (or his adviser) had precedent, again, from earlier Renaissance artists in giving them expression. In other words, we must bear in mind that some subjects were familiar and more or less traditional, even though this fact does not explain why in any given instance certain ones were chosen for depiction and others were not.

Edgar Wind and, after him, other art historians have persuasively postulated that the historical scenes in the ten medallions represent observance, violation, or punishment for violations of the Ten Commandments.[38] According to Wind, the curiously obscured medallion above the *Persian Sibyl* depicted two naked lovers, presumably in an act of adultery, who were later obliterated when the relationship to the Commandment against adultery was no longer recognized. A problem with such an interpretation of the medallions, though not unresolvable, is that the Commandments, as historians have identified them on the Ceiling, do not follow their standard sequence. On the

THE CREATION
OF THE SUN AND MOON

And God said,
Let the earth bring forth grass,
the herb yielding seed,
and the fruit tree yielding fruit after his kind,
whose seed is in itself, upon the earth:
and it was so.

GENESIS 1, 11

The Creation of the Sun and the Moon, *and of the earth. The double scene seems to involve two days of creation, the third and the fourth, on which God made the "two great lights, the greater light to rule the day, and the lesser light to rule the night; he made the stars also", but only the sun, to which*

God points with his right hand, and the moon, conjured into being with his left, are represented. On the left, moving in the opposite direction, God has brought into being on his left the earth, made indirectly, not directly, from the waters already existing; and the earth has been covered with grass and the herb yielding

And God said,
Let there be lights in the firmament
of the heaven to divide the day from the night;
and let them be for signs,
and for seasons, and for days, and years:
... and it was so.
GENESIS 1, 14 – 15

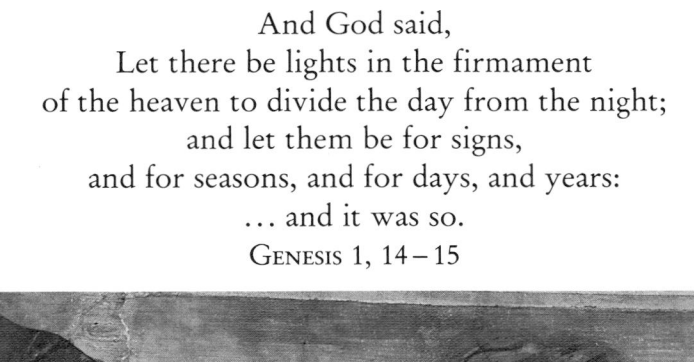

seed, but the fruit trees are not yet in evidence.

The splendid isolation of the Creator in the first scene is modified by the presence of cherubim: "There are together with Him several little angels", says Condivi, "one of whom, on the left-hand side, hides his face, clinging to his Maker".

But the main force of this scene is its monumental vigour, "quite terrible in its foreshortening of arms and legs", as Vasari has it. Particularly the double figure of God moving in opposite directions lends a dramatic sense of zooming.

other hand, if the Ceiling was to represent "almost all the Old Testament", the Commandments would surely be required, even though the *Descent from Mt Sinai* in the fresco by Cosimo Rosselli on the lower wall globally represents them. Salvation was effected through the Law in the period of history "before Grace."

No one doubts that the scenes in the four 'spandrels' of the Chapel represent God acting through His servants to effect the salvation of His people. In the corner to the left of the altar wall, Michelangelo tampered with the original story of the execution of Haman in the book of Esther to have Haman die on a cross rather than by hanging. The raising of the brazen serpent in the desert, with which Jesus in John's Gospel (3, 14 – 15) compared his own "raising" on the cross, covers the opposite 'spandrel'. These two frescoes thus surely relate to the altar below where the sacrifice of Christ on a Cross was celebrated in the mass. Especially admired among the frescoes of the Ceiling for the artistic mastery displayed in them, these two scenes also correlate appropriately with the theology of salvation, or soteriology, implied in the *Jonah*, the *Assumption* on the altar wall, and on the altar itself. The *Slaying of Goliath* and the *Slaying of Holophernes* in the 'spandrels' at the rear of the Chapel depict scenes of salvation familiar in the Renaissance. They both appear, for instance, on Ghiberti's Paradise Doors of the Baptistery in Florence. David was the subject of famous statues by Donatello, Verrocchio, and Michelangelo himself. In the Chapel the two paintings flank the huge coat of arms of the two Della

Detail of the cherubim beside God in the Creation of the Sun and Moon. *One looks up as if God were speaking his creation, as indeed the Bible puts it; the other is shading his eyes from the brightness of the newly created sun – this is the one Condivi referred to (see previous page).*

(Opposite page) Detail of the face of God the Father. Though Michelangelo was something of a specialist in "terribleness", an adjective habitually applied by Vasari, and a quality he was considered to share with Dante, it was anyway traditional to show God the Father as "terrible", and to represent in this way his almightiness.

Rovere popes that hangs over the ceremonial door.

Do these four scenes of danger overcome, besides their generic message of salvation, have political overtones and allude to events contemporary with Julius II and related to him? Critics now assume, for instance, that Michelangelo's *David* in Florence is a symbol of republican sentiment and civic liberty after the driving of the Medici "tyrants" from power.[39] While Michelangelo painted the Ceiling, Raphael laboured to complete his frescoes for Julius in the papal apartments – the famous Stanze. The scenes Raphael painted, especially those in the Stanza d'Eliodoro, clearly suggest the politico-ecclesiastical programme Julius set for his pontificate.

Julius himself, the "warrior Pope", took up the sword and led his armies in various campaigns to subdue "the enemies of the Church". Theologians and preachers during the Renaissance liked to see God operating in their times, just as He had acted on behalf of His people in the sacred history of the Bible. Whether or not an allusion to contemporary events was intended in these four 'spandrel' frescoes, some persons surely would have interpreted them in this sense. In this context neither David nor Judith would represent republican liberties, but would convey, rather, the legitimacy and biblical precedent for the much criticized military involvement of the Pope. Nonetheless, the scenes transcend contemporary particularities in their soteriological import and point to the salvation wrought by Christ.

This brings us to the relationship between Michelangelo and his patron, the impetuous and strong-willed Julius. Our sources for the origins of the programme for the Ceiling break their tight-lipped silence only for the Pope. He is the one person with whom we know that Michelangelo discussed the project. Julius conceived the original plan for twelve apostles, and then gave Michelangelo, the latter maintained, a free hand. But we know there were further conversations in that stormy but affectionate relationship. From the records that survive, it would seem that these conversations centred on the Pope's attempts to keep Michelangelo in his employ, and in them the Pope's impatience to see the work completed surely often erupted . They do not hint that Julius ventured further suggestions, or commands, regarding the programme.

We have no reason to doubt Condivi, however, when he states that Pope Julius loved Michelangelo "with all his heart and with more concern and jealousy for him than for anyone else whom he had around him."[40] Moreover, it was Julius who importuned Michelangelo to undertake the task, and it was his unrelenting demands that produced the Ceiling from that reluctant genius, virtually untried up to that point in the art of fresco painting. Julius was surely not a "learned theologian", and according to a famous story he supposedly said to Michelangelo at some earlier date, "I for my part know nothing of letters".[41] True, the contents of Julius's private library suggest that he was not quite so indifferent to learning as those words indicate. Nonetheless, critics have correctly refused to consider the possibility that Julius himself could have been directly responsible for a detailed, sophisticated, and highly integrated programme. This does not mean that the Pope did not have some clear ideas about how certain stories of the Bible could be used to justify his sometimes controversial decisions and actions.

The four 'spandrels' of the Ceiling depict, in any case, four interventions by God for the salvation of His people, and they thereby suggest His intervention par excellence, the salvation wrought by Christ. The two nearest the altar demand this interpretation. As we have seen, this motive presents itself implicitly in a number of ways in various parts of the Ceiling, but we should not be surprised to find it explicitly stated. That is precisely what the lunettes over the windows and the paintings in the triangular spaces above them do. It is here that we find the *Ancestors of Christ* named and painted.

In the tablets just above the windows in the lunettes the names of the ancestors are clearly inscribed. About the origins of these names there is no doubt. In an alternating sequence that would have begun with the altar wall and that shuttles back and forth across the Chapel, they

THE SEPARATION
OF THE SKY AND WATER

The Separation of the Sky and Water. *This is the third Creation scene, but chronologically it comes before the second, since the expanse of water and absence of any living thing can relate only to the second day. There is a comparable reversal of the chronological order in the third part of the Genesis*

And God said,
Let there be a firmament in the midst of waters,
and let it divide the waters from the waters.
And God made the firmament, and divided the waters
which were under the firmament from the waters
which were above the firmament: and it was so.
GENESIS 1, 6–7

cycle. It may be that Michelangelo wished to reserve the larger field (for in the alternating system of the central part of the Ceiling, the 'bays' with the ignudi and the medallions reduce the size of every other central panel) for the grander composition, and have room to set sun, moon and earth together. How-ever that may be, it may be noted that he did not paint the creation of the plants, fish, birds and animals; perhaps they would have required too much de-tail, and have been unsuitable both to the titanic scale on which he was now paint-ing, and to the pressure he was under from Pope Julius II to finish the work.

follow faithfully the genealogy of Christ from Abraham to Joseph presented in the first 16 verses of the opening chapter of Matthew's Gospel, the first book of the New Testament. The passage ends with the words, "... and Jacob was the father of Joseph the spouse of Mary, of whom Jesus was born, who is called Christ".

From a theological viewpoint, the *Ancestors of Christ* are thus the culmination of the Ceiling, for they point most explicitly to what, in the Christian perspective, was the culmination of the Old Testament, the coming of Christ. The visions of the Prophets (and Sibyls!) foresaw that event. God's "acts" of Creation were done in view of it, and His acts to save His people from great perils adumbrated it. In Christ all the promises were fulfilled – and surpassed.

Christian theology in the Western Church generally pinpointed the effecting of human salvation in Christ's death, resurrection, and ascension. But the preachers in the Papal Chapel emphasized another tradition as well, a tradition vigorously expressed in the Greek Fathers of the Church, whose theology was revived during the Renaissance. They believed that salvation had been effected, inchoately but radically, by the act whereby God became man, the Incarnation. By taking flesh in the Virgin's womb and being born of her, the Second Person of the Trinity already healed the corruption brought about by Adam's sin. Moreover, by God's deigning to take on human flesh, he raised – "promoted" – humanity to a far greater dignity than it had before the Fall.

Therefore, in their soteriology, preachers at the court proposed a somewhat different vision than did St Anselm in the 12th century. According to Anselm, Christ by his suffering and death "atoned for" Adam's sin and appeased God's wrath. Thus Christ "bought back" the human race from its captivity by sin. Anselm's soteriology found great support in the Middle Ages and later in the Reformation and Counter-Reformation. At the papal court in the Renaissance the soteriology of the Greek Fathers tempered the Anselmian viewpoint with a more optimistic message and emphasis. Operative there was not so much a soteriology of atonement as of "promotion" or "elevation" to an even greater dignity than that conferred on Adam in his creation. Pietro del Monte, a distinguished figure in Renaissance Italy, echoed a widespread sentiment in a sermon at the papal court: "And through the Incarnation of His only Son, God concedes this gift to us that we become free men from being slaves and that from strangers we are promoted to sons."[42] The preachers did not want to deny a special efficacy to Christ's death and resurrection, but they tended to give in fact more attention to the soteriology implied in the Incarnation. A sermon in the Sistine Chapel on 1 November, 1492, well expressed their attitude: "... in the Virgin's womb and on the Cross he kissed us and renewed all reality."[43]

The Incarnation restored the "dignity" that Adam had largely lost, and it at the same time raised humankind even closer to the divine. As the prayer recited at every mass stated: "O God, you wondrously created the dignity of the human race, and [through Christ] you more wondrously restored it."[44] Renaissance theologians loved to repeat an ancient theological axiom that more boldly expressed the same idea: "God became man that man might become god." They found this idea in the Fathers of the Church, in medieval theologians like Thomas Aquinas, and even in the "Father of the Renaissance", the humanist Francesco Petrarch.[45] It fitted perfectly with their rhetoric

And God said,
Let us make man in our image,
after our likeness:
and let them have dominion
over the fish of the sea,
and over the fowl of the air,
and over the cattle,
and over all the earth,
and over every creeping thing
that creepeth upon the earth.
GENESIS 1, 26

138

of praise and congratulation directed to God and his "works", particularly the great work that was the Incarnation.

The triangular spaces surely relate to the "generations" indicated by the names in the lunettes below. These generally affectionate scenes of family life correlate with the style of religion proposed by Renaissance thinkers. When these men discussed human dignity and the corresponding obligations it imposed, they turned their attention to human relationships. Thomas Aquinas had earlier proposed that the virtue of love extended in a special way to those to whom one was bound by family ties.[46] The peculiar conjunction in the Renaissance mind of Christianity and the ethical "humanity" found in Greek and Roman literature gave support to this ideal. The Renaissance promoted with new vigour the religious dimensions of a life of public service, but it also insisted on the integrity and affection required in even the humblest dealings of human beings with each other. God was to be found and served not so much by the ascetical practices that characterized much of medieval religion as by service to one's fellows. In the sermons at the papal court, one hears little about pilgrimage, fasting, self-flagellation, and indulgences. One hears a great deal about change of heart, acts of kindness, dedication to the duties of one's state in life, and the spiritual benefits of reading the Bible and the Fathers of the Church.

THE CREATION OF ADAM

The Creation of Adam. *The fourth Creation scene is set in one of the larger fields of the central part of the Ceiling, but even so its great fame is out of all proportion to the amount of space it actually occupies in the whole. Its conception perhaps appears less dramatic if one comes to it from the preceding Creation scenes, in which a similar majestic God is also painted; but this scene of course was imagined and painted first, before the others, since Michelangelo worked from the entrance wall of the Chapel down. Indeed the* Creation of Adam *was very probably the first scene he painted after the break of six months in 1510–1511.*

The humanist Andrea Brenta epitomized this style of piety in a sermon for Pope Sixtus IV in 1483: "Our cult of God is a spiritual one, and it consists in thinking honest thoughts, speaking helpful words, doing good deeds, and storing up in heaven a wealth of piety that no accident or evil fortune can snatch away."[47] Preachers at the court delighted in quoting a line from Cicero and locating it in the context of Christian theology: "Non nobis solum nati sumus" – "We are not born for ourselves alone".[48]

This human ideal pervades the theological vision of preachers in the Sistine Chapel during the Renaissance and was characteristic of it, as opposed to what seems to have prevailed in other parts of Europe at

The standard image of the Creation of Man *before Michelangelo had been a standing profile God the Father extending his hand towards Adam, whom He in effect was raising to his feet. So in general disposition, and in his anticipation of God's infusion of power into his body, Michelangelo's Adam is traditional. However, placing God the Father in a cloudburst, on which Vasari particularly commented, and Adam's wonderfully languid pose – this was special to Michelangelo.*

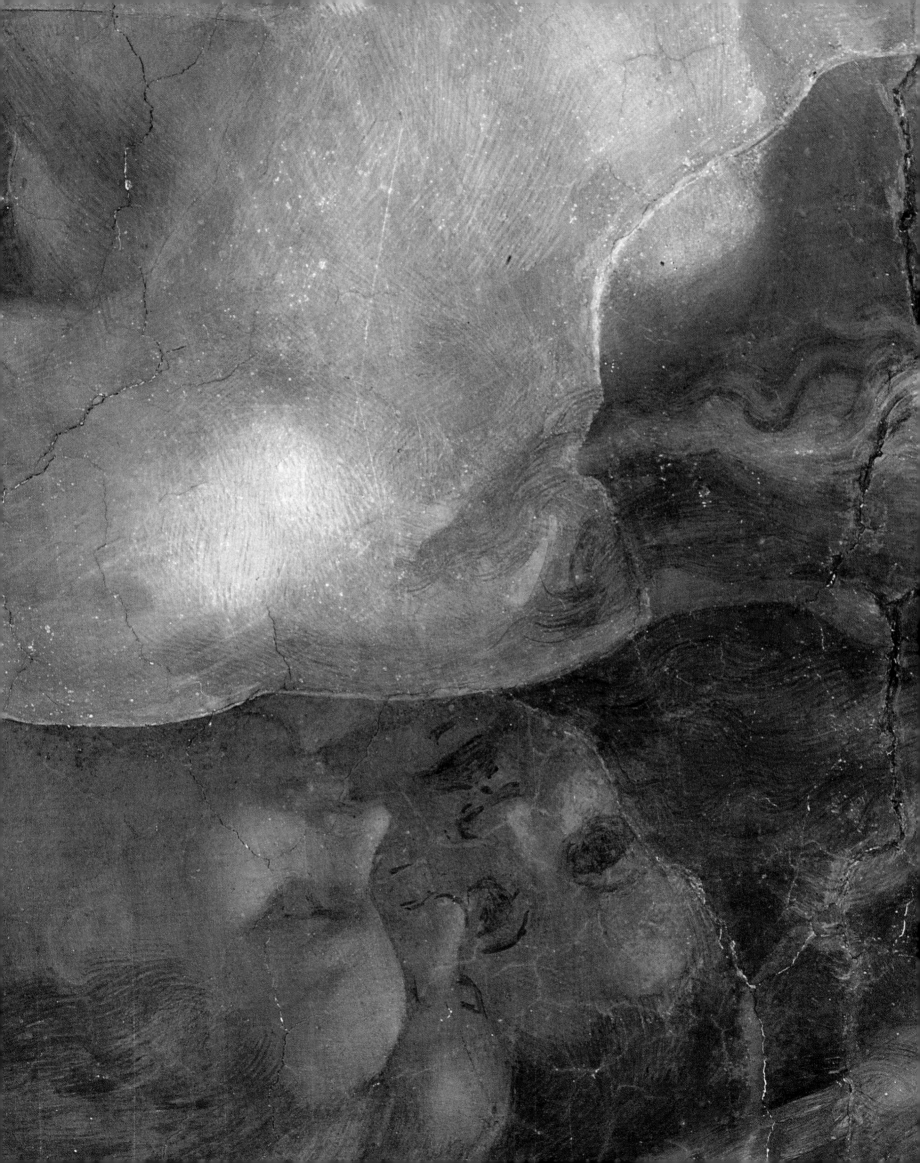

Johan Huizinga described, for instance, a mentality or spirituality of "violent extremes" in France and the Netherlands during this period in his *Waning of the Middle Ages*. Over the course of the years Huizinga has been challenged on a number of points, but much of what he has to say about religion is still supported by contemporary historians, who often find Western Europe "on the eve of the Reformation" to be ridden in its spirituality by a depressing anxiety or morbidity and by a reliance on practices that smack of superstition.[49] The contrast between the spirituality that one hears in the sermons at the papal court and what prevailed elsewhere should not be exaggerated, but recent researches do establish for it a character that was more positive, more serene, more biblical – less prescriptive. The Counter-Reformation later modified that character.

The exquisitely conceived device of isolating the moment of Creation in the convergence of two solitary fingers was an invention, one might say, anticipating that of electricity. But also the design is in the abstract a masterpiece of rhythmic line, of that "disegno" of which Michelangelo was acknowledged master.

(Opposite page) Detail of the largest of the angels surrounding the Creator. Vasari said of the group of God the Father and the angels: God is "borne by a cluster of nude angels of tender age, who seem to hold up not only that one figure but the weight of the entire world".

When the creator of the programme for the Ceiling hit on the idea not only of portraying the ancestors of Christ but of actually inscribing in the lunettes the list of names found in Matthew's genealogy, he could hardly have chosen something that would have excited a more profound response from those who participated in the liturgies of the Chapel. Such inscriptions were unusual in Renaissance painting and especially unusual in Michelangelo. That fact alone calls attention to them and heightens the impact they were intended to have. The list is taken from the opening words of the New Testament, yet it harks back to personages from the Old, thus tying the two Testaments together. Though we know little enough about some of the ancestors named in that list, they were presumed to have been real persons, something that would have appealed to the special interest the Renaissance had in history and narrative. The genealogy points to Mary, to whom the Chapel was dedicated. Most importantly, however, it culminated in the birth of Jesus, that most palpable manifestation of the Incarnation.

Obvious though the general import of Christ's ancestors would be to the Renaissance, some particulars present problems, as usual, to modern interpreters. Michelangelo destroyed the two lunettes on the altar wall some years later when he painted the *Last Judgement*. These contained the first seven ancestors, from Abraham to Aram. If we include these missing seven, we find all 40 of the ancestors of Christ distributed in two series of 20 along the length of the Chapel up to and including the rear wall. Of the original 16 lunettes, 14 survive,

THE CREATION OF EVE

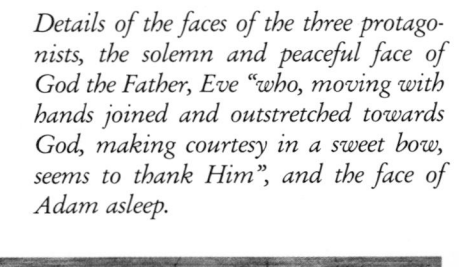

Details of the faces of the three protagonists, the solemn and peaceful face of God the Father, Eve "who, moving with hands joined and outstretched towards God, making courtesy in a sweet bow, seems to thank Him", and the face of Adam asleep.

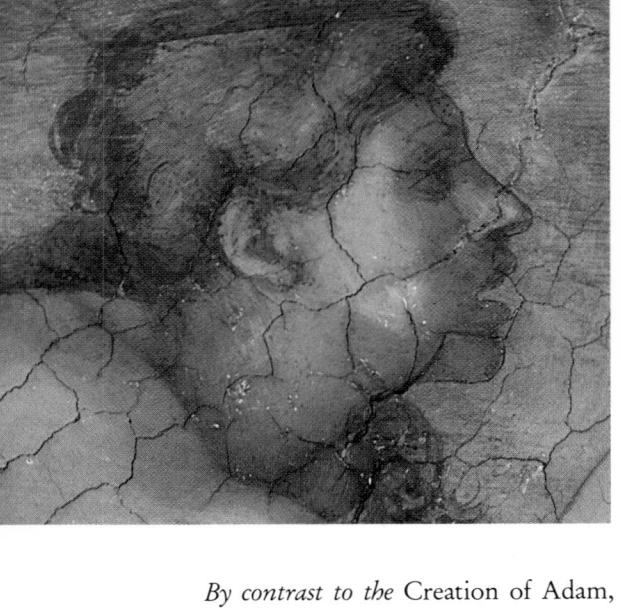

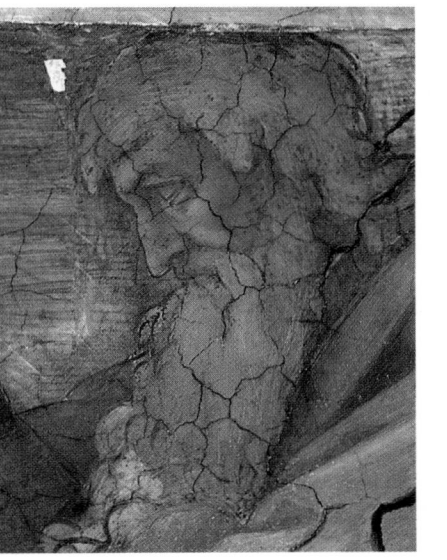

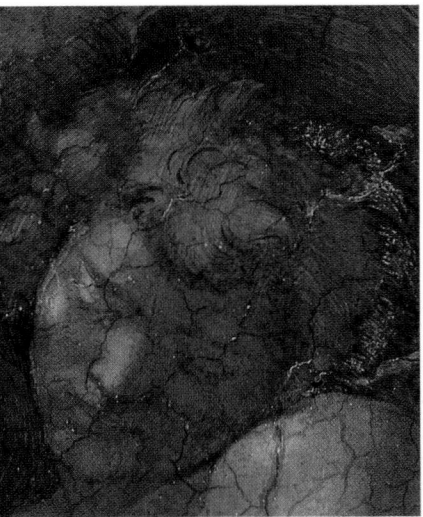

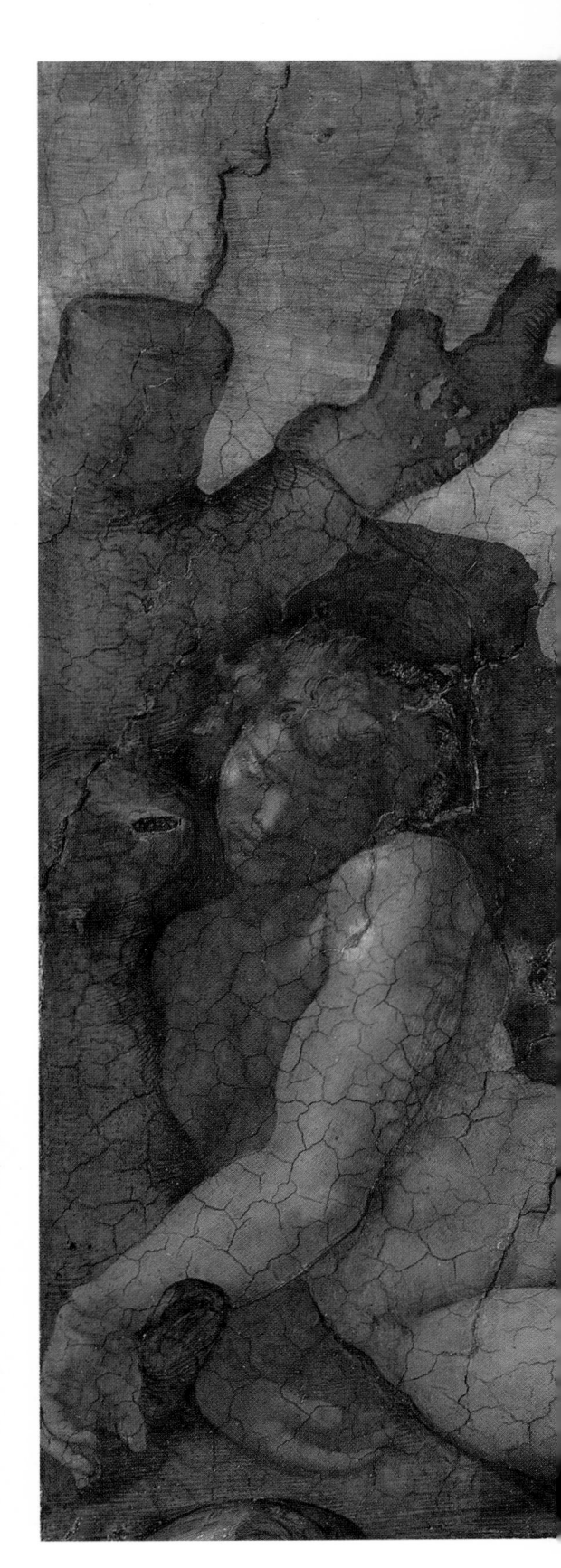

By contrast to the Creation of Adam, painted after the break of 1510–1511, the Creation of Eve belongs to the first campaign, and appears almost archaic. God the Father is shown in the traditional profile; even though he huddles with considerable Giotto-like mass, he has nothing of the majesty of Adam's Creator. For all Vasari's praise, Eve's movement is rather awkward.

Above all the provision of detail – the trees and rocks – and the smaller scale of the figures show this scene to have been painted before the scaffolding was removed and Michelangelo could see that his figures should be as large as he could make them.

divided evenly into seven on each side of the Chapel. For the most part, the number of ancestors inscribed in a lunette corresponds to the number in the lunette on the opposite wall. All this is straightforward enough.

The regular sequence of distribution on the alternating walls, however, shifts pattern with Josias, Jechonias, and Salathiel in the lunette well down the Chapel, just opposite the *Deluge*. Moreover, the numerical distribution of the ancestors is slightly irregular: the lunette on the altar wall near the *Brazen Serpent* contained only three names, whereas the corresponding space on the other side contained four, and

the two lunettes opposite each other near the *Creation of Adam* contain two and three names respectively. The first lunettes on both sides of the Chapel nearest the altar wall are unique in containing only one name each.

Historians have failed to come up with a satisfactory explanation of these phenomena, though they have proposed some suggestive relationships of certain ancestors to nearby narrative scenes. For instance, the name Naasson, in the first lunette on the south wall under the Brazen Serpent, was interpreted to mean "their serpent" or "the serpent is theirs".[50] He is therefore aptly placed, but we must

145

THE FALL AND EXPULSION

And the serpent said unto the woman,
Ye shall not surely die:
For God doth know that in the day ye eat thereof,
then your eyes shall be opened,
and ye shall be as gods, knowing good and evil.

GENESIS 3, 4 – 5

The Fall *and the* Expulsion. *With the Fall, God no longer appeared among men. It so happens that this scene and the following occupy the part of the ceiling over the "place for the people", outside the choir screen (in its original position) of the Chapel. However, given that the Genesis scenes had to start from the altar wall in order to match the order of the Moses and Christ cycles below, this may well be happy coincidence rather than deliberate design on the part of the artist.*

Therefore the Lord God
sent him forth from the garden of Eden,
to till the ground from whence he was taken.
So he drove out the man;
and he placed at the east of the garden of Eden Cherubims...
GENESIS 3, 23 – 24

The Tree of Knowledge divides the scene into 'before' and 'after', emphasized by the parallelism between the serpent wrapped round the Tree who offers the apple to Eve on the left, and the avenging angel who drives out the sinful pair on the right. The rather more anecdotal events, such as the donning of figleaves and the hiding in the bushes, have been left out, for the sake of a tellingly stark opposition. The figure of Eve is one of Michelangelo's most successful, 'difficult' in itself but also suggestive of the gradual awareness of the tempted woman as she turns from forward to back with a look of innocent curiosity. The devil eagerly stretches out the forbidden fruit, lips parted in persuasive words.

The intercrossing of Adam's and Eve's arms, the Devil's arm, and the branches of the tree (detail below) is an example of the kind of complexity that Michelangelo avoided in the second half of the ceiling, partly through necessity (he was under pressure to finish) and partly because he realized that it had comparatively little effect when seen from the floor. He moved from such intricate psychological balance to more dramatic, and simpler, confrontation.

remember that, following the order of the genealogy, he would have been near this scene in any case. I call attention to these details only to indicate once again the interpretative difficulties with which the Ceiling continually confronts us.

The figures in the lunettes, so haunting in their sober contemplation, perhaps suggest the unfulfilled condition of humanity as it awaited its redeemer. Or is there some other explanation? Now that the lunettes have been restored, they will surely be the object of intense study, which will investigate aspects of them that go beyond the theological explanation of the Ceiling that I have attempted here. I have, unfortunately, not had the space adequately to relate the Ceiling to the Chapel as a whole.

Raphael: 'Heraclitus', detail from the 'School of Athens' in the Stanza della Segnatura. In the pensive, clouded person of the "obscure" philosopher (so he was called by Aristotle) it is difficult not to see a portrait by Raphael of Michelangelo, and an imitation by the up-and-coming painter of the older man's style.

Limited though this review has been, I have undertaken it with the persuasion that a presentation of some theological ideas that were operative at Rome in the Renaissance and that we know received expression in sermons delivered in the Chapel itself can enhance our enjoyment of Michelangelo's work. While Renaissance theology surely falls within the broad lines of Christian orthodoxy, it has certain emphases that differentiate it from its medieval counterparts, as well as from those of the Reformation and Counter-Reformation. Even today the Western world is most directly the heir of these last two. We must make some effort, therefore, to place ourselves back into the Sistine Chapel during the Renaissance, if we wish to see the Ceiling with the eyes of Michelangelo's generation.

Renaissance theology continued but gave new emphases to the old tradition that tried to reconcile Christianity with classical culture, and the Sibyls testify to this impulse, as well as to the vast extent of God's plan for the salvation of the race both "under the Law" and "under Grace." Although the Creation narratives from Genesis were hardly new in Christian art, the Renaissance would take special delight in them. The misery of man, sinful and fallen, was not a neglected theme in Renaissance thought, but his dignity, especially as created "in the image and likeness" of God and as "more wondrously" restored by Christ, emerged in the era with new prominence. Renaissance thinkers, while insisting on the historical immediacy of stories and persons from the Old Testament, would also invest them with Christological significance. In a fashion peculiar to themselves, they developed their Christology in a decidedly "incarnational" style of theological thinking that Michelangelo's *Ancestors of Christ* would validate for them. One way or another, soteriology pervades all aspects of Christian interpretation of the Bible. Though not therefore a peculiarly Renaissance concern, it was strongly operative and forces us to look at the whole of the Ceiling with that perspective. In sum, the Renaissance would have seen the Ceiling as pointing in its totality to the salvation, restoration, and even divinization of humanity – in the Church, through the Incarnation and sacrifice of Christ.

All the theology in the world, of course, will not explain the Sistine Ceiling or exhaust the appreciation of those who have had the opportunity to see it, either during the Renaissance or today. Whatever its programme and whoever originated it, the Ceiling in the final analysis is the result of the creative act of one of the greatest artists of all time. Like any great work of art, it is accessible to any sensitive human being. Like any great work of art, too, the more it is studied the more jealously it guards the secret of its greatness. The ultimate mystery of the Sistine Ceiling is locked in the mystery of Michelangelo's genius.

(Left) Raphael: 'Tiburtine' Sibyl, *detail from the Chigi Chapel in Santa Maria della Pace in Rome.*
Like Michelangelo's, these Sibyls, too, have genii *who inspire them. Like Michelangelo's* Cumaean *and* Persian *Sibyls, Raphael's is also represented as an old woman, turning imperiously over great Michelangelesque knees.*

(Right) Pontormo: St Veronica, *detail of the fresco in Santa Maria Novella, Florence. Pontormo shares with Michelangelo a concern to render the figure with maximum impact.*
Since the cleaning of the lunettes of the Sistine Chapel, it has been realized that Michelangelo's influence was also strong on Pontormo's colour.

Sixtus IV's chapel had been conceived as a setting for the most solemn ceremonies of the Church. Nothing was too fine, too magnificent, too impressive for it: the celebrants were to be exalted and inspired, heart and soul, to the utmost degree. Circumstances have decreed that this building, though its exterior, occluded by other buildings of the Vatican complex, counts for nothing, offers the richest available "reading" of the Roman pontificate at that auspicious moment we have been engaged in analysing. The whole era, the whole Renaissance even, is encapsulated here. The Sistine Chapel can transport us back instantly to the great days of Julius II and Leo X: we have all its elements – the magnificent floor, its splendid furnishings, its marble screen, its cycle of tapestries, the serene frescoes of its walls, the majestic figurated argument of its vault, and the colossal frescoed symphony of its altar wall. Nothing is lacking, except the music that was then so important a part of sacred ceremonial.

Alas, "poor music" fades away as soon as it is born, according to Leonardo. That did not mean that the master should not excel at the lyre in his youth, in which he was not unusual among artists of his time.

ANDRÉ CHASTEL

FIRST REACTIONS TO THE CEILING

Too often there is no thought of the song and instrumental music in which princes and prelates, together with their ladies and "cortigiane oneste", took such delight. It was not only at Ferrara and Mantua that concerts and recitals and services with hymns were appreciated, but also at Rome; we are particularly well informed for the pontificate of Leo X, himself a competent player and a devotee of music sacred and profane. Not for nothing had he associated with Heinrich Isaacs

Raphael: The prophet Isaiah, *fresco in Sant' Agostino, Rome. This was the figure that Vasari said Raphael went off and painted in a kind of fury under the impact and spell of a preview of the Sistine ceiling. It is a good story, and the resemblances to Michelangelo's Prophets* are obvious.

149

And the Lord said unto Noah,
Come thou and thy house into the ark;
for thee have I seen righteous
before me in this generation.
GENESIS 7, 1

The Deluge. The eighth scene of the Genesis cycle should actually be the seventh, but this inversion of chronology seems not to have troubled anyone and the advantages of using a larger field for a subject like the Flood are self-evident – particularly since, early on in the painting of the Ceiling, Michelangelo has set forth a full panoply of figures.

… I will cause it to rain upon the earth
forty days and forty nights;
and every living substance that I have made
will I destroy from off the face of the earth.
GENESIS 7, 4

Though difficult to read in detail from the ground, the action is clearly enough organized. On the left, streaming up towards the figure clinging against the wind to a tree, are refugees loaded with their belongings who hope to find safety on higher ground. In the middle of the picture, there are those who hope to escape in a boat that is evidently too flimsy. On the right is another refuge, where a crowd shelter beneath a makeshift tent; towards it a man carries his stricken or dead companion or relative. In the background, solid and square against the elements, the Ark.

during his youth in Florence. Under his predecessor Julius and in the time of Alexander VI Borgia Roman choirs directed by Flemish masters were also widely esteemed.

Carnival in Rome was always an occasion for new songs, for serenades of varying degrees of decorum and for endless dancing to musical accompaniment. The latest thing in the time of Leo X was to bring in the musicians to enliven the end of a meal at home. Cardinal Luigi d'Aragona, the companion of Leo at hunt and feast, presented him with a small organ that excited remark among the chroniclers for the number of its "voices". Accomplished musicians were regaled with

Details of the Deluge: *(Above) Detail from the point of refuge on the right: two figures who hold out helping hands to the man carrying in his stricken companion.*
(Below) Another detail from the same area of the painting: the figure who curls or huddles on the rock. From the detail one can savour the expression of numb endurance and blank despair so brilliantly conveyed.
(Right) Detail of the man and his stricken companion: since he is old, and the man he carries is young, it would be natural to think of a father carrying his son, which would not decrease the pathos.
(Far right) From a vantage point of safety near the Ark, this briefly suggested figure looks out in a pose of ease.

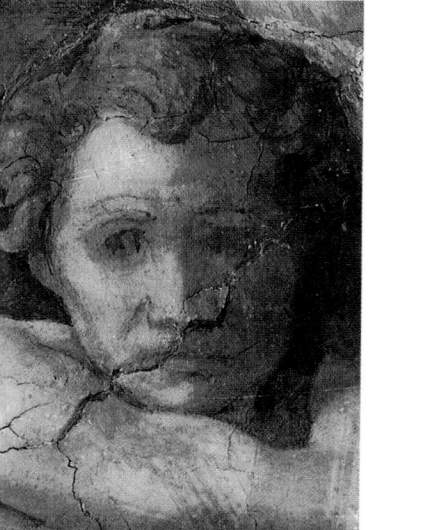

favours, including ecclesiastical benefits. The Sistine Chapel was the place in which to hear the best in sacred music, directed by a master of high renown with a choir of, at one point, more than 30 voices. The tradition was upheld; it did not falter under Paul III. A German visitor, named Rot, would describe with wonder several years later (1554) the productions put on by Palestrina at San Giovanni in Laterano and St Peter's. While looking at Michelangelo's Ceiling we must also try to imagine the music, slightly shrill to our ears, that sounded here on days of pontifical mass.

Given the political importance of Rome, and the coming and going of envoys and political emissaries, there was certainly rapid diffusion of news, and the novelty was not always political. The despatches of Venetian ambassadors, collated in the diary of Marin Sanudo, and local chronicles of all kinds bear witness to the efficient circulation of cultural developments, too. The years 1510–12, however, were not propitious in this regard. The incredible energy of Julius II was devoted not only to pressurizing Bramante for a new St Peter's, Raphael for the Stanze and Michelangelo (postponing the tomb) for the Sistine Chapel ceiling, but also, after the unexpected developments following on the alliances made in 1509, to "throwing the barbarians out of

Italy". He was compelled to convoke the Fifth Lateran Council at the end of 1512, insisting that reforms, should there be need of them, could be instituted only by the authority of the Pope.

After all, there was no Press, so we should not be surprised if during these times of crisis the unveiling of the Ceiling did not give rise to much comment. The unveiling of the *Last Judgement* in 1541 was a very different matter. In Julius II's time there was no procedure, or virtually no procedure, for the announcement of such things. The development of such a procedure was the result precisely of the great artistic initiative of Julius II and Leo X.

Detail of the boat in the centre of the picture. Condivi alludes gently to the cannibalistic fury of the scene: "… the boat, full of many different people, is already taking in water because it is overloaded and because of the violence of the waves, it has lost its sails, it is beyond aid or any human act or rescue; it is a wonder to see the human race perish so squalidly in the waves".

THE SACRIFICE OF NOAH

This scene is actually the seventh on the Ceiling, the *Flood* which precedes it being the eighth, and this may have contributed to Condivi's and Vasari's confusion (a sacrifice of Cain and Abel would have been chronologically in the right place). Compared to Botticelli's scene of sacrifice in the *Purification of the Leper* below,

Though Noah (detail above) is set central in the scene, the real emphasis is evidently on the gathering together of the "clean beasts" and the "clean fowls". One youth hands to another, astride a ram, a fowl; the rest handle other animals or busy themselves with the lighting and fuelling of the altar.

And yet according to Condivi, the dust had hardly settled when all Rome burst in to see the Ceiling after the Pope. He may be right. In his enthusiasm Vasari presented a more embellished version:

Sentissi nel discoprirla correre tutto il mondo d'ogni parte, e questo bastò per fare rimanere le persone trasecolate e mutole

The whole world came running when the vault was revealed, and the sight of it was enough to reduce them to stunned silence

The world of art-lovers and dilettanti passed under the vault and

Michelangelo's composition seems much more sophisticated, with a complex interrelationship of the figures in a much denser format. The sources are very obviously classical reliefs showing sacrifices, rather than a strictly biblical tradition; Noah is conceived in the mould of some Augustus or Numa.

The Sacrifice of Noah. *This scene is somewhat rare in art, which probably explains why both Condivi and Vasari misidentified the subject. Vasari in the first edition of his* Lives *speaks of a sacrifice of Moses; Condivi in his subsequent* Life of Michelangelo *describes it as a Sacrifice of Cain and Abel, "the one grateful and acceptable to the Lord, the other hateful and reprehensible", and in this Vasari followed him in his second edition. However, though it is clear that a sacrifice is going on, it seems unlikely that is performed by Moses, and certainly impossible that it is Cain and Abel's, who are nowhere to be seen. However, the problem did not take long to solve, since the Bible quite clearly describes Noah sacrificing (Genesis 8, 21): "And Noah builded an altar unto the Lord, and took of every clean beast, and of every clean fowl, and offered burnt offerings on the altar. And the Lord smelled a sweet savour ..."*

looked up in the course of the following years, that much is true. But we have no information about reaction to the vault at the time of its unveiling. It was probably not until the early years of Leo X's pontificate that Michelangelo's fame reached the rest of Europe.

However, we do possess one significant document of the interest Michelangelo's ceiling excited. About the middle of July 1512, Alfonso d' Este, Duke of Ferrara, having come to Rome to make his peace with the Pope on the eve of an attack on the French, asked to go

His Excellency very much wanted to see the vault of the Great Chapel which Michelangelo was painting: (it was arranged) and the Duke went up to the vault with several people, who, however, one by one went down and left the Duke alone with Michelangelo; he could not see enough of his figures and covered him with compliments, making it clear that he would very much like a picture, indeed insisting and promising him money; and Michelangelo promised to do one for him ... When the Duke came down, they wanted to take him to see the Pope's apartments and the figures Raphael had painted but he did not wish to ...

This episode is somewhat extraordinary. It marks the beginning of a devotion to Michelangelo that the Duke of Ferrara never relinquished (as he proved in 1529, when he welcomed the artist in flight from Florence). The last sentence has been taken as a proof of rivalry and tension between the artist of the Stanze and the artist of the Ceiling. But the explanation, as suggested by John Shearman, may be simply the lack of time. Anyhow this text confirms the hold that Michelangelo's art was beginning to exert on the great of this world.

However it would be foolish to expect that everyone at the papal court – theologians, prelates of all kinds, diplomats – should, instead of attending to state matters, have regarded as most important what was after all not crucial. Even after the Sistine Chapel had become a monument, witnesses do not mention it. Better yet, the German visitor Johannes Fichard in the account of his voyage to Italy published in 1536 attributes the frescoes of the Sistine Chapel to Raphael. The mistake is revealing. More familiar to us are criticisms emanating from within certain camps within the Vatican. Vasari reports the reactions of the Dutch Pope Hadrian VI (1522–23). Just as the popes of the Early Christian church had committed every antique statue to destruction, "Hadrian had started to talk of wanting to cast down to the ground the Chapel of the divine Michelangelo, for the reason that it was a stew (*stufa*) of nudes; he looked with distaste even upon paintings and statues of good quality, and called them sinful, worldly, shameful and abominable". A mere ten years had elapsed since the ceiling had been finished. Vasari certainly enjoyed dramatizing the passing aspersion cast upon Michelangelo's vault by the ex-tutor of Charles V, but Hadrian undoubtedly took no pleasure in celebrating mass beneath the ring of his *ignudi* – or even in being in Rome at all. As for the reaction of artists to the ceiling, Vasari did not miss the opportunity of relating rather maliciously that at the first, partial revelation of the Ceiling in 1511 Raphael "vistola, mutò subito maniera, e fece a un tratto per mostrare la virtù sua i profeti e le sibille dell' opera Pace" – "when he saw it, he straightway changed countenance, and painted as fast as he could, to show his own mettle, the *Prophets* and *Sibyls* in Santa Maria della Pace". The tale has its value but is not quite accurate; to find an immediate, direct response in Raphael's art to the partial unveiling of the Sistine ceiling, one has only to travel a few paces to the *Stanza della Segnatura* and the figure of Heraclitus in the *"School of Athens"*, or the saturnine *penseroso* generally so identified. The fact that this figure is an addition, absent from the cartoon in the Ambrosiana Gallery, confirms the deduction. It has a monumentality and a strength of modelling out of keeping

Details of the Sacrifice of Noah. *The woman beside Noah seems to react to a sputtering or similar of the fire in front of them; the garlanded figure in front of her (the garland betrays the classical sources for the sacrifice!) is handing over the "clean bird" to the youth astride the ram.*

(Below) Detail of the head of the man lighting the altar fire. His contorted pose became standard for people performing this task in sacrifice or related scenes.

Detail (left) of the man with a ram on the left of the picture. In the second half of the Ceiling Michelangelo had neither the time nor the inclination to paint such figures as this, very carefully drawn and intricately designed; though his subsequent figures are so much more energetic, they have lost the comparatively relaxed peacefulness of this leisurely and communal scene.

Detail (above) of the head of the youth astride the prone ram. A classic profile of Michelangelo's early style, the hair brisked up in the authentic manner of classical busts.

with the other figures in the fresco. At the very least, it is a spiritual portrait of his colleague, who was known for his over-arching temperament and his moody self-absorption. It is probably also a physical likeness, consistent with the infiltration of a gallery of contemporary heads into the crowd of antique thinkers. This indeed constitutes the earliest known reaction to Michelangelo's masterpiece — or to half of his masterpiece; it is a bold, critical and intelligent tribute to the art of the older man, whom all Rome would set up as Raphael's rival.

Another work of Raphael's, his fresco of *Isaiah* in Sant' Agostino in Rome, though this was painted after the unveiling of the complete Ceiling, aroused Vasari to relate another story, though its details make it rather suspect:[2] while Michelangelo was away,

> *Bramante, who had the keys of the Chapel, out of friendship towards Raphael let him have a look in order that he could get some idea of what Michelangelo was up to. That glimpse was enough to make him re-do from scratch his prophet* Isaiah *in Sant' Agostino, above Andrea Sansovino's* St Anne: *in that work, because of what he had seen of Michelangelo's, he re-vamped and re-scaled his style and gave it monumentality*

The placement of the two *putti* or angels, the copious drapery, the forward thrust of the knee, the movement of the arm are indeed very close to Michelangelo's style. In 1512, Raphael deliberately altered his style: the Stanza d' Eliodoro shows him seeking a kind of vehemence that would without doubt have been less intense without the example of Michelangelo's painting. It is therefore tempting to see in the end of 1512 a particularly significant moment, and to see again in the *Sibyls* of Santa Maria della Pace, as did Vasari, the echo of Michelangelo's ceiling. However, it is really only the "Tiburtine" *Sibyl* seated on the right, with her book on her knees, turning towards her *putto* of inspiration, that recalls the gravity and, though more calm than they, the torsion of the Sistine figures; Raphael's other *Sibyls* are sweeter, and, engaged in active conversation with their "daimons", have more of the femininity of the Stanza della Segnatura *Parnassus* Muses.

Leonardo da Vinci, in Rome from 1513 to 1515, has left us no report of what he thought of the Sistine Chapel. But we are familiar with his strictures of 'over-muscled' nudes — which he compared to bags of nuts — a criticism directed at the anatomical exercises of Florentines such as Pollaiuolo but also Michelangelo. The date of the last appearance of this criticism in his notebooks dates from 1513–14, so it may be that it should be related to the Sistine ceiling, as Lomazzo and later authors imply. There is no sign of any copy after or influence from Michelangelo's ceiling — one drawing of a nude at Windsor (inventory no. 12648) looks as if it could be an echo of the *ignudo* above the prophet Joel, but its dating about 1503–04[3] would exclude any connection with the Chapel. Anyway Leonardo had experimented with a similar pose even earlier, for which the inspiration might have been a classical cameo. It is possible also that Michelangelo might have found in a classical work of art of one collection or another the starting-point for his own figure. Michelangelo's ceiling was the first of such dimensions ever to have been painted. Its fictive architectural membering was too original not to have been exploited by other painters involved in similar problems in the subsequent development of ceiling painting. By 1519 Perino del Vaga had taken over elements from the design invented by Michelangelo for the barrel vault of the chapel at San Marcello where he painted a *Creation of Eve*.

The last of the Genesis cycle, situated immediately by the entrance wall, the story of Noah's drunkenness was traditionally an example inculcating respect for authority and for one's elders. Noah, having, as the Bible relates, and as Michelangelo shows on the left, "begun to be a husbandman", then became drunk on the wine made from the vines

And Noah began to be an husbandman,
and he planted a vineyard:
And he drank of the wine, and was drunken;
and he was uncovered within his tent.

GENESIS 9, 20 – 21

The four great compositions in the corner fields or 'spandrels' and the figures of the lunettes seem to have had a particular importance for connoisseurs. Independent of the fictive architecture, they stand free as if they had no part in the general scheme and present themselves more immediately to the spectator's gaze. The figures in the four 'spandrels' were also destined to a par-

he had planted, in which state he was seen, in his nakedness, by his son Ham. Ham told his brothers Shem and Japheth who reverently, without looking, laid a drape over their father. But Ham's son Canaan was accursed by Noah for Ham's sight of his nakedness.

ticular *fortuna*. There is evidence of it in the notes that Paolo Giovio began to make about 1525 for a work about painting. He dwells on just these figures in his manuscript:[4]

> *Called by Julius II with the offer of a huge sum of money to paint the Hall of the Sistine Chapel in the Vatican, Michelangelo left there the testimony of his perfection in art, completing it in a very short time. Although he had to paint it stretched backwards, he used a gradually diminishing light to suggest some figures in the distance, almost hidden, for instance the body of* Holophernes *in his tent, and in others, for instance* Haman *on the cross, he gave such emphasis to the light, in contrast to the shade, that even knowledgeable artists were induced to believe in the truth of the figures he painted, and to see what was flat as solid. Among his outstanding male figures there is to be seen in the middle of the Ceiling the image of an old man flying to heaven, depicted with such rhythm* (symmetria), *that, though one might gaze at him from different parts of the Chapel, he always seems to turn and to persuade one's deceived eyes that he is moving.*

What were most important for Giovio were the modelling or "rilievo" of the forms, and the skilled handling of light, and colour. Contemplating the lunettes, Michelangelo's fellow artists could not help but be impressed by the broadness of execution and simplicity of his composition, by which his subjects were rendered easy to perceive and appreciate. The cleaning of 1982–83 has also revealed aspects of Michelangelo's genius, or simply of his technique, that would have been grasped immediately by professional artists, above all the speed of his hand, his "fa presto", evident in the large size of the *giornate*. Then the incredible variety of poses, profiles, gestures, expressions and so on, constituted a repertory of 'types' without parallel (in these there also seems to re-appear an equivalent to the comic or bizarre figures on friezes or in ornamental sculpture and to the fantastic, for which Michelangelo had a taste). His colours must have been gazed at by the painters with fascination – their quality, the subtle, exhilarating relationships of the complementaries, and, above all – it impressed everyone – their consistent brightness. No less revolutionary were the shimmering effects, the shifts, greens which gave way to yellows in the folds, purples verging into blue; but it was their unprecedented luminosity that Giovio indicated as the most astounding aspect of the Ceiling.

Michelangelo had sent packing his entire team of Florentine assistants, but the frescoes still were a matter of passionate interest for Tuscan artists, in particular for Rosso and Beccafumi, who we know went to Rome, and for Pontormo, whose visit is hypothetical. According to Vasari,[5]

> *In his youth Rosso made drawings after Michelangelo's cartoon and there were few masters with whom he was willing to learn, having formed his own ideas, inimical to their style*

One can easily picture it: Vasari is describing the excitement of the young artist (born in 1495) studying the cartoon made by Michelangelo for the *Battle of Cascina* (1505), which had inspired him with a vision of a new, extraordinary style of painting – "a style more vast in its power, more ravishing in its beauty", as Vasari also put it. Rosso was certainly primed to seek out, study and draw lessons from the plentiful treasures of the Ceiling. We may imagine that he already had some knowledge of them in Florentine workshops, where there was a premium on new effects of bright and shifting colour, although he did

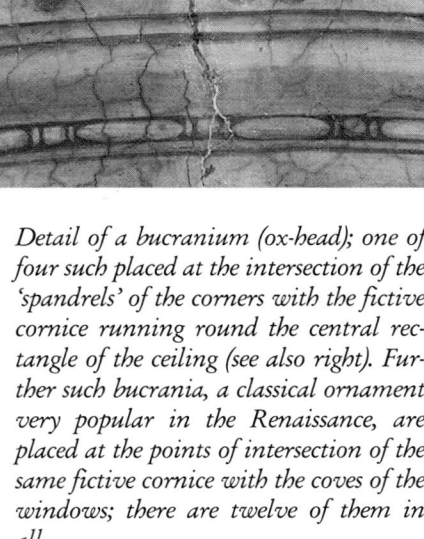

Detail of a bucranium (ox-head); one of four such placed at the intersection of the 'spandrels' of the corners with the fictive cornice running round the central rectangle of the ceiling (see also right). Further such bucrania, a classical ornament very popular in the Renaissance, are placed at the points of intersection of the same fictive cornice with the coves of the windows; there are twelve of them in all.

Either side of the bucrania are placed fictive bronze nudes, mirror images of one another. Their function may safely be said to be to fill up the space and to enrich the architectural syntax − nothing more.

The detail (below) is of one of the pairs of putti, these in fictive marble, who serve

as miniature Atlas figures supporting the fictive cornice that runs all the way round the central rectangle. These occupy the point of intersection between the field in which the Prophets and Sibyls appear and that of the fictive bronze nudes over the window coving. They are slightly more prominent than the bronze nudes: these were mentioned by Condivi, the bronze nudes were not.

161

JUDITH AND HOLOPHERNES

The 'spandrels' of the Ceiling: Judith and Holophernes, *situated on the 'spandrel' between the entrance wall and the left-hand side of the Chapel facing the altar. The whole 'spandrel' (above) is divided into two scenes, on the left Judith and her maid departing with the head of Holophernes, on the right the headless corpse sprawling in the general's tent. The detail (below) shows Judith's head as she turns back to look for the last time at the corpse and at the same time covers over the head in the basket; thus she unites the two parts of the picture in a dramatic moment of her daring mission and escape.*

not go down to Rome until 1523, on the accession of the second Medici Pope, Clement VII. There he saw Michelangelo's masterpiece, from which there followed, as is known, disaster – in Vasari's words, "he painted the least successful of all his works". His *Creation* in Santa Maria della Pace is indeed a bad pastiche of the Sistine ceiling. The pace in Rome was too much: the Florentines were too receptive, and lost their heads. The Antique, so many masterpieces and above all the painting and sculpture of Michelangelo sent them wild. It is nonetheless true that Michelangelo's Ceiling marks the advent of the new bright, shimmering painting.

Even in the phase of Quattrocento art when high tonality was the mode, with Domenico Veneziano and Piero della Francesca, there had never been such vivid, bold and exhilarating contrasts of tone such as one sees in the figures of the lunettes of the Sistine Chapel. In this lower part Michelangelo showed his "sprezzatura", and the disregard of local colour was a manifesto of the new style. This attractive "maniera" was being tried at a moment when, in Rome as in Florence, there was just coming into vogue a sombre style, or at least a darkening of the palette, stemming, it is remarkably clear, from the principles and example of Leonardo. The 'argument' between these two men extended even to technique and in a sense encompassed the entire evolution of Renaissance painting.

About Pontormo we have no exact information, but the hypothesis of a Rome journey advanced by Roberto Longhi is attractive, especially because his links with Michelangelo later in his career are extremely close. It is indeed difficult to suppose that this precocious adept of high tonality painting would have been infected with the new style in Florence, without having felt the need to go to Rome. It is true that he did not like travelling, but his well-known secrecy is a feature of his later career. In any case, when his talent had brought him to the forefront and he was given the opportunity to paint a *Veronica* above the entrance arch of the Pope's chapel in Santa Maria Novella, its audacious design and high-keyed colours placed him firmly in the camp of "Michelangelism". But full comprehension of the reactions of the new generation to the Sistine ceiling is impossible without better information of the workshop of Andrea del Sarto, that crucible through which passed both Rosso and Pontormo, and of the contacts and exchange between Rome and Florence. An anecdote in Vasari's *Life* of Perino del Vaga reveals that his colleagues in Florence cross-questioned him about "news from Rome" – this was in 1524. In 1515, the solemn entry *alla romana* of Leo X into Florence would have brought together all interested parties.

According to Vasari, the young Beccafumi had rushed down to Rome much earlier:[6]

> *In Rome the chapel of Michelangelo and the works of Raphael of Urbino were available to see. Domenico, who wanted nothing better than to learn, realized he was wasting time in Siena ... and went to Rome*

He must have gone then, to see these novelties, after 1512. In the months he spent in Rome Beccafumi achieved nothing of importance, apparently, but he assimilated these models to the point that he became "fiero nel disegnare, copioso nell' invenzioni e molto vago coloritore" – "forceful in his drawing, inventive and versatile, and a very attractive colourist". If we possessed a better chronology of his work, we might be able to point to pictures in which the lesson of the Ceiling had been directly applied.

Few of the drawings made by Michelangelo for the Ceiling, which must have run to the hundreds, have survived – with the exception of those for the lunettes. Destruction, theft, wear and tear – there are many possible explanations. Such drawings in any case were sought out by artists to copy from. A red chalk drawing of the *Adam* of the Ceiling in the British Museum is generally attributed to Salviati in his first period in Rome, about 1532–34. There are other Renaissance copies, notably a sheet with the *Sons of Noah,* finely modelled, also in the British Museum, and another, again in red chalk, but more delicate, of the *Family of Josiah* from one of the lunettes, which are

definitely not by Salviati. Salviati "discovered" the work of Michelangelo at the same time as Vasari, but, more impressionable and less eclectic than his friend, he went so far as to take direct copies after Michelangelo's drawings, for which there was already a demand. Michelangelo's *David and Goliath* was imitated by Salviati in the Palazzo Sacchetti in 1553, using a drawing (now in the Pierpont Morgan Library in New York) which differs in some respects from the painting itself. In the same cycle, Salviati also used Michelangelo's *Judith,* showing Holophernes in his tent and Judith already on her way back with her servant carrying his head. As was apparent from Giovio, it was particularly the 'spandrel' compositions that attracted attention; Rubens, much later, made a drawing of the *Brazen Serpent.*

The detail (above) shows the splendidly craggy profile of Holophernes before it is discreetly covered over. The composition of this scene does not reflect the Bible narrative very closely, but follows the traditional 15th-century portrayal of this subject, as it had been handled, for instance, by Botticelli and Mantegna. Michelangelo has not exploited the unusual shape of the field for his composition, either, but essentially treated it as a rectangle with more or less superfluous extra corners.

163

DAVID AND GOLIATH

Very commonly paired with Judith and Holophernes, David and Goliath *are located in the neighbouring 'spandrel', the one between the entrance wall and the right-hand wall of the Chapel facing towards the altar. Here, however, Michelangelo has adapted his composition rather more to the shape of the field, setting a triangle, David over the corpse of Goliath, against the inverted triangle of the field. Once again with good 15th-century precedent, Michelangelo shows David not killing Goliath with his sling, but cutting off his head after his stone has struck him down. Both Judith and David, examples of virtue overcoming its enemies despite apparently hopeless odds, could have been given a variety of more specific meanings if necessary. The detail (below) shows two soldiers of the onlooking armies.*

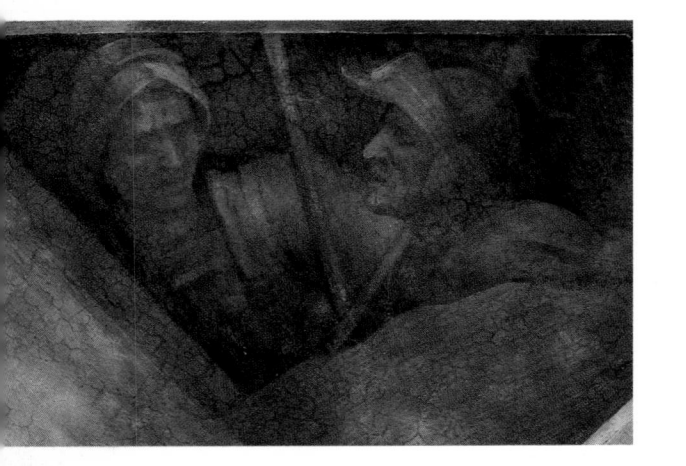

Unlike Raphael, Michelangelo made no attempt at all to disseminate his designs by means of copyists and engravers. However, "the exhibition in 1505 of his cartoon for the *Battle of Cascina* determined the way of things for the future. Engravings after elements or details of the cartoon were indispensable aids in the assimilation of the lessons of the master" – of Michelangelo, be it noted; no such engravings were made after the *Battle of Anghiari* of Leonardo opposite, of quite different style. Even if the production of engraved copies after the Sistine ceiling was less precipitate, nevertheless the number of printmakers who were attracted to the Ceiling in the course of the 16th century and after was considerable. "The first was Marcantonio Raimondi, some time before 1527. The scenes he chose were (thrice) *Paradise,* the *Drunkenness of Noah* and one of the *Families* of the lunettes (once each). These are all figure studies, a partial reproduction, essays as it were. At this period the faithful reproduction of pictorial compositions in engravings was extremely rare."[7]

There are few prints after the Ceiling before the 1540s; but from that period on they multiplied, with the production of "suites" of more or less faithful figures by Giorgio Ghisi, then by Enea Vico, Benasone and others – often copying the copies. In 1551 Jerome Cock published in Antwerp sets of the *ignudi,* the *Prophets* and the *Sibyls,* without doubt based on other drawings made *in situ.* There were also represented some other famous scenes: the *Creation of Adam* bears an inscription which might have amused Michelangelo: "Hieronimus de grandi pinxit / gaspar Ruina fecit". The intermediary had insisted on inserting his own name!

According to a remark at the end of Vasari's *Life* of Perino del Vaga, who died in 1547, Perino collected drawings and among them "the complete chapel of Michelangelo, drawn by Leonardo Cungi dal Borgo San Sepolcro, most excellently done; all which designs, with some other things, were sold by his heirs." The draughtsman is almost unknown, and the drawings have disappeared, but, given the importance Perino attached to them, they must have been good ones of their kind and quite possibly were the basis for a well-known series of six engravings of the five great figures of the left (south) side of the ceiling and the *Delphic Sibyl.* However, according to the conclusions of Michal and Lewis,[8] this series should be dated to about 1570–72, despite the fact that the name Piero Facchetto and the date 1549 appear on several of the prints. Facchetto, born in 1539, could not have been the publisher and one cannot attach much weight to these inscriptions. Competition between publishers was sharp and would explain the date being brought forward. Vasari, after mentioning the engravings after Michelangelo's drawings published by Lafreri, adds that four of the *Prophets* of the Ceiling had also been engraved, but were so badly drawn and printed that "it would be better not to mention" the names of those responsible. It has been supposed that he meant the 63 prints of Adamo Scultori, which do indeed deserve to be forgotten, but attest a considerable demand.

The importance of Giorgio Ghisi's six engravings after the Ceiling is partly that they created an independent *fortuna* for the *Prophets* and *Sibyls* they reproduced: these now took their place, along, for instance, with the marble *Moses* from Julius II's tomb, in a repertoire of monumental figures. But also these engravings provided together with these great figures the minor figures beside them and at their feet – the *genii* behind who reflect the onset of their inspiration, the *putti*

THE BRAZEN SERPENT

Occupying the 'spandrel' between the altar wall and the right-hand side of the Chapel facing the altar, the Brazen Serpent offers a typological parallel that was very often drawn to the central

drama of Christianity and the mass, the Crucifixion. When the people of Israel were afflicted by plague, Moses set up a brazen serpent (detail below) that cured those who looked at it; Christ, according to St John's Gospel, would in the same way give eternal life to those who believed in Him. Michelangelo has exploited both the subject and the field (detail, opposite) to give a virtuoso demonstration of writhing nudes, of the kind that was much appreciated by Mannerist artists: Vasari called them, "still more beautiful and divine ... than all the others".

who 'carry' the cornice, the figures in the segments between them, the *putti* who bear their tablet and all the diverse and delightful personages of the coves over the windows. The role and influence of Ghisi's engravings in this format – putting into circulation all these secondary inventions of such vitality – cannot, I do not think, be overestimated. One can see, for example, how the ramping figures in the segments repeat the poses of the *ignudi* above them; and they are nude like them, a little shocking like them in their freedom of

movement, and are occupied like them in holding up or in handling garlands, ribands or other ornaments.

All the details of handling and modelling in the engravings can be checked today against the original. It is particularly interesting to do so, making due provision for the copyist's translation or interpretation in another medium, now that the frescoes have been restored. The transcription into black and white accentuates or rather exaggerates even the nature of the drawing, rendering it more exuberant, more insistent. In the fresco the ramping figures are held back on the wall by their brown colouring; in the engraving, they come right forward. In the fresco the *putti* of both levels merge into the architectural

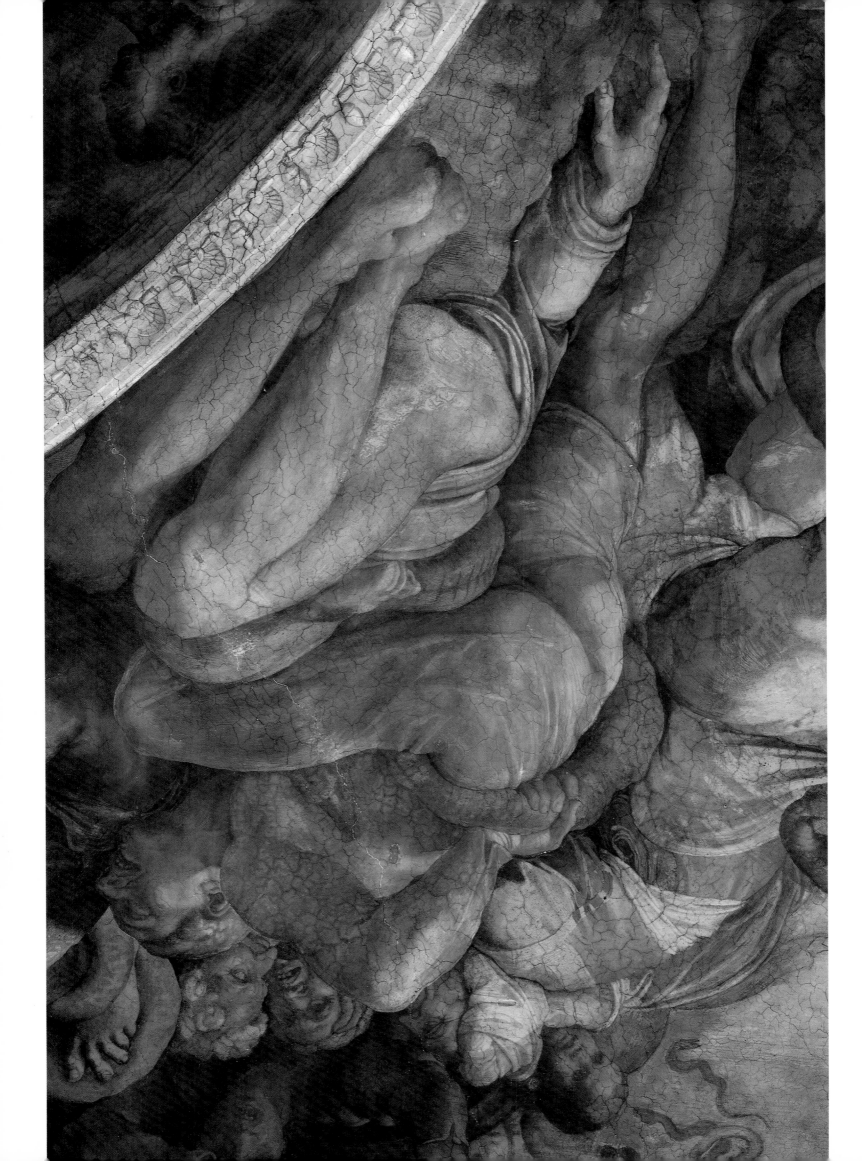

THE PUNISHMENT
OF HAMAN

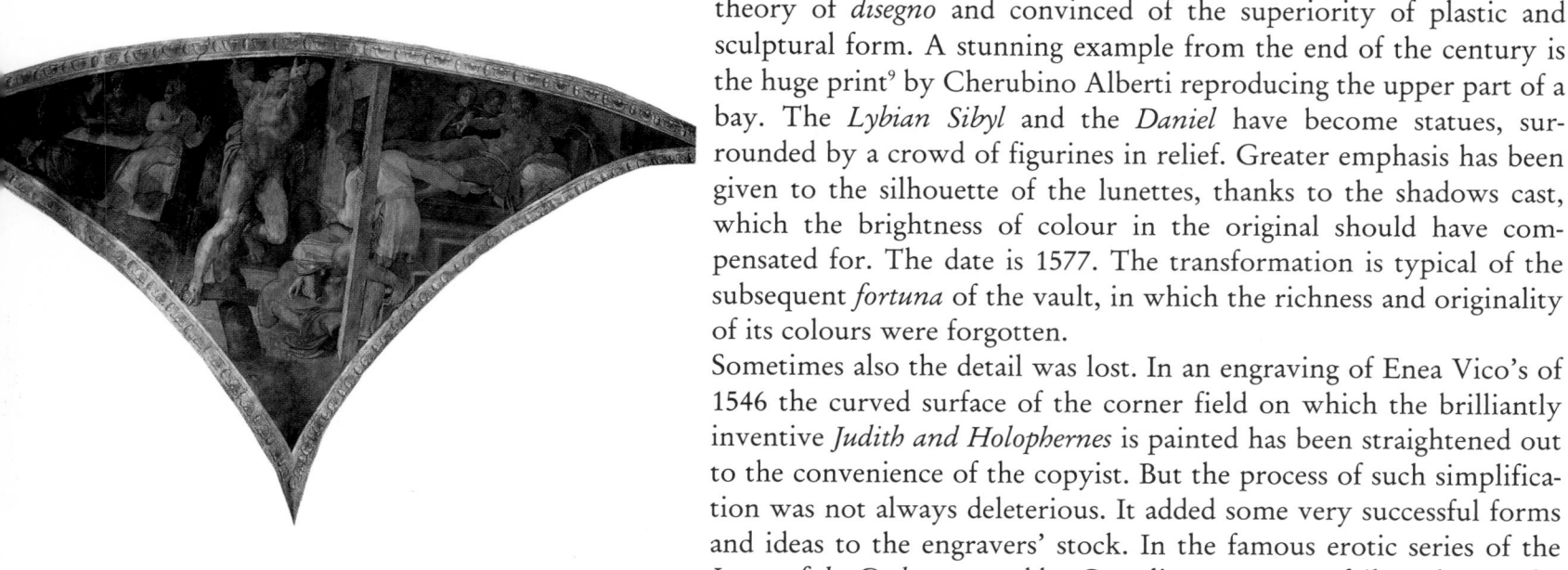

framework; when engraved, they take on greater relief and a usurping importance. The light, shimmering colours of the minor scenes in the lunettes suspend the figures in an unreal atmosphere; their stark intensity in black and white makes it possible to appreciate the variety of their poses and characterization, though it imbalances the whole. In the fresco itself, the first place and firmer presence of the *Sibyls* and *Prophets* is incontestable.

Such a development must not be minimized. The translation into black and white of the delicate colour system of the frescoes was easily accepted by Tuscan or Roman artists imbued as they were with the theory of *disegno* and convinced of the superiority of plastic and sculptural form. A stunning example from the end of the century is the huge print[9] by Cherubino Alberti reproducing the upper part of a bay. The *Lybian Sibyl* and the *Daniel* have become statues, surrounded by a crowd of figurines in relief. Greater emphasis has been given to the silhouette of the lunettes, thanks to the shadows cast, which the brightness of colour in the original should have compensated for. The date is 1577. The transformation is typical of the subsequent *fortuna* of the vault, in which the richness and originality of its colours were forgotten.

Sometimes also the detail was lost. In an engraving of Enea Vico's of 1546 the curved surface of the corner field on which the brilliantly inventive *Judith and Holophernes* is painted has been straightened out to the convenience of the copyist. But the process of such simplification was not always deleterious. It added some very successful forms and ideas to the engravers' stock. In the famous erotic series of the *Loves of the Gods* engraved by Caraglio, one cannot fail to observe the debt of the couple of *Mercury and Hersa* to Michelangelo's *Judith*, that of *Vertumnus and Pomona* (drawn by Perino del Vaga) to the *Libyan*

The detail (below) shows an episode in the involved intrigue after which the king eventually ordered Haman's death.

On the 'spandrel' between the altar wall
and the left-hand side of the Chapel facing the altar, the Punishment of Haman, like the Brazen Serpent, was commonly used as a 'type' of the sacrifice of
Christ; the parallel between Haman's
mode of death and Christ's is obvious,
though it involves in fact a distortion of
the biblical narrative, which had him
die on the gallows.
The two parts of the composition are divided and joined by the central,
dramatic figure of the agonized Haman,

compositionally counterpointing the
shape and curve of the spandrel (detail
left). On the right, the king, Ahasuerus,
is shown on his bed, where he could not
sleep, and therefore looked again into his
records, after which he turned against
his vizier Haman (detail, above). One of
the most successful elements of the painting is the inclusion of two onlookers between the king's bedroom and Haman's
death, who serve to set the suffering
nude into greater illusionist depth
(detail, below).

Sibyl. This series came out in 1525 and the years following: we can see
that the straightening out of the corner fields had begun early on, and
this in turn is a sign of the interest of these compositions for artists,
who to a degree made Michelangelo's work more freely available by
removing them from the sacred to the profane. Indeed the propaga-
tion of the striking "moti" with which the Ceiling is abundantly
provided had no end: they are a fundamental determinant of the
whole of Western art. But to pursue their further *fortuna* would take
us outside the perspective of contemporary reaction to the Ceiling.

THE GENERATION
OF JESUS CHRIST

(see page 120)

Between the 'pendentives' descending either side of the windows and under the rectangle of the Ceiling proper, marked by the fictive architectural cornice, there is an irregular space divided up into three triangles. Two of these triangles are occupied by nudes in fictive bronze (see page 120). The third was coupled by Michelangelo with the lunettes flanking the window, and given over, with them, to the representation of the Ancestors of Christ. *While the Ancestors were represented in the lunettes in pairs, triplets or even once, on the destroyed altar wall, in a foursome, the cove above (if there was one) was occupied by the family of the Ancestor concerned. In the cove shown opposite, over the last window on the left-hand wall facing the altar, between the prophet* Daniel *and the* Libyan Sibyl, *the* Family *depicted is that of Jesse, David or Solomon.*

Or, as Condivi put it: "But in the space which is under (i.e., in) the lunettes, and also in the space above, which is shaped in a triangle, there is painted the entire genealogy, or we should say generation, of the Saviour." "Generation" was what Matthew had called it in the first sentence of his Gospel.

The book of the generation of Jesus Christ, the son of David, the son of Abraham.

Abraham begat Isaac; and Isaac begat Jacob; and Jacob begat Judas and his brethren;

And Judas begat Phares and Zara of Thamar; and Phares begat Esrom; and Esrom begat Aram.

And Aram begat Aminadab; and Aminadab begat Naasson; and Naasson begat Salmon;

And Salmon begat Booz of Rachab; and Booz begat Obed of Ruth; and Obed begat Jesse;

And Jesse begat David the king; and David the king begat Solomon of her that had been the wife of Urias;

And Solomon begat Roboam; and Roboam begat Abia; and Abia begat Asa;

And Asa begat Josaphat; and Josaphat begat Joram; and Joram begat Ozias;

And Ozias begat Joatham; and Joatham begat Achaz; and Achaz begat Ezekias;

And Ezekias begat Manasses; and Manasses begat Amon; and Amon begat Josias;

And Josias begat Jechonias and his brethren, about the time they were carried away to Babylon:

And after they were brought to Babylon, Jechonias begat Salathiel; and Salathiel begat Zorobabel;

And Zorobabel begat Abiud; and Abiud begat Eliakim; and Eliakim begat Azor;

And Azor begat Sadoc; and Sadoc begat Achim; and Achim begat Eliud;

And Eliud begat Eleazar; and Eleazar begat Matthan; and Matthan begat Jacob;

And Jacob begat Joseph the husband of Mary, of whom was born Jesus who is called Christ.

So all generations from Abraham to David are fourteen generations; and from David until the carrying into Babylon are fourteen generations; and from the carrying away into Babylon unto Christ are fourteen generations.

MATTHEW 1, 1 – 17

(Opposite page) The Family *of Jesse, David or Solomon.*

Though there are six windows on each long wall of the Chapel, only the middle four have coves; the others abut the 'spandrels' of the corners. There are in fact 14 sets of Ancestors, but only eight families; the Family of Jesse *is shown on the previous page, the other seven are here.*

Though the coves are not very prominent, Michelangelo was concerned as always to provide variety. But, though his invention did not flag, it is noticeable that some of these figures show marked signs of depression, exhaustion or despair, which can be related to Michelangelo's own emotional state while the painting went on.

We may perhaps think of these family groups as 'extra legem', beyond the pale of divine law, or more precisely as 'sub lege', subject to the Covenant, but not yet 'sub Gratia' – redeemed by Christ's sacrifice.

The long and arduous way of redemption, as a historical as well as an actual experience, is perhaps portrayed in the psychological reaction of these groups, as if they were in an intermediate state between ignorance and complete grace. Michelangelo varies the attitudes of the nameless figures as much as possible, although they are without exception in a sitting or reclining position; and the sex and age of the persons are fully identified by the way he poses the bodies, thus lifting them out of complete anonymity. Nevertheless, when we compare these with the daring perspective solutions of the *ignudi* on the vault, or the lunette figures, we may be reminded of the dwellers in the cave of Plato's *Republic,* incarcerated in surroundings where light appears only as a reflection, a far-away echo in the mind.

But the figure on the previous page, squatting in a frontal position, seems to pierce the darkness, eyes straining towards the future.

Following page:
Michelangelo: the lunettes of the Sistine Chapel: the Ancestors of Christ. *The Gospel of St Matthew begins with the genealogy of Jesus Christ, "son of David, son of Abraham". The intention was to insist that Christ was the pre-ordained, indeed royal successor to the Patriarchs and Kings, born to the leadership of Israel. The genealogy is divided into three sections, each of 14 generations, from Abraham to David, from David to Jechonias ("about the time they were carried away to Babylon") and from Jechonias to Jesus Christ.*
Each lunette contains a central tablet

where the names of the Ancestors are inscribed, in groups of three, two or, rarely, one. Two of the lunettes were destroyed to make way for the Last Judgement, so that the series, instead of beginning with Abraham, begins with Aminadab. Like the figures of the popes, the Ancestors are arranged chronologically but advance from the altar down the Chapel on both sides at once, alternating from side to side. Though they are simply representative figures, almost ciphers, they have been given sometimes tremendous power and expression by Michelangelo: as Vasari said: "I cannot describe the variety of them, of their drapery, the heads, their look and expression, and the infinity of bizarre and novel inventions, beautifully judged for their role".

173

Hitherto these lunettes had not aroused much more than a passing mention, largely because of the extremely dirty condition in which they have long remained. After the recent cleaning, they have emerged as fascinating and sometimes extremely beautiful examples of Michelangelo's fresco style, ringing and resonant in their bold colour, dramatically painted in simple, sure, broad strokes.

These Ancestors, which had never, so far as is known, been painted before, were in one sense an ingenious solution to a problem of space that needed to be filled; in another sense they could serve as shorthand for the rest of the Old Testament for which there was no space on the Ceiling. Starting originally, on the altar wall, with Abraham, Isaac, Jacob and Judas, and continuing to Jacob and Joseph, the spouse of Mary, these names, sometimes famous, sometimes entirely obscure, served as a compendium of the entire story of the Bible, and might have justified Condivi's statement that Michelangelo painted on the Ceiling "almost all of the Old Testament".

174

The *Last Judgement* was unveiled on All Saints' Day's eve 1541, about five and half years after Michelangelo had mounted the scaffolding and started to paint his representation of this final act of human history on the end wall of the Sistine Chapel. However, the series of events that led eventually to the painting of the work had their beginning much earlier, probably in the summer of 1533. These events are not clear in all their aspects, and the documentation we possess, though plentiful, is not sufficient to provide unambiguous answers to our questions about the original nature and purpose of Michelangelo's commission and the exact intentions of his patron, or about the first reactions of the artist and the way in which the programme of the new work was eventually arrived at.

Having been pardoned by Clement VII for his active support of the anti-Medicean Republic of Florence, Michelangelo spent a long time in Rome, from August 1532 to June 1533, before returning to Florence with the task of bringing to completion the work in progress on the New Sacristy of San Lorenzo. It would seem that the idea of

PIERLUIGI DE VECCHI

MICHELANGELO'S LAST JUDGEMENT

(Opposite page) Detail of the Christ of Michelangelo's Last Judgement, *on the altar wall of the Sistine Chapel.*
The magnificent, ambiguous, titanic figure of Michelangelo's Christ commands not only the fresco in which it occupies the pivotal position, but the whole Chapel. The significance of the gesture made by Christ, or rather the movement that integrates Christ's entire figure, is manifold; it does not correspond to any conventional iconographic sign language, but combines reminiscences of Christ raising his standard in Resurrection with others – damning gestures, the gestures of emperors, and so on.

the new undertaking was conceived soon after his departure from Rome if, as Johannes Wilde first convincingly proposed,[1] its first traces can be identified in a letter sent to Michelangelo by Sebastiano del Piombo on 17 July 1533. Sebastiano writes[2]:

> *Our Lord has told me that I should let you know on his behalf ... that you should be of good cheer, because he has decided, before you return to Rome, to work as much for you as you have and will continue to do for his Holiness, and to give you a contract for something beyond your dreams ...*

The Pope could have communicated his intentions to the artist directly about two months later, when there was a meeting between them at San Miniato al Tedesco,[3] through which Clement VII passed on his way to Nice. Probably Michelangelo showed much less enthusiasm about the project than the Pope or Sebastiano had expected: judging by what Condivi and Vasari have to tell us, he was even quite strongly opposed to it, and it would conflict with the undertakings he had given the Della Rovere in a new contract of April 1532 for the tomb of Julius II. On the other hand two further factors came to

View of the altar wall with the Last Judgement *in the context of the Chapel as a whole.*
Originally the three tiers into which the 15th-century decoration of the Chapel divides the walls continued unaltered across the altar wall; indeed the decoration as it were emanated from the altar wall, where both the

cycles of Christ and Moses on the walls and the story of Genesis by Michelangelo on the ceiling began. The disruption to the old scheme caused by the insertion of the Last Judgement *is immense; correspondingly the impact of Michelangelo's fresco is all the greater, requiring the spectator radically to re-adjust.*

177

Engravings from W. Y. Ottley, Italian School of Design, *published in London in 1823, representing the two lunettes once on the altar wall and painted by Michelangelo with the first seven Ancestors of Christ; these lunettes were destroyed together with the windows they surmounted when the entire wall was remade for Michelangelo's fresco of the* Last Judgement. *Ottley evidently ob-*

tained the designs from drawings or engravings that have since been lost. They can provide only a schematic idea of the originals, but they confirm what one would have expected, that these figures, among the last to be painted in the Ceiling campaign, were bold, monumental and venerable. They represented not only mere names but also Abraham, Isaac and Jacob.

(Opposite page) Michelangelo: The Last Judgement.

make the project seem more attractive – Michelangelo's dislike and fear of the new Duke of Florence, Alessandro de' Medici,[4] and a growing dissatisfaction with the work in the New Sacristy, which was dragging on and on and was increasingly being devolved on to assistants.

Between October 1533 and May 1534 Michelangelo was once more in Rome and in that time probably discussed and finalized an agreement with the Pope. The first sign of the artist's commitment to the new project had come in a letter of 20 February 1534 from an agent of the Gonzaga in which he reports that the Pope[5] "ha tanto operato che ha disposto Michelangelo a dipinger in la cappella e che sopra l'altare se farà la resurrectione, sì che già si era fatto il tavolato" – "has managed to persuade Michelangelo to paint in the Chapel and so above the altar there will be the *Resurrection,* for which the scaffolding is already prepared". However, work had not in fact yet started, and two days after Michelangelo had finally settled in Rome, having passed the remainder of the summer in Florence, Clement VII died (on 27 September 1534) and Michelangelo, presuming that the death of the Pope meant the end of the project, was thinking again of being able to dedicate himself completely to the tomb of Julius II. He was again disappointed: the newly elected Pope, Paul III Farnese, who had long been a fervent admirer of his art, took up his predecessor's project with, if anything, greater enthusiasm, refusing to accept any excuses and even threatening to tear up the contract Michelangelo had made with the Della Rovere.[6] Forced against his will to go back to his studies and other preparations for the fresco, Michelangelo created delays and in every means in his power put off the moment when he had to start painting. The rendering of the wall for painting was not begun until April 1535 and took a very long time, both because of the need to fill in the two windows which opened through it and especially because the wall, in accordance with the specific requirements of the artist, had to be cut away to a depth increasing from top to bottom, in such a way that it sloped forward, and then this surface had to be covered over in a "scarpa" – "embankment" – of bricks "ben murati e scelti e ben cotti" – "well laid, selected and well made" – in such a way that it should be as regular and uniform as possible.[7]

No sooner had these preparations been completed, than an argument broke out between Michelangelo and Sebastiano del Piombo over the proper fresco technique to be used (*a fresco* according to Michelangelo, in oils according to Sebastiano), and so also about the final surface of the wall. Although Condivi is silent about the affair, Vasari reports it in full, though not in Michelangelo's *Life* but in Sebastiano's.[8]

This incident is confirmed by documents: between January and March 1536 the "incrostatura" that Sebastiano wanted was removed and replaced by the surface required by Michelangelo. After which, when one last obstacle, the purchase of what to the mind of the artist was the necessary quantity of ultramarine blue, had been overcome, the painting of the fresco could be got under way in the first weeks of the summer of 1536.

More than 400 years later, it is no simple task to reconstruct with any certainty the steps by which, starting from the original concept and intentions of Clement, the artist arrived, after discussion, modification and transmogrification, at the extraordinary image we see today.

Vasari, alone among our sources, reports that Clement intended to have Michelangelo paint both the end walls of the Chapel.[9] But on the

other hand the letter already mentioned from the Gonzaga agent, of 20 February 1534, asserts that the Pope had finally succeeded in persuading the artist to paint a "Resurrection" over the altar, which has led several scholars to suppose that at that time the intention was simply to substitute for the fresco altarpiece of the *Assumption* by Perugino a *Christ's Resurrection*,[10] a subject for which there are several studies by Michelangelo datable to the early 1530s.[11] This supposition, however, seems to be extremely dubious and particularly unconvincing considering that the Chapel was dedicated to the Assumption and that, in one of his studies for the *Judgement*,[12] Michelangelo was intending to leave untouched the fresco immediately over the altar even when on the other hand he had already anticipated destroying some of the other 15th-century frescoes on this wall.

In fact "Resurrection" can be understood readily enough as short for "Resurrection of the Dead" or "of the Body" and therefore to mean a *Last Judgement*, although perhaps the element of resurrection was particularly emphasized, as it had been in Signorelli's frescoes for the San Brizio chapel in Orvieto Cathedral.

If Vasari is correct, then, the initial project envisaged the painting of two large frescoes representing the *Last Judgement* and the *Fall of the Rebel Angels* on the end walls and was subsequently reduced, presumably in accordance with the artist's wishes, to a *Last Judgement* alone on the altar wall. Vasari also says that Michelangelo made drawings for the *Fall of the Rebel Angels* as well, and it is in fact possible to find at least an echo for such studies both in the preparatory drawings for the *Judgement* and in certain elements of the fresco itself.

In any case Clement's project necessitated the first action one could call destructive that had been taken since the Sistina had been built. The Sistine Chapel was the setting for the most solemn papal ceremonies and had evolved, in accordance with its special role and thanks to the employment of some of the greatest artists of the time, into a fully harmonious and coherent structure, coherent both iconographically and architecturally or decoratively. Even the frescoes of Michelangelo's Ceiling had transformed, but not disturbed or contradicted its overall unity, which had been sealed finally by the superb series of tapestries designed by Raphael and hung by Leo X when the future Clement VII, his nephew, already occupied a leading position in the Curia.

The new project necessitated not only a disturbance to the internal environment of the Chapel, in so far as the lighting conditions were to be altered, but also the destruction of an element of the 15th-century cycle – the effigies of the earliest popes, including *St Peter* himself, the first two episodes in the cycles of Moses and of Christ and even, in the end, the *Assumption* over the altar – and of two of the lunettes painted by Michelangelo himself at the time of the Ceiling, showing the first two *Ancestors of Christ*. Thus the entire iconographic programme of the Chapel, which had been built up in stages but with marvellous consistency, so as to express with remarkable rhetoric the ideology and belief of the Roman Curia in the last years of the 15th century and the first years of the 16th – this was now brutally mutilated on the initiative of a pope and by the hands of an artist who together had seen the increase and fruition of the ideal of the "renovatio" of the "eternal city" under the governance of St Peter's successors, but who also had lived through the dramatic events that led, amid extreme religous bitterness and great agonies of conscience, to

The Last Judgement, *12th century, painted in Rome, now in the Vatican Gallery.*
Fundamental elements of the iconography of the Last Judgement, which appeared first in the illuminations of manuscripts in the 11th century, are the Majestas Domini, *or the Lord enthroned in glory, deriving from Matthew's Gospel, and St John's vision of the Apocalypse. The image is best known perhaps from the tympana of portals of numerous churches and cathedrals.*

(*Below*) *The* Last Judgement, *fresco in the church of Sant' Angelo in Formis, near Capua. The patron was Abbot Desiderio of Montecassino, and it was painted in the second half of the 12th century.*

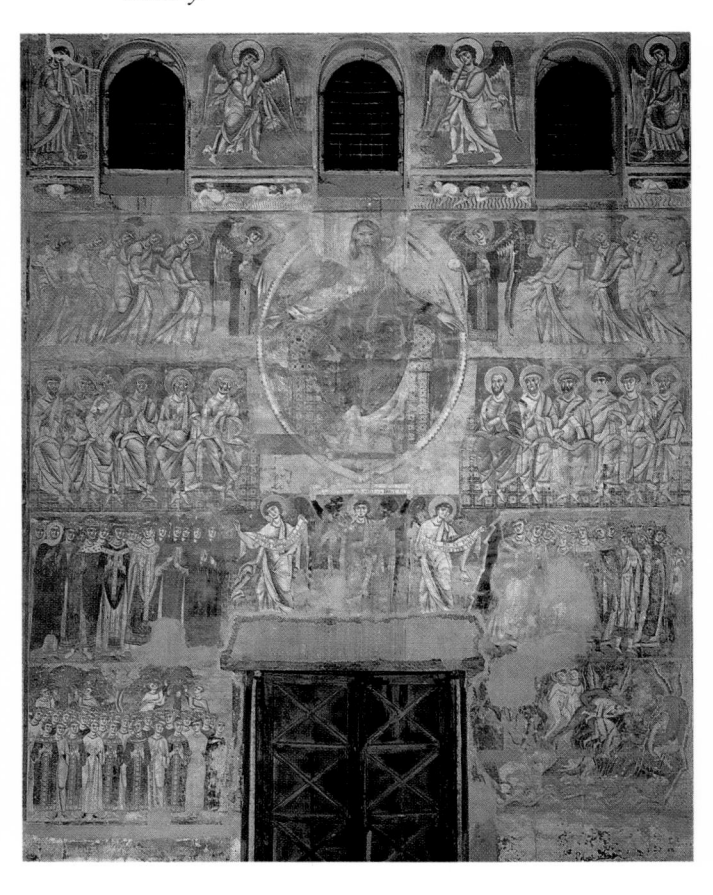

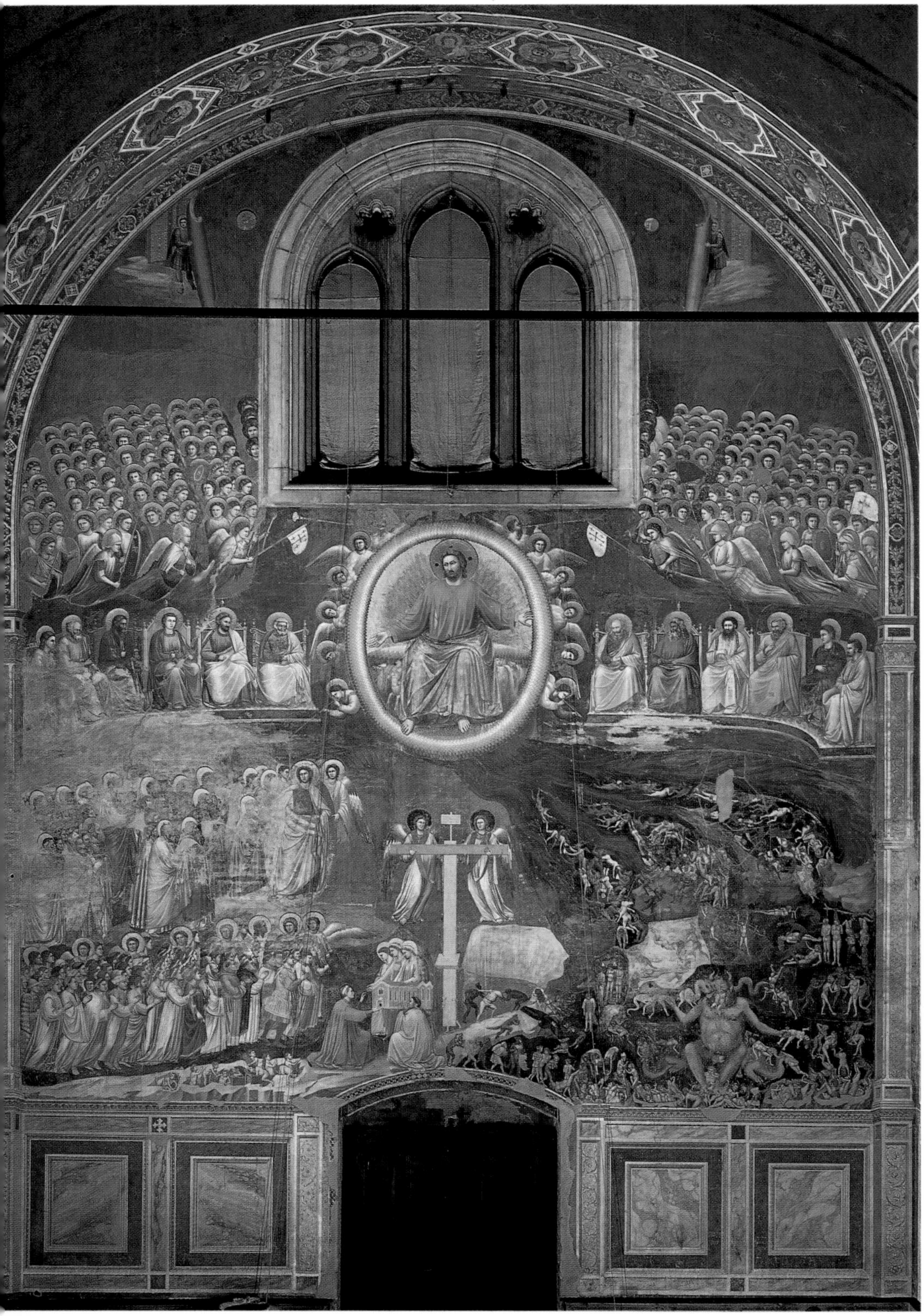

(*Left*) *Giotto:* Last Judgement, *on the entrance wall of the Arena Chapel in Padua, very early 14th century. As always, the dominant figure is God, "enthroned in glory", while around and beneath the remaining personnel are ordered in tiers or bands. In Giotto's fresco particular prominence is given to the Cross and Instruments of the Passion, in the lower centre, just next to which Scrovegni, the patron, offers the church to recipient angels.*

the toppling of the "caput mundi" and the pillage of the see of Christ's vicar, in which part at least of Christendom had identified the aspect of a "new Babylon".[13]

The consequences of the new project, such a radical disturbance of the order both formal and doctrinal of the Sistina as it stood, must necessarily have been foreseen and accepted by the Pope, whose decision in itself constitutes recognition of a dramatic change of direction. The choice furthermore of subjects as pregnant with menace and as terrifying as the *Judgement* and the *Fall of the Rebel Angels* reflects, in addition to their primary significance as "mementoes" of death and punishment, a desire, as André Chastel[14] has acutely observed, on the part of Clement VII to register in symbolic form the catastrophe that had overtaken his pontificate.

Considering the destruction involved, and recalling Michelangelo's

constant tendency to involve himself so personally in the content of his work, we can perhaps better understand his reluctance and hesitation before accepting the commission, and his relief when it seemed that the death of Clement would free him from it.

The determination of Paul III to carry through, at least in part, the programme of his predecessor, was motivated by several considerations, but in the first place by his desire to have for himself the benefit of Michelangelo's art. It is therefore reasonable to suppose that Michelangelo had a rather freer hand with Paul III than he had done with Clement VII, so that he was able to make some significant choices about the iconographical details and the general arrangement of the project.

The identification and relative importance of the Scriptural and literary sources Michelangelo may be presumed to have used — in particular that of Dante's *Divine Comedy* — is still controversial, but there can be no doubt that, setting out to paint a subject that was relatively rare in Renaissance Italian art, Michelangelo looked hard at earlier large-scale representations of the *Last Judgement* and adapted himself, at least in the beginning, to the traditional composition of the subject; indeed there remain clear traces of the traditional composition in the completed fresco. Very probably Michelangelo knew the mosaics of the Baptistery of Florence, Orcagna's frescoes in Santa Croce, those of Nardo di Cione in the Strozzi Chapel in Santa Maria Novella, and the cycle in the Camposanto in Pisa; perhaps also Cavallini's *Judgement* in Santa Cecilia in Trastevere in Rome and that of Giotto in the Arena Chapel in Padua, and Giovanni da Modena's frescoes in San Petronio in Bologna; he certainly knew the cycle painted by Signorelli in the Cathedral of Orvieto and the fresco by Fra Bartolomeo once to be seen in Santa Maria Nuova in Florence.

The iconographic tradition of the *Last Judgement*, whether it was painted in fresco or carved on the tympana of portals, invariably held to a rigorous compartmentalization of the composition into tiers. The subject itself had evolved as a kind of "assemblage" of episodes round the nuclear figures of Christ the Judge, the Deesis and the gathered apostles; each of the episodes — the Resurrection of the Dead, the Presentation of the Instruments of the Passion, Paradise, Hell, and so on — though now one, now another might receive greater emphasis in the overall scheme, was an independent and self-suffcient unit. Such an evolution was enough to determine the compartmentalization of the subject, which in western art, from Carolingian times on, progressively ossified and crystallized into an arrangement of rigid symmetry, resembling the articulation of the façade of a church, and serving indeed as a metaphor of the fixed and preordained hierarchy of the universe and of Christian dogma.

Such a composition was the point of departure also for Michelangelo's fresco, though he impetuously overturned the traditional scheme, even if its memory as it were lingers in the fresco, and opted for the even more impressive image of a cataclysmic Last Day. The study in the Musée Bonnat of Bayonne (Corpus 346 recto), for the upper part of the fresco, immediately reveals his intention to maintain the figure of Christ the Judge in a position of pre-eminence, absolutely central, while the ring of apostles and saints around him, reflecting an innovation of Fra Bartolomeo's earlier composition, shows the old, two-dimensional scheme being developed into a more complex spatial arrangement. But the design sketched on another sheet, now in the

(Below) Michelangelo: Study for the Last Judgement *(Corpus 346 recto – Bayonne, Musée Bonnat). Black chalk, 345×290 mm.*
The horizontal format betrays the fact that Michelangelo was at first thinking in terms of the traditional tiers, though they were obviously never rigid. In the centre is Christ, surrounded by the Elect.

Below: Michelangelo: Study for a group of elect to the left of Christ (Corpus 348 recto – Bayonne, Musée Bonnat). Black chalk, 179×329 mm.

(Left) Michelangelo: Study for the Last Judgement *(Corpus 347 recto – Florence, Casa Buonarroti). Black chalk, 418×297 mm.*

Datable to 1533–1534, the drawing shows that Michelangelo did not at first envisage removing the 15th-century decoration and his own lunettes on the altar wall. The top of Perugino's altarpiece is drawn in below. Compared to the previous study, the movement of the scene has become vertiginous, and the old convention of distribution in tiers has been almost completely eliminated.

(Above) Michelangelo: Study for the Resurrection of the Body, in the lower part of the Last Judgement *(Corpus 351 recto – Windsor Castle). Black chalk, 278×420 mm.*

(Below) Study for a risen figure. This figure can be found on the lower left of the painted fresco, captured in the slow movement of awakening to the sound of the angelic trumpets (Corpus 360 recto – London, British Museum). Black chalk, 293×233 mm.

Casa Buonarroti in Florence (Corpus 347 recto), represents a much more advanced and revolutionary idea, breaking precedent with extra-ordinary audacity, and almost deliberately ignoring Scriptural sources. The figure of Christ, to whom the Virgin turns with a gesture of urgent invocation, is still more terrible and dominant, but the ascent of the Blessed on the left has been transformed into a tangled mass of figures who appear to struggle with as much violence and feeling as the Damned, hurled into the abyss on the lower right. In the middle, below, the frame of Perugino's *Assumption* is detectible, and in this early stage it was to be spared, together with the *Ancestors of Christ* in the lunettes at the top of the wall.

The arrangement of the composition in tiers has been definitively rejected in this design, and replaced with a markedly dynamic one, formed of linked and contrasted groups or isolated figures.

Between this sketch and the final design the disturbing turmoil of the Blessed of the left-hand side, recalling a scaling of Olympus by Giants,[15] was moderated and in general both the asymmetry and the violent movement up and down of the Florentine sheet attenuated. In contrast, the central figure of Christ has become even more majestic and insistent, and His commanding gesture seems to occasion and

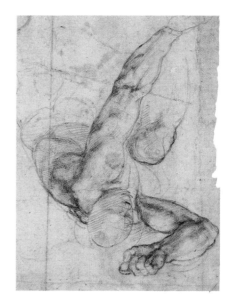

(Above) Study for an angel (Corpus 352 recto). Black crayon, 396×263 mm.
(Below) Study for an angel (Corpus 359 recto). Black chalk, 264×182 mm.

(Above) Michelangelo: Study for a devil of the Last Judgement, at the extreme right of the group of Damned (Corpus 359 verso — Corsham Court, Wiltshire, Methuen collection). Black chalk, 264× 182 mm.

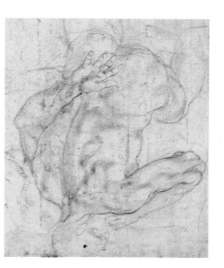

sweep along with it the physical and emotional disturbance of the nearly 400 figures in the fresco, in all their involvement with one another and their movement back and forth. But the decisive step was taken by Michelangelo when he extended the *Judgement* over the whole wall, thereby destroying the *Assumption* over the altar and the two lunettes belonging to the cycle of the Ceiling. If he had not sacrificed them, the terrible fascination that the *Last Judgement* continues to work over those who stand before it would have been almost entirely lacking. With this step Michelangelo did not merely mutilate the previously existing iconographic scheme, he interrupted the rhythm and continuity that as it were enclosed the huge space of the Chapel. Deprived of all articulation, vertical or horizontal, the wall of the *Judgement* now literally cuts into the ring of the side walls and the ceiling, denies its function to close off, and generally exposes what had been a seamless, ordered harmony to the presence of a "second reality".[16] This effect is also powerfully accentuated by the extraordinary illusionistic depth of the *Judgement*, suggested by its foreshortenings, by the vanishing perspective of the groups of figures, by the sudden jumps in scale, and, though these have been diminished by deterioration in the course of time,[17] by the relationships of colour and light; but again what is most vital to it is the complete absence of any means by which the eye can judge the spatial distances or resolve the ambiguity between extension across surface and extension into space. There is a powerful inherent contrast between the dynamic, expressive and symbolic protagonist, Christ the Judge, constituting the unifying nucleus of the whole scene, striking the eye like a bolt of lightning, and the simultaneous complexity and multifariousness of the rest of the wall, which the arbitrary variation of the scale of the different zones serves to compound, while the individual scenes, so rich in movement and expression, invite the eye to dwell, to explore gradually, to unravel through time.

It is precisely in its relationship to the real space of the Chapel, opening out an extension of indeterminate dimensions in a contained, measured box, that the *Last Judgement* shows most clearly, most immediately and most brutally the lesion it constitutes to the harmony of the building that had evolved in the previous decades.

From the iconographic tradition of the *Last Judgement* Michelangelo took over virtually all the essential elements of his fresco, but, whether in order to achieve maximum force and immediacy or because some particular interpretation dictated it, he abandoned the old clear division between the zones of Heaven (with Christ the Judge flanked first by the Virgin and the Baptist, who intercede for us (the Deesis) and then by the deliberating "bench" of apostles, surrounded by the ranks of angels, saints and patriarchs) and the zone of the earth, with the Resurrection of the Dead and the division into Damned and Blessed. The angels who carry upwards the instruments of Christ's Passion, the proof of the sacrifice of God incarnate, were also traditional elements, though they were included in the fresco only when Michelangelo realized that he needed to extend the *Judgement* across the whole wall and into the lunettes.

These angels, nude and wingless, figures of extraordinary beauty, are perhaps of all the figures in the *Judgement* the closest in feeling to those of the Ceiling. Nevertheless they, too, are affected by the hurricane unleashed by the arm of Christ the Judge, and seem to have to fight against the force of the elements in order to raise aloft the

184

Cross and the Column. Their poses and movement, which aroused severe censure from critics of the fresco, look incoherent when they are compared to tradition, and are quite incomprehensible if they are seen outside the particular context of Michelangelo's fresco and the active part they have to play there.

In earlier images of the Judgement Christ had been represented generally, according to the words of St Matthew, "seated on the throne of Glory" between the apostles, themselves seated on the thrones of the twelve tribes of Israel. He is shown with arms open, the marks of the nails visible on His hands, or alternatively with His right palm turned up and His left palm turned down, signifying the calling of the Elect and the dismissal of the Damned: "Come ye blessed of my Father, inherit the kingdom prepared for you from the foundation of the world ... Depart from Me, ye cursed, into everlasting fire prepared for the devil and his angels."[18]

The regal and judicial paraphernalia, and the thrones, were rejected by Michelangelo even in the sketch in Bayonne. They were incompatible with his intensely dynamic conception for the end of time, in which the figure of Christ would no longer be static and motionless, seen straight on "in maestà", but would be shown in the act of rising or moving forward (a certain ambiguity as to His precise movement seems deliberate), with His arm raised over His head and His left arm bent towards the wound in His side.

There are indeed precedents for this gesture in the tradition of the *Last Judgement*, specifically in Tuscany, from the 14th-century fresco in the Camposanto in Pisa to the example painted by the Florentine Dello Delli in the apse of the Old Cathedral in Salamanca. But the pose of Christ in the Sistine *Judgement* also has antecedents in Michelangelo's own earlier work, in fact it is a recurrent motif of his. In different forms, it is found in the figure who stands out against the tangled mass of bodies in his youthful *Battle of the Centaurs* in the Casa Buonarroti, in the colossal bronze statue of Julius II for the façade of San Petronio in Bologna (which was destroyed, but descriptions of it survive: the Pope was shown raising his arm in fierce blessing, or warning, or even – according to the ironic interpretation of Julius II himself – cursing),[19] and in the figure of Juppiter hurling a thunderbolt in his drawings of the *Fall of Phaethon*.[20] It is also probable that a suggestive part was played in the formulation of the final image by the traditional pose of Christ the Redeemer, in resurrection[21]. So, not only the complex movement of the figure, a *contaminatio* of "judging" and of the *Parusia* or Return of Christ in glory on the clouds at the end of time, but also Christ's gesture in the fresco is deeply ambiguous. The iconographic precedents, the similarity to the comparatively recent drawing of Juppiter fulminating in the *Fall of Phaethon*, and also the attitude of the figure in the preparatory sketches, all lead one to suppose it to be a gesture of fearsome condemnation, but the face of Christ is impassive and certainly not wrathful. The attenuation in the fresco of the violence of the second drawing, giving way to a gentler action by which all the figures are conjoined in one single movement, leads one to interpret it rather as a kind of imperious signal of the end of the world. It initiates and actuates the cataclysm of the last act of human history, and preludes its final regeneration.

In Michelangelo's *Judgement* the traditional element of the Deesis, the Virgin and St John the Baptist interceding on either side of Christ, is

Michelangelo: Study for the Last Judgement, *detail (Corpus 350 recto – London, British Museum). Black chalk, 385×251 mm.*
The sheet contains several studies of different sizes. The central group is a study for the struggling mass of the Damned.

lacking. This is perhaps surprising, given that it had been a central element of the subject and fundamental to the teaching of the Church. However, the Virgin has been included by Michelangelo near Christ, indeed within the luminous circle which surrounds His figure, and at the centre of the ring of saints. In the Casa Buonarroti drawing she is clearly turned to Christ in an act of supplication; in the fresco it is not nearly so clear what her attitude is, and it is has been variously interpreted. The idea that she draws close to her wrathful Son in fear, though supported by the descriptions both of Vasari and of Condivi,[22]

The two lunettes, left and right, at the top of the Last Judgement. *As Condivi explained, the two lunettes are given over to the presentation of the Cross and the Instruments of the Passion, an element of the Last Judgement seen previously, for instance, in Giotto. But what had had there a calm, static demonstration, is here subject to the general turbulence of the entire fresco, indeed is one of its most violent passages. We can only presume that Michelangelo divided what was usually a unitary scene in order to accommodate the shape of the field.*

is difficult to accept, but it is equally difficult to see her movement as one of intercession. A more attractive idea is that Michelangelo intended to express the absolute unity of Justice and Mercy in the *Judgement,* and that is what their close relationship means; there was some precedent for the idea in the *Judgement* of the Camposanto in Pisa, where the figures of the Virgin and of Christ, each in a mandorla of equal size, appear side by side between the two "benches" of apostles.

Round Christ and the Virgin throng the multitude of saints, prophets and patriarchs, divided into compact groups, but ranking back into great depth. Several of the saints hold the instruments of their martyrdom, sometimes with such pronounced excitement that it has been imagined that they may be seeking vengeance against the damned responsible.[23] Such an interpretation is absurd, but reflects an aspect of

Michelangelo's fresco that even today strikes the spectator with some force, and that is that rare indeed are the expressions of joy or exultance on these faces, but almost universal is a profound disturbance, tension and commotion. Even among the blessed rising to Heaven, there is a preponderance of expressions of agony and of terrible oppression, of fear, bewilderment, torturing doubt, as if their reawakening, their resurrection, was one of pain and anguish rather than of spiritual peace, as if they felt dread instead of the warmth naturally associated with the notion of eternal joy in paradise. From

this point of view again, as well as that of the vehement characterization of the saints, Michelangelo's fresco has no precedent.

The lower, or earthly, part of the action was reserved traditionally for the Resurrection of the Body and the separation of the Blessed from the Damned, destined for Paradise and for Hell. Often this part, and particularly the depiction of Hell, was richly developed, as at Pisa; in the Strozzi Chapel in Santa Maria Novella Paradise and Hell occupy each of the side-walls. Signorelli at Orvieto had dedicated the entire lower part of the wall to the resurrection of the dead, and Michelangelo followed, no doubt partly because it gave him ample opportunity to indulge his mastery of the foreshortened and contorted human body. Awakened by the trumpets of angels, the dead struggle free heavily and with difficulty from the clods of their deserted strand, like the last survivors of a horrendous catastrophe; gradually freeing them-

Perhaps particularly these two lunettes raise questions of what might be called the "Mannerism" of the fresco: just what purpose does this frantic energy serve, beyond the demonstration of Michelangelo's consummate skill conveying it? It was certainly along lines similar to this that criticism of the Last Judgement *moved, even if it tended to concentrate more on what is for us the less important issue, why should all these figures be nude?*

187

Details of the two lunettes, left and right, at the top of the Last Judgement. (Right) Angels in flight holding the Crown of Thorns.

Detail of the lower left of the left lunette and the ranks of Old Testament figures beneath it. Typically Michelangelesque is the intensity of the gaze of the seemingly crazed woman with her hair bound in a band. The figure above, labouring under the Cross, is in the titanic mould of Michelangelo's heavyweight figures of this period.

selves from the clinging earth, they ascend slowly towards the community of saints, some of them driven by an irresistible power, others needing support and submitting fearfully to the effects of Divine Will. Condivi in particular was aware that the emotions of the Blessed were ambiguous:[24]

> ... you see the tombs on the earth opening up at the sound of these trumpets, and the human race emerging in diverse and marvellous postures; for some of them, according to the prophecy of Ezechiel, have regained only their skeletons, others are half clothed in flesh, others entirely. Some are naked, some are still wrapped in the

(Left) Angels in flight bringing down the Column, whose motion balances that of the group of the left lunette. The detail (below) shows one of these faces of pure, passionate intensity.

Detail of the group at the lower end of the Column. Particularly audacious is the rodeo figure of the muscled nude struggling with the apparently bucking foot of the Column. Motion, violent motion, seems to have become an absolute necessity for Michelangelo.

shrouds in which they were buried, and others are trying to unwrap the shrouds. And there are also some who do not seem yet to have woken, and, looking up to Heaven, are still doubtful of the destiny Divine Justice has for them

The right-hand side of the lower part features prominently a furious skirmish, in which sinners attempt to rise up towards the ranks of saints but are violently repelled by armies of angels and pulled or dragged downwards by devils. Below them, the bark of Charon will convey them to the abyss of Hell.

There can be little doubt that Michelangelo drew inspiration, at least

189

(Opposite page) Detail of the left-hand side of the Last Judgement, just under the lunette: Old Testament figures. Names have been given to some of these figures, but few of them bear attributes by which they may be recognized, and their emotional reaction rather than

their historical or religious significance seems to be the point.
(Above) Further details of the same. There is no complacency in this fresco: even those here, who have no punishment to fear, fear anyway, such is the awesome splendour of the Lord.

for the two figures of Charon and the judge of the underworld, Minos, from Dante's *Divine Comedy*, which he had loved from his youth and knew extremely well. These mythical and literary figures, however, hardly serve to diminish the brutal violence of the way in which the damned are beaten and dragged in indescribable tumult and tragic confusion to their doom. The gleam of the infernal flames, the revolting, bestial forms of the devils, the desperate gestures of the damned, the extremity of the emotions they feel at their plight, shown on faces reduced to masks or spectres – all this cannot be read as mere scenery or as an objective, uninvolved illustration of some fable or myth. Although Michelangelo avoided the kind of torments that the damned traditionally were shown suffering, revealing instead their internal feelings – desperation, remorse, brutalization, a terror of a psychic rather than physical annihilation – there is no doubt about the presence of Hell and Damnation in his *Last Judgement*.[25]

Even before the fresco had been "unveiled", there was controversy, voices being raised on both sides. But less than three weeks afterwards, opinion could at least be summed up, and Nino Sernini could write to Cardinal Ercole Gonzaga:[26]

> ... although the work is of such beauty as Your Illustrious Lordship may imagine, there are indeed those who do not like it; the Theatines are the first to say that the nudes are not fitting in such a place, showing their parts, even though Michelangelo has exercised considerable tact in this, and there are scarcely ten in the whole multitude where you can see sexual organs. Others complain that the Christ has no beard and is too young, and hasn't the majesty that He should have, and in general there is no shortage of carping, but the Very Reverend Cornaro, who went to study them for a long time, seems to have it right, saying that if Michelangelo were willing to give him in a picture just one of those figures, he would gladly pay him whatever he asked, and I agree, because I do not believe one can see the like of it anywhere else

So, despite the appreciation of an eminent cleric such as Cornaro, from the beginning there were voices to raise accusations of obscenity and indecorum. Hostility and criticism must have been aroused in the Curia even before the artist had finished the fresco, and there is proof of it in the amusing story of the Master of Ceremonies Biagio da Cesena who for his harsh criticism of Michelangelo's frescoes was portrayed by the artist as Minos: the episode, corroborated by other sources, is narrated by Vasari.[27]

Biagio's objections repeat almost to the letter those of Hadrian VI to Michelangelo's Ceiling *ignudi*, and undoubtedly do not reflect merely a personal opinion. Such views were also common outside the papal court, and were voiced most aggressively and eloquently by Aretino.[28] His accusation of obscenity and of sacrilege is cleverly compounded by the imputation of vanity in the achievement of "perfection in painting". There already appears in Aretino's letter the threat even to destroy the frescoes.[29]

The accusations of obscenity led soon enough to accusations of heresy. In a letter dated 19 March 1549,[30] an unnamed Florentine, enraged by the installation of Bandinelli's statues of *Adam* and *Eve* (which he called "ugly, bestial figures") in Florence Cathedral, and also of a copy of Michelangelo's Vatican *Pietà* in the church of Santo Spirito, pointed to Michelangelo as the one primarily responsible for all the works of contemporary art he considered obscene.

Details of the upper central part of the Last Judgement: (below) Christ the Judge with Mary beside him, who "drawing her mantle to her, sees and hears such ruin", as Vasari had it; (far below) detail of the flayed skin of St Bartholomew, to Christ's lower left.

The letter ends with the prediction that the Almighty will send "his saints to cast down these idols to the ground". Pope Paul III was also included in his vituperative attack; he was deemed guilty for protecting the artist and for tolerating his sacrilegious art in his Chapel.[31] Eventually still more formidably armed, articulate and dangerous opponents entered into the controversy, some of them well versed in doctrine and in positions of eminence – men such as the famous Do-

minican preacher Ambrogio Politi il Caterino[32], whom Michelangelo himself had gone to hear with Vittoria Colonna at San Silvestro al Quirinale, or Giovanni Andrea Gilio, whose *Dialogue*[33], or rather indictment, which was written within Michelangelo's lifetime though not published until after his death, marshalled and systematically developed all the various accusations of indecency, of offense against religion, of sin against tradition and truth, to which the Last Judgement had given rise.

The persistent pressure to destroy the fresco had little effect in the pontificates of Paul III and his successor Julius III, but the climate altered significantly to the prejudice of the artist with the accession of Paul IV. Paul IV urged Michelangelo that he "acconciasse" – "should

(Above) Detail of the group ranging behind the gigantic figure on Christ's right, identified as St John the Baptist. There are identifications made for these figures, too, but it is guesswork, since they have no attributes.

(Above) Detail of the group ranging behind St Peter, who moves forward towards Christ bearing the Keys. St Paul may be identified just by the fact that he is beside St Peter; however, he is usually shown bald.

(Below) Details of heads: (left) that of the figure identified as John the Baptist; (right) the head of the figure identified by his grill as St Lawrence, at Christ's lower right.

(Below) Details of heads: (left) this figure is alleged to be a portrait of Michelangelo's servant Urbino, while St Bartholomew (right) is alleged to be a portrait of Pietro Aretino, who admittedly had a beard, but was not bald.

tidy up" – the fresco, receiving the sarcastic reply[34]: "dite al papa che questa è piccola faccenda e che facilmente si può acconciare; che acconci egli il mondo, chè le pitture si acconcian presto" – "tell the Pope that this is a small thing and can very easily be tidied up; in the meantime he should tidy up the world, for pictures are readily tidied up". In the pontificate of Pius IV the continuing bitter attacks led eventually to the decision taken at a session of the Council of Trent at least to "emendare" the fresco[35].

Daniele da Volterra, who was given the task of 'censoring', proceeded with the greatest possible discretion (he was a sincere and fervent admirer of Michelangelo), and went no further than the covering of a few figures with drapery, although he could not avoid completely repainting the figures of St Catherine and St Blaise, which had been singled out particularly in the attacks. However, Daniele's 'censor-

Details of the upper right section of the fresco: the ranks behind St Peter. Once again identification is quite arbitrary, although the bearded figures may reasonably be taken for Patriarchs.

ship' was not enough to dispel the threat of total destruction which re-surfaced in the pontificates of Pius V, Gregory XIII and probably again of Clement VIII, and other purificatory adjustments to the fresco were much less discreet or respectful[36].

Besides criticism on moral or doctrinal grounds or occasionally mixed in with it, there had also appeared from the beginning criticism on

(Right) Two further details of heads. The one in the detail on the right holds up a cross: he is the Good Thief, who has been in Paradise since the Crucifixion.

formal grounds. The opening of Aretino's famous letter, mentioned above, had included the words "studying the complete drawing of your *Last Judgement*, I had managed to find the supreme grace of Raphael, and his exquisite gift for invention"; this was the line taken in the reactions that appeared to Vasari's celebration of the fresco in the first (1550) edition of his *Lives*, particularly in the writing of Lodovico Dolce[37], representing the artistic climate of Venice and the Veneto. The work of Raphael was held up as an ideal of harmony, proportion, grace and variety, and systematically presented as the positive to the negative of Michelangelo's *Last Judgement*, which was criticized in particular for its "mancanza di certa temperata misura e certa considerata convenevolezza, senza la quale niuna cosa può avere grazia nè istar bene" – "lack of a certain measured proportion and a certain well considered decorum, without which nothing can be graceful or look well". Michelangelo's "disegno", his virtuosity in the representation of the human body in movement and in an infinite variety of poses, which Vasari regarded as the fulfilment of "perfection in painting", was now paradoxically enough condemned as monotonous, as mere anatomical exhibitionism.[38] The position taken by Aretino and Dolce was widely endorsed even outside the Veneto; in

Details of the heads of the Seven Angels who sound the Last Trump, according to the Apocalypse, and who have also brought the books in which the names of the Blessed and the Damned are written.

Details (above) of the angels with the book of the Blessed and (top) of the angel with the book of the Damned. It has been observed that the book with the names of the Damned is considerably larger than the book of the Blessed.

fact, generally speaking, despite Vasari, throughout the second half of the 16th century the *Last Judgement* was compared unfavourably with Michelangelo's own paintings on the Ceiling of the Sistine Chapel.

The almost excessively dynamic composition of the fresco may still be disquieting and difficult to accept today; it certainly would have appeared all the more so in the 16th century. It is precisely in the dynamism of the composition that we should recognise the most innovative and original aspect of the *Last Judgement;* it is this that created the "rupture" or lesion to the development of figurative art up to that point.

There is little point in trying to discern this rupture in the figures, in the style in which Michelangelo has represented the human body, for all that that is his greatest achievement. In the style of the figures, on the contrary, there is an obvious continuity with what had gone before; even though the numerous figures of the *Last Judgement* appear to differ from those of the Ceiling, particularly in their proportions and in their idealization or lack of it, it is not difficult to trace a perfectly coherent and consistent development in Michelangelo's own drawing and sculpture that leads from one to the other. The rupture, both with his own development and with the course of contemporary art, must be recognised instead in the structural principles of the complex composition, involving in particular the complete abandonment of an architectural (or fictive architectural) framework to contain and counterbalance the physical and psychological restlessness of the figures, such as had been present not only in the Ceiling but also in the projects for the tomb of Julius II, the façade of San Lorenzo and the Medicean tombs in the New Sacristy.

Vasari replied to such criticism in the second edition of his *Lives* in 1568, making a powerful and impassioned effort to bring out the fundamental qualities of Michelangelo's art, with particular reference to the *Judgement* and the expressive benefits of Michelangelo's violent distortion and movement of his figures. He had already in the first edition not rested his case solely on the perfection of the "disegno" and on the "terribilità" of the effects, but also praised the qualities of colouring and finish that set the *Judgement* apart from Michelangelo's previous work[39]: " . . . and one of its extraordinary beauties is the unity and consistency in the actual painting of the work, so that it looks as if it had been painted all in a day and is finished with all the finesse of an illumination in a manuscript".

For all his articulate and acute perception of the artistic values of the fresco, Vasari was not able to give a very satisfactory or lucid account of its content or significance. In this respect one can see in the emotional reaction of all camps[40], whether bitterly opposed or expressing reservations or lauding to the skies, a common sense of unease or even bewilderment, which only subsequently, after rationalization, was formulated within the various critical positions.

The subsequent accusations of obscenity, or pedantic cataloguing of improprieties, or offenses against "decorum", against "truth" or against the "letter" of Scripture, and also the subsequent rejections of the fresco on purely formal grounds, all these should be seen to be rooted in the unease and dismay that the *Judgement* inevitably aroused: all the criticisms come down to a complaint that Michelangelo had treated intolerably, indeed had upended, the essential principles and norms of their common language and culture.

Even the defenders and supporters of the work praise it in terms that, though often enthusiastic, are seldom penetrating, and in most cases show very distinctly signs of hesitation or uncertainty before its less familiar and more disturbing aspects. Vasari and Condivi tend to transfer on to details which they pick out – sometimes quite inappropriately – the tragedy and violence that actually is an effect of the overall composition of the *Judgement*, that stems from its general, indeed systematic exasperation and exacerbation of its expressive means. It is in fact a tendency both of its critics and of its supporters

to make very one-sided statements on the basis of this or that aspect or detail, as if more or less consciously they were performing an act of collective disassociation from the deeper meaning of the whole. All these accusations of obscenity, of heterodoxy, of lack of decorum or proportion, serve as a kind of exorcism of the "subconscious", but actually more immediate, significance of the fresco, which after all presents the image of an irresistible and global catastrophe taking place in the privileged area of the ultimate expectations of humankind, in other words the painful and frantic shipwreck of humanity in the port of paradise. With the denial of this last intellectual and moral

The Sounding of the Last Trump, detail of the lower centre of Michelangelo's Last Judgement. Vasari described it: "Under the feet of Christ the Seven Angels of whom St John writes, with their seven trumpets, sound out the judgement, making the hairs of the heads of spectators stand on end, so terrible is the sight of them. And among them there are two angels, each holding the Book of Lives in their hands."

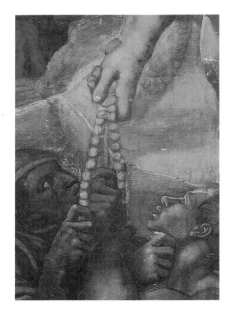

(Above) Detail taken from the section shown on the opposite page, the lower left-hand side of the Last Judgement, showing the Blessed making their difficult way up to Heaven. The detail shows the rosary by which one figure hauls up two more.

refuge, humanity can only wait in fear for the fulfilment of the promise of the resurrection of the Blessed at the hands of the "Son of Man" at the end of time.

The same tendency as it were to "repress" the message of the *Last Judgement* is also apparent in Vasari's and Condivi's description of certain of its details. These depart from the terrifying and threatening elements of the subject, rather than from Michelangelo's way of representing it[41]. For instance, the impassive face of Christ the Judge becomes a "faccia orribile e fiera" – "terrible and fierce face", turned menacingly on the Damned – "ai dannati si volge maledicendogli". The Virgin is described as "timorosetta in sembiante e quasi non bene assicurata dell' ira e secreto di Dio" – "timidly apprehensive in expression as if no longer sure of God's anger and intention". The saints display the instruments of their martyrdom "per rinfacciare ai rei i benefici di Dio, de' quali sieno stati ingratissimi e sconoscenti" – "in order to hurl in the face of the guilty the goodness of God that they have rejected and ignored".

Their interpretations were revived and developed in the course of the 19th century, when there was an impassioned re-appraisal of the fresco in Romantic terms. Moreover in the work of artists such as Géricault and Delacroix there can be found an intuitive appreciation

Details of the section shown on the opposite page. The mastery by which Michelangelo has achieved convincing, and energetic, movement through the air, upwards rather than downwards, certainly makes this one of the most stupendous passages of the fresco, though it is not the most violent.

of some of the more profound aspects of the fresco, even though these were arrived at largely by means of the concept of Michelangelo's "terribilità"[42].

More recent contributions to our understanding of Michelangelo's fresco have been analytic: there have been fundamental studies of its compositional elements, notably from the point of view of Michelangelo's own artistic progress (evident in his sketches and drawings) and

from that of his precedents and sources. Studies and contemporary reaction and philological contributions of various kinds have also fuelled a debate that is still warm over the "real meaning" of the *Last Judgement*, and particularly over its relationship to contemporary theological and religious controversy and the various Reform movements both within and without the Church[43].

In the context of the religious movements of its own time, the *Last Judgement* has been read at various times as perfectly in line with the official doctrine of the Curia; as directly inspired by ideas of internal Reform – and particularly those of the "Viterbo circle"; as conta-

minated by Lutheran sympathies; as more or less explicitly anti-papal on the model of Savonarola; or even as a scarcely concealed manifesto of heresy. It has been seen as a representation of the final destiny of humankind in the key of the *Dies Irae* – a threatening and pulpit-thumping admonition to meditate on the insuperable human propensity to sin; it has also been seen as a re-assertion of the power "to loose and to bind" on the part of the Pope. Alternatively it is an expression of hope for eternal life founded on the Resurrection of the Body; or an affirmation of the doctrine of Justification by Grace Alone, or of the doctrine of Predestination, either in Protestant or in orthodox terms, or the negation of the doctrine of Hell and of eternal punishment for the Damned.

In such a dense thicket of contradictory interpretations, many of

200

which are supported by coherent argument, by learned citations from Scripture, or by reference to the theological debate that preceded or followed the fresco's execution, clear light by which to orientate oneself is not easy to come by. One is assailed by the feeling, even by the conviction, that any attempt to grasp under one exclusive aspect, or to 'tie down' the "real meaning" of the fresco in its religious significance is irremediably doomed; that it is doomed in fact, paradoxically, by opting for any one aspect or ingredient, to a partial statement of the extraordinary complexity of its content. Michelangelo's fresco, one can say with certainty, cannot be forced or enclosed or imprisoned in the narrow space of one single religious viewpoint. However, one of the most important results to have emerged from several recent studies of the fresco is the decisive rejection of any reading centred too one-sidedly on its terrifying aspects; the presence of positive aspects – passion and trepidation, tender affection, pride in the resurrected body – has been established. Another result of equal importance has not usually been stated so explicitly, and that is the admittance that there are contradictions and ambiguities inherent in the work itself, and not to be explained away: some obvious examples are the gesture and movement of Christ, the attitude of the Virgin, the attitudes of the "impassioned" saints who surround them, and the fact that there are figures who rise, or who are driven up, by a force stronger than their own will or consciousness, and figures who struggle forcefully with the power by which they are seized.

Similarly, a close analysis of the fresco with the aim of revealing its doctrinal content or contents reveals from any point of view numerous inconsistencies. Also, some of the reasons for which the

Despite the fact that he had tradition on his side, it seems that it was these nudes by Michelangelo as much as any others that caused offence. Perhaps it was because these are some of the most violently contorted and frenetic poses of the fresco, notably in the detail (far left). Against those moving upward and in, are set others moving out from distance (detail, immediate left).

Details of the bottom left of the fresco, showing the Resurrection of the Body. It was an essential part of Christian doctrine that at the end of the world the spirits of the dead would be reunited with their flesh in Heaven.

fresco has been argued to represent doctrines such as that of Justification by Faith Alone or, on the contrary, by Deed (because the saints brandish the instruments of their martyrdom), or to allude to the debate on Predestination, or to contain an attack on the Curia (because the Mouth of Hell and its terrifying demons are placed exactly over the altar of the Chapel) are just too tenuous or, at best, are based on details of the work, from which it is not valid to proceed to a global statement about the entire meaning of the fresco.

The circumstances of the commission, taken over by Paul III after the

Detail of a head (below). The bodies are shown in various stages of recomposition: some are still skeletons, some are fully repaired.

death of Clement VII, as related above, and the behaviour of the artist (at least as described by our sources) both before and during the execution of the fresco make it likely that Michelangelo was given considerable freedom and initiative. Although this was an important work by virtue of its size and position, Michelangelo enjoyed an enormous fame and prestige, and so was probably responsible not only for the form but also for the "invenzione" of the *Judgement*.

However, while working out the eventual form of the fresco, Michelangelo was not suspended in a vacuum. He must have been affected, and so therefore must have been his art, by his contact with people who were profoundly involved, personally and spiritually, in the religious debate of their time[44]. This is not to speak of his own conscience, of his own sensitivity and dismay at one of the worst crises to which either the papacy or Christendom had ever been subject. It was a crisis indeed that eventually overtook all the ideals of Renaissance art and culture.

Michelangelo overturned the traditional scheme for the representa-

*Details of skeletal heads (left and above).
Further details of the lower left section of
the Last Judgement (below).
Michelangelo has been fairly traditional
in his representation of this standard element of the Last Judgement; it was here
entirely proper to show naked bodies,
since it was the doctrine of the reuniting
of the soul with the body that was chiefly
to be illustrated. Of course he has used
the resources of his art to make the scene
macabre, as well as galvanized with
action.*

tion of the *Last Judgement;* he dissolved and exploded the order and
balance which had been representative of a fixed hierarchy in the
cosmos and of an immutable doctrine that did not recognize or permit
doubt. He had introduced for a moment a vision of a titanic storming
of a Christian Olympus, before arriving at the eventual fresco. It is
difficult not to read the *Last Judgement* as an analogy of the collapse of

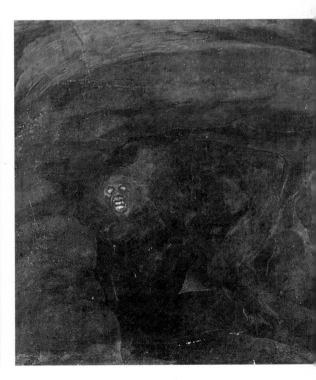

old values and of a conflict which had forced upon his time a new and painful palpitation of conscience. In fact this is the only way in which the *Judgement* may be said to be genuinely "catastrophic": the dynamic composition imposes a dominant emotional tonality into which individual iconographic items are subsumed. The details themselves are sometimes incoherent or mutually contradictory, because left over from a previous scheme that is now discarded, or because deliberately sought out and calculated as such.

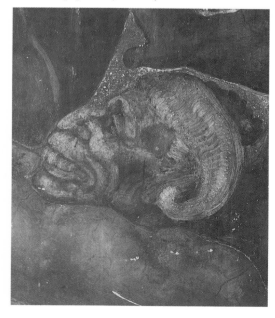

In the years during which the fresco was planned and executed, the tragic episode of the division of Western Christianity into sects was by no means decided or closed; and on the other hand a subsequent dark age of intolerance and bigoted repression had not yet opened. The movement for Reform within the Church, led by Cardinals Pole and Contarini, was more prepared to listen, was more open to suggestion from the ideas of the Protestant Reformation at this time; indeed the hopes of this movement for a settlement were at their highest in these years preceding the definitive rift of the Diet of Ratisbon. However, in reality the rift was already irreversible: too many certainties had been challenged, and the disturbance to the old order could not be contained.

Michelangelo's *Rime* provide ample testimony that he was personally and very emotionally involved in the contradictions, uncertainties and spiritual trials of his time; that he felt an obscure and oppressive sense of guilt, living under the fear of a "second death"; that he came to feel with increasing conviction that the things of this world are vanities – and especially art; that he was conscious of the weakness of human nature exposed to the enticements of sin; but also that he was

Charon (left) does not seem dependant directly on Dante's "demon with smouldering eyes", though he owes a great deal to medieval artistic precedent. This is a demon unsoftened by rationalism or humanitarian apologetics, but an old-style figure of terror.

Michelangelo added to the medieval conception of Hell a new psychology of pain. Often his creatures do not physically suffer, but show in their dehumanized, maddened faces a suffering consciousness, or semiconsciousness, of extraordinary conviction.

The figure (detail far left) of Minos, wound in a serpent, is another inhabitant of the classical underworld introduced by Dante into the Christian Hell. In this figure the features of Biagio da Cesena, whom Michelangelo maliciously incorporated among the Damned after he had criticized the work in progress, have traditionally been recognized.

Detail of the skin held by St Bartholomew, to the lower right of Christ in the fresco, in which the features of Michelangelo himself (detail opposite page) have been convincingly recognized. The skin is the traditional attribute of St Bartholomew, the instrument of his martyrdom: he was flayed. His privileged position so close to Christ is presumably due to the implicit reference to the Resurrection of the Body: the saint has received a new skin, whole and intact. Michelangelo, however, introducing a self-portrait into the features of the old skin, thereby expressed the fact that he was outside paradise, unrejuvenated, sinful, and not reconstituted. There is also a tradition that sees the saint's features as those of Pietro Aretino, who had criticized, or we might say 'torn into' or 'flayed' the Last Judgement, *and thus Michelangelo was the flayee; but this is obviously anachronistic.*

capable of sudden trust in divine mercy, that he had moments of hope, leaps of the spirit, enthusiasm; he sometimes was inspired by meditation on the sufferings of the Redeemer to fervent plea[45]:

> *O Flesh, o Blood, o Cross, o mortal agony, my sin through You was made just, even the sin of which I was born and that was my father*

In the confessional of the *Rime* we find told over precisely the same spiritual and emotional states that found more dramatic and more universal form in the fresco of the *Last Judgement*. Is it probable that Michelangelo, personally tormented by doubt and oscillating emotionally between the waste of his obsession with sin and a "second death" and the rapture of warm invocation of the Redeemer, should be concerned objectively and dispassionately to illustrate coherent and articulate doctrinal truths (be they orthodox, less than orthodox or heterodox) on the altar wall of the Sistine Chapel? Is it not preferable to believe that he wanted to project a universalized image of the hopes and fears by which the minds of his contemporaries were riven, by which he himself was riven, as the burning sincerity and passion of the *Rime* show beyond doubt?

Certainly in the fresco all is objectified in monumental terms and his individual drama has taken on cosmic proportions. And yet the artist also wanted to leave a trace or hint of his personal drama in the enigmatic self-portrait roughed out on the skin of St Bartholomew, destined to remain unnoticed and unrecognised for centuries.

St Bartholomew holds up his own skin just as the other saints display the instruments of their martyrdoms, but his skin hovers suspended directly above the abyss of Hell. Also, this skin is not actually needed by St Bartholomew, who has recovered his body intact in resurrection. This is yet another ambiguous motif, once again very difficult to "decode" convincingly presupposing a single message pervading all, and one which has given rise to contradictory and sometimes fantastic explanations.

Why should we dismiss the idea that Michelangelo, after painting the skin simply as the attribute by which the saint should be identified, was then struck by its position directly above the abyss, and obeyed an irresistible impulse to place exactly there the contradictory "signature" of his own personal hopes and fears? Though the idea cannot be proved, obviously, because such impulses leave no trace, and usually are not taken into account in iconographical explanation, still it cannot on the other hand be refuted. And it is at least possible to demonstrate that the association of "skin", or better "old skin which is exchanged", i.e. a renewal amounting to eternal life, was one which had been made before by Michelangelo in a similar context, when he composed the following stanza of a *sestina*[46]:

> *Passing like an old serpent through a narrow place, leaving my old armour, I may be renewed, taken up into life, abandoning my old ways and every human thing; covered by a surer shield, I know that, faced with death, the world is less than nothing*

In the verses immediately before Michelangelo had reported with a shudder that his propensity to sin — "la trista usanza" — his evil ways and old habits, had now deprived him of "la gratia che 'l ciel piove in ogni loco" — "the Grace which descends everywhere". So it is quite possible that the skin of St Bartholomew alludes, in a serendipitous addition, to the old skin a serpent sloughs in order to obtain a new one, just as the old artist aspired to renewal and regeneration with the just on the Day of Judgement.

The recent cleaning of Michelangelo's fourteen surviving lunettes has not only revealed unfamiliar aspects of the artist as a painter; it has served also to resolve a number of issues which have concerned art historians for over a hundred years. As Fabrizio Mancinelli shows, access to the lunette level of the chapel walls has clarified what kind of scaffolding the artist employed. The cleaning itself has permitted a complete reassessment of the pictorial style of the lunettes and of the way in which Michelangelo carried them out.

Evidence about Michelangelo's activity in the Chapel is much less complete than we should like, but there is enough to suggest when he began work there, when he suspended his activity, and when he completed the project. The written sources do not, however, tell us how

MICHAEL HIRST

„IL MODO DELLE ATTITUDINI"

MICHELANGELO'S OXFORD SKETCHBOOK FOR THE CEILING

Michelangelo: Study for the figure of Abraham, one of the destroyed figures of the altar wall lunettes (Corpus 172 recto – Oxford, Ashmolean Museum). Charcoal, 140×145 mm.

he carried out the programme. These sources are of different kinds. There are the letters written by and to the artist. To these can be added a few *ricordi* (receipts or memoranda) one of which documents the formal commissioning of the work (the contract for the ceiling is lost). Of equal importance are three entries in the diary kept by the papal Master of Ceremonies, Paris de Grassis. These are all sources from the period when the decoration was being painted. To them must be added the later evidence of two drafts of a letter of the artist of December 1523, and, finally, the accounts written by Condivi and Vasari.

Michelangelo's own initial *ricordo* of 10 May 1508, which acknowledges receipt of five hundred ducats from Cardinal Alidosi, states that he is beginning work on that day.[1] But this statement, concerned with recording money received, cannot be taken literally. From a letter written to Michelangelo from Rome in May 1506, we know that Julius II was contemplating asking Michelangelo to paint the Ceiling two years before the work was begun.[2] And there is implicit evidence in the letters that he was concerned with the project by December 1507, whilst still in Bologna, working on the bronze statue of the

Pope. On 21 December he sent to Florence a letter to be forwarded to Cardinal Alidosi in Rome to which he attached great importance (its text has not survived). At the same time, he expressed his intention to go to Rome as soon as his affairs in Bologna allowed.[3] The contract of May 1508 was, therefore, the result of lengthy negotiation. And already in the previous month, a letter of an old friend of Michelangelo's, the painter Francesco Granacci, shows that Michelangelo had made approaches about obtaining artists as subordinate collabo-

rators or assistants for the undertaking.[4] The work of preparing the surface of the vault and of constructing the scaffolding began in May.[5] But the building of the scaffolding was still creating serious disturbance in the chapel in June, as we know from a comment of Paris de Grassis in his diary.[6] Negotiations over the hiring of assistants, entrusted to Granacci in Florence, proved a protracted business; one of those who would join Michelangelo in Rome was still to be found in Florence on 5 August.[7] Late in the same month, we find the artist

Michelangelo: Study for a figure of the destroyed lunette of Esrom and Aram *on the altar wall (Corpus 172 verso – Oxford, Ashmolean Museum). Charcoal and ink, 140 × 145 mm. These were among the last works Michelangelo painted for the Ceiling.*

Michelangelo: Study for a female figure (Corpus 160 recto – Firenze, Casa Buonarroti 24 Fr).

Michelangelo: Study for the woman in the Naasson *lunette (Corpus 172 verso – Oxford, Ashmolean Museum). Charcoal, 140 × 145 mm. A source for the figure in a classical representation of a Muse has been claimed.*

still requesting materials for his painting from Florence.[8] The artist cannot have begun to paint the vault before the late summer or the early autumn of 1508.

That Michelangelo worked throughout the winter of 1508–09 is clear from his letters; the notorious episode of the development of mould on work he had already completed, referred to by both Condivi and Vasari, is implicitly mentioned in his well-known letter of late January 1509, where he complains that painting is not his profession.[9] Painting came to a provisional end in late July or August 1510, when the artist had completed what he himself called "the part he had begun" ("… la parte che io chominciai").[10] In mid August, Pope Julius set out for Bologna, leaving the artist, in his own words, without instructions and without financial provision to continue; he explains in a letter that he requires more money both for further scaffolding and for undertaking the painting of the other part of the work.[11] Despite two journeys by the artist to Bologna to solicit funds, in late September 1510 and midwinter of 1510–11, adequate money was not forthcoming; the Pope's resources were directed towards his military operations rather than art. In February 1511 Michelangelo even contemplated a third visit.[12] Pope Julius returned to Rome only in June 1511. On 14 and 15 August, he attended vespers and mass respectively in the Chapel and saw the recently uncovered ceiling murals (in the words of Paris de Grassis: "… picturas novas ibidem noviter detectas …").[13]

We do not know when the first scaffolding had been removed to allow for the August viewing; nor do we know when the preparation of the scaffolding for the second part of the work took place; Michelangelo's *ricordi* for this later period have not survived. Indeed, there are no specific references to the progress of the second part of the work in any of the written sources. In his letters, the artist writes only of his ill health and the exhaustion provoked by the demands of the work. All that we do know is that the completed decoration was seen by Pope Julius and 16 cardinals at vespers on the eve of the Feast of All Saints, 31 October 1512. Michelangelo had reported that he had finished the work in a letter to his father written a few days earlier.[14]

What the written sources fail completely to tell us is what Michelangelo did in each of his two campaigns of work. This has led to much speculation in the art historical literature. Critics of the late 19th century, led by Wölfflin, concluded that Michelangelo had painted all nine Genesis scenes and the prophets and Sibyls in the earlier of his painting campaigns, and that he had then retraced his steps to the east (entrance) end of the Chapel in order to paint the triangular areas and the lunettes in the second phase.[15] Modifications were subsequently made to this thesis, the chief one being that he had painted everything other than the lunettes by the summer of 1511. It therefore followed that between 1511 and 1512 he was engaged exclusively on painting the lunettes.[16] Support for this theory of how the work proceeded was adduced from a remark of Michelangelo's own in the draft of a letter of late 1523, mentioned above, that he had made the cartoons for the "teste" (ends) and the "faccie" (faces, sides) of the chapel after his journeys to Bologna.[17]

These earlier views were questioned by Wilde who argued that all parts of the painted programme were carried out concurrently as the artist proceeded from the entrance end of the Chapel to the west (altar) end. He proposed that the break of 1510 came at a point in the programme between the *Creation of Eve* and the *Creation of Adam* and pointed out how many features in the part of the work up to this point were modified or changed by the artist in the part that follows.[18] The interpretation finds support in a remark of the artist's biographer, Condivi. Writing of Pope Julius's impatience to see the work, he relates how, when the decoration was half done, the Pope insisted on its being uncovered; and Condivi states that this was the part from the door to half way along the vault ("cioè dalla porta fin a mezzo la volta …").[19] There seem to be no good reasons for doubting that this unveiling, described by Condivi in his life of the artist, is the one "documented" by De Grassis in his diary as that taking place in August 1511, after the Pope's return to Rome.

The new evidence revealed by the current cleaning adds further support for this view. Mancinelli's reconstruction of the kind of scaffolding adopted shows that the artist could have painted the histories, prophets and Sibyls, triangular spandrels, and lunettes, from the same structure in the same phase of the work. And one of the most remarkable consequences of the cleaning of the surviving 14 lunettes is the discovery that Michelangelo did not use cartoons at all for this part of the decoration.[20] This fact throws serious doubt on the reliability of Michelangelo's letter of 1523 already mentioned about the making of cartoons for "teste" and "faccie". It must be emphasized that this letter was not written as a careful record of how the ceiling had been painted although some modern critics have accepted it as such. Its purpose was to provide a vindication of Michelangelo's financial probity. Its evidential value is poor on several counts. For example, Michelangelo informs his correspondent that Pope Julius had ordered him to paint in the chapel down to the 15th-century narrative frescoes ("… insino alle storie di socto …") which is inaccurate, for there was no intention of destroying the cycle of popes above the narratives.[21] Again, he writes of an initial plan to paint the twelve apostles in the lunettes ("nelle lunecte …") when he should have written pendentives.[22] That Michelangelo took trouble to inform Condivi more carefully about the painting of the Chapel 30 years later is understandable for he knew that Condivi's account was to be published; he may even have checked his *ricordi* to attempt to establish its accuracy.

This brief survey of chronology is relevant for an attempt to understand and date the surviving fragment of a sketchbook of Michelangelo's at Oxford. It consists of eight leaves, now in the Ashmolean Museum. Our first notice of their existence is in Ottley's *Italian School of Design* published in 1823. Ottley, painter and collector, must have bought them in Italy during his extensive stay there from 1791 to 1801 but he does not state how he acquired them. When he bought the leaves, the sketchbook must have been already broken up; at a date which cannot now be established, the leaves were opened out and four of them glued together to form a sheet four times the size of the original pages. They were reproduced in this misleading form by Frey and were separated again, restored to their original size, only in 1953.[23]

The leaves show only slight differences in size. That they have been marginally trimmed can be deduced from the appearance of a black chalk study (Corpus 173 recto); there are now no traces of any stitching holes which might have indicated how the book was bound. Yet the losses are clearly small. None of the surviving leaves now measures more than fourteen centimetres high and just under fifteen centi-

Melpomene, one of the nine Muses, detail from a Roman sarcophagus now in the Louvre. There is a striking resemblance to the female figure in the Naasson lunette (see also p. 256).

metres wide, and there can be little doubt that the book was always a very small one by the standards of the period.[24] Although the leaves will be discussed here with the numbers given to them by Parker and De Tolnay, it cannot be assumed that this sequence is the original one. Indeed, there is evidence to suggest that it is not. A scrutiny of the offsetting in black chalk visible on several sheets, where the chalk on one pages has marked off on the facing one, reveals, for example, that what is now Parker 306 *verso*, Tolnay 173 *verso* was once a *recto*, facing Parker 305 *verso*, Tolnay 172 *verso*; the latter study is clearly visible on the other, offset in reverse. And that there were other leaves now lost can be proved by the existence of an offset on another of the

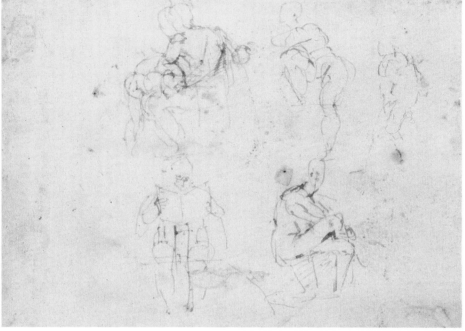

Michelangelo: Study for the lunette of Esrom and Aram, *reworking an earlier study (Corpus 168 verso – Oxford, Ashmolean Museum). Charcoal (the large figure); pen and bistre (the smaller figures), 140×142 mm. Clearly identifiable, top right of the drawing, are studies of the prophet* Jonah *on the neighbouring pendentive.*

Above right: Study for figures not carried out (Corpus 171 verso – Oxford, Ashmolean Museum).

sheets (Corpus 166 recto) from a black chalk study which no longer exists.[25]

Michelangelo's employment of sketchbooks can be inferred from evidence other than this Oxford fragment. But when he took one up, it appears to have been for a specific purpose, and this seems to be true of the one of which the Oxford leaves were a part. All the sheets now surviving can be related to Michelangelo's work for the Sistine ceiling programme. Fifteen of the 16 pages reveal very clearly their nature – they contain studies devoted to inventing or developing figure motives for the decoration; and the sixteenth (Corpus 171 recto) can also be related to the work in a slightly different way. Many of the small studies are of figure motives which the artist did not use in the ceiling as painted. But those inventions which can be matched convincingly with figures in the programme as carried out are ones which relate to the area of the decoration at the later (altar) end of the Chapel, the area which, if Wilde be right, was painted after the pause of 1510–11. Suggestions have been made which do not conform with this observation but these proposed contexts are not convincing. For example, it has been suggested that the study in the upper left corner of Parker 304 verso, Tolnay: Corpus 171 verso is for the woman on the left of the *Ezechias-Manasses-Amon* lunette. The argument is, however, unconvincing, for the drawing shows a figure turned towards us, not one turned away in *profil perdu;* the action of the left arm is different and *pentimenti* in the drawing have been misinterpreted as the sleeping child of the mural. This little study, in fact, was never employed in the painted programme at all.[26]

As the sketchbook is no longer complete, we cannot exclude the possibility that studies for earlier parts of the programme once did exist on leaves which no longer survive. But given the exclusively "late" context of the studies which we possess and which relate to painted motives, the chance that the lost sheets contained such drawings seems slight. As mentioned in greater detail below, the surviving sheets are concerned with the planning not only of late lunettes but of the last of the Genesis scenes to be painted and include also studies for *Jonah* and the *Libyan Sibyl*, carried out at the end of the programme.

The nature of the sketches suggests, therefore, that Michelangelo made them at some point between the suspension of work in the Chapel in the summer of 1510 and its resumption in late summer/ early autumn of 1511. It is difficult to be more precise. However, as often observed, Michelangelo wrote "15 September" ("dì quindici di sectebre") in the upper corner of one of the sheets (Corpus 166 recto); the lines he drew in after the date show it is a *ricordo*, although what it records we cannot say. *Ricordi* which can be found on some of the artist's drawings are usually of the same approximate date as the drawings and it may be the case that these Oxford studies were made around the period of September 1510, after Michelangelo had suspended painting in the chapel and was awaiting the financial provision to continue which the letters show to have been long delayed. An alternative dating of September 1511, after the unveiling of the first part of the ceiling in August, cannot, however, be excluded. In fact, the second part of the painting was probably begun at the end of September 1511, for Michelangelo had two audiences with the Pope, the first on 30 September, the second on the following day, and was paid a further installment of money at the same time.[27]

With the exception of two leaves to be discussed later, the drawings fall into two general classes. The most numerous are very small studies, initial *concetto* sketches, where the artist was concerned with inventing figure motives; the other drawings are rather larger, done to study the anatomical implications of the poses worked out in the *concetto* drawings or to clarify a detail. The latter seem to have been made from life.

The invention drawings, mostly drawn in pen and bistre ink, vary in scale from the smallest which measure about 3.5 cm or even less (just over one inch) to those which are about 5 to 6 cm. There are just over 60 in all and it seems to be the case that less than half were actually used in the frescoed decoration. Of those that were, the majority are for the late lunettes, in particular for those of *Jesse-David-Solomon*, *Roboam-Abia*, *Salmon-Booz-Obed*, *Naasson*, and the two lunettes of the altar wall which were later destroyed to make way for the *Last Judgement*. In a number of cases, Michelangelo worked and reworked a motive which he subsequently did not use. A case in point is the figure reading a book, seen frontally, drawn either seated or standing, who appears not less than four times on one page (Corpus 166 verso) and once on another (Corpus 171 verso). The figure may have been intended for one of the altar wall lunettes; in the event, the motive of the figure holding the book with both hands appears in a part of the decoration for which no preparatory material exists in the sketchbook, in the corner 'spandrel' of the *Crucifixion of Haman*, and then in a subordinate rôle.

Michelangelo: Study for figures of Prophets *(Corpus 166 recto – Oxford, Ashmolean Museum). Charcoal and pen and ink, 140×132 mm. The upper figure is clearly provided with a book; the lower figure has crossed legs.*

213

Michelangelo: Study for the hands of Booz, in the upper sheet, and studies for the Booz *and Aminadab* lunettes, *in the lower sheet (Corpus 167 recto – Oxford, Ashmolean Museum). Pen and bistre, 135×145 mm. Booz is the figure with a stick, who is figured as an old man. The small frontal figure in the centre of the lower sheet can be identified with one in the lunette of Aminadab; the baby shown here has, as in a previous case, been suppressed in the fresco itself.*

Studies for the Roboam/Abia *lunette (Corpus 167 verso – Oxford, Ashmolean Museum). Pen and bistre, 135×145 mm.*

Ottley, the first identifiable owner of the drawings, regarded these diminutive figure studies as at least partly made from nature, the result of Michelangelo's observations, sketchbook in hand, in the streets of Rome. J.C. Robinson, who first attempted a systematic study of the leaves, rejected the hypothesis; he saw that they were "rapid conceptions, some of them entirely momentary and original" which sprang from Michelangelo's imagination.[28] In many cases, Michelangelo rapidly drew in alongside the figure studies the curved arcs of the framing lines of the lunettes, scarcely the result of study outside the workshop and evidence that the little figure sketches were not separable, for the artist, from their projected context. Nevertheless, in one case, to be discussed below, Ottley was almost certainly correct (Corpus 171 recto).

That Michelangelo drew in the lunette lines allows us to appreciate how one figure could be tried out for one side of the lunette and then moved to the other. A good case are the jottings for the bearded pilgrim-like figure painted on the right of the *Salmon-Booz-Obed* lunette. He appears, hat on back, turned to the left on one sheet (Corpus 170 recto) and then reappears, armed with a stick and now in the direction of the painted figure, in another (Corpus 167 recto). A comparable change overtook the sleeping figure painted on the left of one of the altar wall lunettes. The pen invention appears on one sheet, planned for the right side of the lunette (Corpus 170 verso). It was elaborated in a black chalk study (Corpus 172 recto). And then the artist changed his mind and reversed the motive, sketching this variation in black chalk on another sheet (Corpus 168 verso) where the orientation is as in the fresco. There were clearly many such changes.

When Ottley first mentioned the Oxford leaves, he recognized that not all of the studies were made for lunettes. On a page which is now, unfortunately, one of those most difficult to read (Parker 31r, Tolnay 168r), he himself noted three studies for the figure of God the Father in the last Genesis scene to be painted, that of *God dividing Light from Darkness* (Corpus 168 recto). In fact, there are in all six studies for the figure in the sketchbook, for on another sheet (Corpus 172 recto), there are three others, minute and at first sight seemingly inchoate jottings below and to the right of the black chalk study; these seem to have preceded the other three. Those on the sheet described and reproduced by Ottley are of great fascination. In two of them, God is drawn vertically and whilst it may be argued that Michelangelo drew these with the sheet turned laterally, the diagonal hatching lines show this was not the case; in other words, the artist experimented with a figure drawn along the axis of the chapel before establishing the final lateral design drawn on the upper right. This little sketch, about 5.5 cm across, is an astonishingly complete draft for the mural scenes as painted; even the framing lines are drawn in.

On the verso of this last (Corpus 168 verso) there are other significant studies. Two seem to be studies for *ignudi*, one to the right of the *Libyan Sibyl*, flanking the final *Creation* scene. Above, to the right of centre, are two further tiny studies, one of which is for the prophet Jonah and this sketch is supplemented by a further study for Jonah on the upper left of another sheet, Parker 303r, Tolnay 170r. Returning to the verso, we may consider the little drawing on the upper left. This sketch has always been interpreted as another study for the *Division of Light from Darkness*, with which it has no connection. It is this writer's impression that it constitutes Michelangelo's first thought for the figure of the *Libyan Sibyl* (compare the detail on top of Corpus 168 verso with the mural). The figure, turned to the left, is drawn reaching up, the left leg drawn back more acutely than in the definitive design. A bald description of these tiny studies does little justice to their exceptional character. Drawn in varying shades of bistre and with pens of differing breadth, they show a seemingly limitless inventiveness. Varying in scale as we have seen, sometimes articulated with a few strokes, sometimes given more substance by very rapid hatching, they could have served as inspiration for Giorgio Vasari's characterization of initial sketches written in his *Preface to Painting:* "Sketches ... we call a certain kind of initial drawings made to establish the form of the poses and the first arrangement of the work" (... "Gli schizzi ... chiamiamo noi una prima sorte di disegni che si fanno per trovar il modo delle attitudini, ed il primo componimento dell' opra").[29]

As a class of drawing, these Oxford sketches are not a novelty in Michelangelo's work, nor is it a type confined to sketchbooks. We find a very close precedent in a series of tiny studies on a sheet in the Uffizi, done to establish the motives of mother and child for the marble group of the *Madonna and Child* now in Bruges.[30] Michelangelo may have made extensive use of this type of initial study when planning the earlier parts of the ceiling. We find similar small-scale sketches in black chalk for figures of *ignudi* on a sheet now at Haarlem, almost submerged beneath red chalk studies from life drawn over them; their scale is the same (Corpus 136 verso).[31] But we cannot fail to note that they are all essentially studies of individual motives, made to create what Vasari calls "attitudini". The little studies for the *Division of Light and Darkness* just discussed were made for the one narrative in which Michelangelo reduced the subject to a single figure, eliminating even the accompanying angels of the earlier *Creation* scenes. It is also, we may note in passing, the one Genesis scene where Michelangelo employs a kind of illusionism, for although the figure of God the Father is not steeply foreshortened, the form is designed as if seen from below.[32]

If we now turn to the other class of drawing represented in the sketchbook, we find that there are examples of this larger kind of study on six of the 16 pages (Corpus 167 r, 167 v, 168 v, 169 r, 172 r, 173 r). Three are in black chalk, the rest in pen and bistre. The most elaborate is the chalk study we have already encountered, done for the sleeping figure in the altar wall *Phares* lunette (Corpus 172 recto). Developed from the tiny pen sketch on another sheet (Corpus 170 verso), the figure is lit from the right, appropriately so for the right lunette of the altar wall. Michelangelo first began to draw this study on a smaller scale and then enlarged it and the drawing fills the sheet more completely than any other in the sketchbook.

All the other drawings of this kind are in pen and ink. Two are particularly interesting for they show (Corpus 167 recto and 167 verso) Michelangelo elaborating on a larger scale motives sketched in on the same sheet; in 167 recto we find details of the left arm and right hand of the tiny figure drawn below. On the other (167 verso) we see him exploring the anatomy of the figure so graphically sketched seated and slumped forward, destined to be the male figure on the right of the *Roboam-Abia* lunette. He then returned to this figure on another sheet (169 recto; the sequence seems here quite clear), inclining him still further forward as in the mural. Below, Michelangelo then rapidly drew the two legs and right foot for a different

Michelangelo: Studies for the prophet Jonah *and for the* Ezekias/Manasses/Amon *lunette (Corpus 170 recto – Oxford, Ashmolean Museum). Pen and bistre, 138×143 mm. The female figure for the* Ezekias *lunette is in particular studied here.*

Studies for the lunette (Corpus 170 verso – Oxford, Ashmolean Museum). Pen and bistre, 138×143 mm. On the sheet appears the pen invention for the sleeping figure planned for the right side of one of the altar wall lunette, later reversed.

figure, the bent "pilgrim" on the right of the *Salmon-Booz-Obed* lunette. From the way these two studies are drawn, it seems to follow that Michelangelo made them from life, drawing the upper form for one figure and the legs for the other from the same model. Such an economy of means can be found elsewhere among the drawings for the Ceiling made from a model. A further observation can be added: many of the *concetto* sketches, despite their miniature scale and brevity, show the forms clothed, whereas the larger studies show the figure nude. The contrast is particularly striking in 167 verso.

Two further drawings remain to be mentioned, neither of which fits quite comfortably into the broad categories here described. One is the black chalk drawing (172 verso) for the standing woman on the left of the *Naasson* lunette. It is one of the most beautiful studies in the sketchbook, and the motive one of the most monumental in the entire series of lunette figures. One can, indeed, trace the genesis of the invention from the earliest ideas in pen to this later sketchbook drawing and then go on to the black chalk male nude study which followed on a sheet now in the Casa Buonarroti (160 recto). In the sketchbook chalk study the figure already holds a mirror in the left hand but the artist has not yet established the motive of the head resting on the right one. Considering the sequence, we are led to ask whether the Casa Buonarroti sheet (a small one measuring fifteen by just over twelve centimetres) could not be a stray leaf from the same sketchbook as the Oxford series. The answer seems to be a negative one, for the texture of the paper and the chain lines are different.[33]

A further observation can be made. We can follow, in the Oxford drawings and in the Casa Buonarroti one, the emergence of a motive with unusual clarity. Yet, although the final solution of the painted image was not, in all details, present at the start, the painted figure, and even details of her dress, relate extremely closely to an antique prototype, one of the nine Muses on a well-known sarcophagus now in the Louvre. The Louvre version of this relief was certainly not known in the sixteenth century, for the sarcophagus was discovered only two hundred years later; nevertheless, the striking resemblance suggests that some version was known in our period.[34] If the relation is accepted, we find here a pattern we encounter elsewhere in Renaissance art, the phenomenon of the final solution adhering more closely to an antique prototype than the initial idea.

The other sketchbook drawing (171 recto) has always been something of a puzzle. Representing a bent old man supported by a stick and accompanied by a dog, the study seems to lack the immediate relation with the ceiling decoration displayed in the other leaves. A further curious feature of this drawing is that its design was adopted over 50 years later for the image on the reverse of Leone Leoni's medal of Michelangelo, which suggests that the artist still had the sketchbook in his own possession in 1560 (the medal was finished by March 1561).[35]

This black chalk genre study is the only one in the sketchbook as it now survives which could answer to Ottley's description of having been sketched in the streets of Rome. Its brief Rembrandt-like recording of outdoor life is rare among Michelangelo's drawings of any period. But that he drew it with no other purpose in mind is doubtful. The way in which the bent figure relates to the bent figure on the right of the *Salmon-Booz-Obed* lunette can scarcely be coincidental. The view seems to be correct that this was a nature study transformed by the pen sketches into the motive which came to be painted.

Michelangelo: Studies for the altar wall end of the Ceiling (Corpus 168 recto – Oxford, Ashmolean Museum). Pen and bistre, 140×142 mm. The study for God the Father in the first panel of the Genesis cycle, the Separation of Light and Darkness, *is in the centre of the sheet. The woman in profile at the bottom resembles that of the* Jesse/David/Solomon *lunette.*

Perhaps, therefore, this was one of the earliest drawings to have been made in the book which really was initially employed as Ottley suggested.

How many different preparatory stages intervened between the initial drawing exemplified in the Oxford *taccuino* and the actual painting of the lunette figures we cannot say. Michelangelo departed from tradition and from his own practice elsewhere in the ceiling programme in abandoning the use of full-scale cartoons for the lunettes. And it may be that his approach to designing these monumental figures was a more improvised one throughout the whole process of creating them: that, in other words, he made fewer preparatory drawings of all kinds. No studies comparable to the Metropolitan Museum one for the *Libyan Sibyl* exist for lunette figures, but we cannot presume from this lacuna that none was ever made. Some lunette details, for example the head of the old man who stares at us so forbiddingly from the left of the *Jacob-Joseph* lunette, suggests very strongly the adoption of a head study made from life similar to those which survive for the heads of *Zechariah* and the *Persian Sibyl*.

As it happens, three preparatory drawings in black chalk exist for one of the lunette figures from the earlier part of the series, the mother who holds one child in her lap and rocks with her foot the cradle of another. Two, made from life, are on a sheet now in Turin (Corpus 155 verso). And there is a third drawing for the figure, an exploratory study certainly not from life and wrongly identified as an *ignudo* study, on a sheet now in the Casa Buonarroti (Corpus 146, detail on lower left part). These studies give us some idea of how Michelangelo carried further the process of clarifying his inventions; but the evidence is too slight for us to reconstruct the process of the genesis of the lunettes in detail.[36]

There is a further consequence of the fact that the sketchbook is for the second part only of the ceiling decoration. The sheets do not show us how Michelangelo came to invent the basic form of his lunette composition. This solution is now so familiar to us, and was so frequently followed by artists of later generations in both Rome and Florence, that we are liable to take it for granted. But how bold his answer to a difficult compositional problem was, can be readily appreciated if we consider the recent attempts by painters of an older generation than Michelangelo to confront the problem, where figures are cut by the frame or, if depicted full-length, are crowded uncomfortably into the wall space available. The work of Pintorrichio is a case in point.

The frescoes of his immediate predecessors can have been of little help to Michelangelo when he came to confront the problem of lunette compositions. If there was a source of inspiration, it is likely to have been an antique one. It was long ago noted that one of his lunette figures, the expectant mother on the left of the *Roboam-Abia* lunette, he derived from a male river god on the Arch of Septimius Severus.[37] And it seems to have been from these antique compositions over the flanking openings of the Severus arch that Michelangelo gained his initial inspiration, converting the keystone into the murals' inscribed tablets. The design of the tablets themselves is of great elegance. And we may note in conclusion that the introduction of the slim half-baluster anticipates Michelangelo's use of a similar very personal form in his first real architectural project, the marble façade of the chapel in Castel Sant'Angelo of a few years later.

Michelangelo: Study for the writing figure in the Asa/Josaphat/Joram *lunette (Corpus 161 recto – Oxford, Ashmolean Museum). Red chalk, 205×213 mm. Doubts have been raised that this drawing is in fact autograph.*

(Below) Michelangelo: Study for an ignudo, *the one to the right of the Persian Sibyl (Corpus 136 recto – Haarlem, Teyler Museum). Red chalk, 279×214 mm. On the left of the sketch, a separate study for the right arm.*

217

THE PAINTING OF THE LUNETTES

FABRIZIO MANCINELLI

The restoration of Michelangelo's frescoes in the Sistine Chapel has brought to light (and will continue to bring to light) a totally new artist, a colourist quite different in character from the unnaturally sombre figure who has in the past fascinated generations of historians, connoisseurs and fellow-artists. This new character of Michelangelo makes much better sense of his historical position, and particularly of the influence he exerted almost immediately on his contemporaries and especially on the Florentine Mannerists Rosso and Pontormo.

The cleaning of the frescoes has led to the surprising conclusion that the kind of suggestive painting by shadows for which Michelangelo was admired until a few years ago was essentially the product of candle-smoke and still more of glue-varnishes applied possibly even before the 18th century. These were presumably intended to allow a better reading of the frescoes through the dirt, but quite soon deteriorated, so that the French traveller De la Lande could exclaim:[1]

The whole ceiling … is monotonous, its colour tends towards dull red and grey; however, this defect is compensated by the design

The intuition that the original colours must have been quite different

MICHELANGELO AT WORK

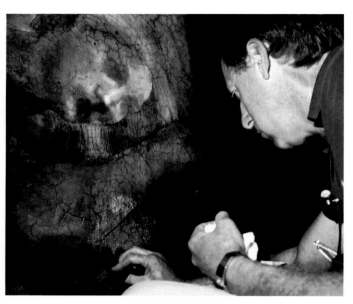

Above, a restorer at work on the Ami-nadab lunette. Opposite, the contrast between the Roboam/Abia lunette restored to the original splendid colour and the Salmon/Booz lunette on the right still uncleaned.

218

from those that could be seen can be found sporadically in the writings of the more perceptive scholars of Michelangelo, from Wilson to Biagetti and Wilde[2]. But clear and conclusive evidence of the original colours was established for the first time in recent times by the extraordinary photographs of the Japanese photographer Takashi Okamura, taken just before the restoration and published in a book of 1980, unfortunately in a small limited edition and not widely seen[3]. The eye of the camera, in itself much more acute than the human eye, and aided by much stronger light than is usually available in the Chapel, revealed beneath the dirt and deteriorated glue-varnish the tangible existence of what the restoration that continues today is gradually retrieving.

Although the book with Okamura's photographs and the restoration that is now proceeding came about independently and for different reasons, the two are complementary, and Okamura's book is today a valuable record of what for centuries had masked the true nature of Michelangelo's painting; if the cleaning had not gone ahead, it would have been the sole means by which to achieve a proper or effective analysis of his work.

Besides the recovery of the original chromatic quality of the frescoes,

PERSICHA

S·ANICETVS·SIRVS·SE·AN·XI·M·II·
D·IIII·MAR·CORONATVR·AN
XPI·C·I   XVI·M·VIII

TGINVS·GRECVS·EX·ATHENIS
SE·AN·IIII·M·III·D·IIII·N·AR·CORON
ATVR·AN·XPI·CLXIIII·M·XDXX

the restoration, as is usual, has also made possible a thorough examination of the technique of Michelangelo; it has also provided some definite answers to certain unsolved problems, in particular the debated matter of the kind of scaffolding the artist used. These emerged from the cleaning of the lunettes of the Chapel, completed in November 1984, but also the operations that are proceeding on the ceiling proper are producing very valuable information, much more valuable than had been anticipated before the operations began.

THE PROBLEM OF THE SCAFFOLDING

T he first problem facing Michelangelo before he could begin painting the ceiling of the Chapel was the construction of a scaffold.

In the absence of any concrete evidence, relying only on the indications of the sources – Paris de Grassis, Condivi, Vasari – scholars have formulated divergent and contradictory hypotheses about the nature of the scaffold Michelangelo used. For the most part they have arrived at their theories not so much by an analysis of the technical problem itself, but rather as a consequence of their (varying) stylistic assessment of the sequence in which the frescoes of the Chapel were painted. They thereby inverted the proper relationship between the two kinds of evidence, for all that they are closely interlinked and even to some extent interdependent.

The two principal theories go back to Tolnay and to Wilde (reflecting an earlier hypothesis of Wölfflin). Tolnay[5] maintained that Michelangelo used one, first, scaffold to paint the whole ceiling proper and a second scaffold to paint the lunettes; Wilde,[6] following more exactly the testimony of Vasari[7] and Condivi,[8] supposed that Michelangelo painted the two areas together, using one scaffold to fresco one half of the Ceiling, from the entrance wall to the *Creation of Adam*, and a second scaffold for the second half. However, when it came to the nature or structure of the scaffold, all camps have departed from the premise that the scaffolding rested on the floor of the Chapel:[9] recently, for example, Gilbert[10] suggested that Michelangelo used a mobile tower, though this idea was criticized immediately, for different reasons, by Joannides[11] and by Hartt.[12] Hartt has also formulated an alternative hypothesis based on the same considerations as the theory advanced in 1982 by myself[13] and here re-stated in more detail.

Scaffolding had not been a problem in the time of Sixtus IV, when the artists responsible for the decoration had first painted the ceiling. (Possibly the artist concerned was Pier Matteo d' Amelia, the author of a coloured design for the ceiling that survives. The ceiling was painted a deep sky blue and spangled with gilt stars.) At that time the Chapel was still in course of construction and was not therefore in use; and the ceiling undoubtedly was decorated before the walls were painted. Under Julius II, however, the Chapel was one of the crucial sites for the liturgy and ceremony of the Curia: it was therefore necessary to devise a structure which would not prevent or obstruct the use of the Chapel during the course of the work, which would certainly continue for a considerable period. That this was the problem to be resolved emerges clearly from an attentive reading of the sources.

The Pope, naturally enough, at first entrusted the task to the palace architect, who at that time was Bramante. Bramante, according to

Detail of a sketch by Michelangelo (Florence, Uffizi, Gabinetto dei disegni e delle stampe) of God the Father in the Creation of Adam; *the detail shows a diagrammatic sketch for the scaffolding used for the painting of the Ceiling.*

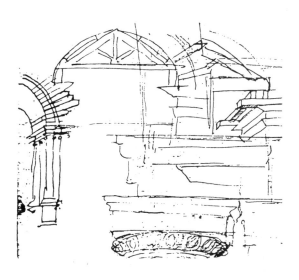

Giuliano da Sangallo: Sketch for the construction of a vault (Florence, Uffizi, Gabinetto dei disegni e delle stampe). At the top there is a representation of the kind of centering used for the construction of an arch or barrel-vault.

Condivi,[14] "not knowing what to do, bored through the ceiling in several places, and let down through the holes ropes on which to hang the scaffold". According to Vasari[15], "he made it hanging entirely from ropes, boring through the vault". A hanging structure of this kind obviously would not cause obstruction in the area underneath. Whether Bramante in fact created such a hanging scaffold, as Vasari and Condivi say, or whether he merely designed one, is a question that must remain open: for either during the restoration carried out by Biagetti or earlier, the upper surface of the vault of the ceiling was covered over with a rendering of mortar which has erased all trace of any holes that might have been bored through. Whether projected or installed, Bramante's structure, however, did not find favour with Michelangelo, who asked his colleague in particular "how he intended, once the painting of the vault was finished, to stop up the holes; Bramante replied, 'We'll think about that later', and that there was no other way of doing it" – so Vasari reports.[16] At this point the Pope removed the matter from Bramante's hands and let Michelangelo construct the scaffold in the way he thought best. Vasari continues:[17]

> Così ordinò di farlo sopra i sorgozzoni che non toccasse il muro; che fu il modo che ha insegnato poi, ed a Bramante ed agli altri, di armare le volte e fare molte buone opere
> He got them to support it on the brackets (sorgozzoni) in such a way that it should stand free of the wall; and this was the method that Bramante himself and others took over from him for the centering of a vault soundly and efficiently

Condivi adds that Michelangelo made it "so well counterweighted ("tessuto") and constructed that the greater the weight put on it, the firmer it held".[18]

Thus Michelangelo resolved the problem of constructing a scaffold that would not obstruct passage in the Chapel by placing his structure on brackets ("sorgozzoni"), that is, on a type of support that may be defined technically[19]: "a piece of wood in the form of a girder or block which, resting on its lower side on a bracket or console, or inserted in a hole in the wall, and projecting outwards on its upper side, bears the beams constituting a scaffold, cantilever, floor, platform or anything else of the kind that by its means extends outwards from the face of the wall". These "sorgozzoni" or brackets were installed immediately above the cornice that runs beneath the lunettes; it is to this cornice that Paris de Grassis alludes implicitly when he writes for 10 June 1508 that "construction was proceeding on the topmost ("altis") cornices of the Chapel".[20]

In the course of the restoration it was possible to establish the exact location of the "sorgozzoni". It emerged that the greyish fascia or frieze, painted a secco, that ran round the bases of the lunettes had been put there later, on the occasion of works carried out by Pope Clement XI (1700–21); it is was clearly of the same date as the decoration of the surrounds of the windows, which bear his coat of arms. Once this restorative intonaco layer had been removed, it could be seen that it had hidden a layer or band of arriccio about 25 cm high, which was blackened by smoke and covered by the dirt of the two previous centuries. Michelangelo evidently had not been able to lay an intonaco on which to paint over this arriccio because of the presence of the scaffold. On the level of this band, one beside each window, there opened a series of irregular holes broken into the wall. These perhaps had been made originally for the 15th-century scaffolding,

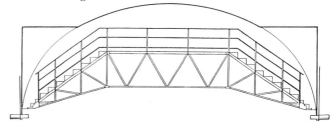

Essentially the design adopted for the scaffold for the cleaning of the Ceiling is a reconstruction, though with modern materials, of the scaffolding used by Michelangelo for the painting of the Ceiling.

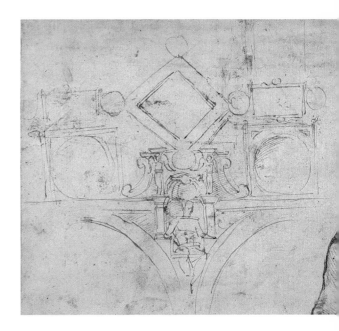

Michelangelo: Study for the design of the Sistine Chapel ceiling (London, British Museum). The central part of the Ceiling was to be filled in with a geometric motif, and there was no idea at this, first stage of painting the lunettes as well. The figures on thrones were to be apostles; though they survived in the subsequent design, they became Prophets and Sibyls. Michelangelo referred to the first design himself: "The first plan for the work was for twelve Apostles in the lunettes (meaning what we call the 'pendentives'), and for the rest some compartments full of ornaments, in the usual way ... I told the Pope that just Apostles, it seemed to me, would turn out a poor thing ... Then he gave me a new commission in which I was to do what I thought best, and I was to paint as far down as to the stories below".

but if so had been enlarged in order to receive much more massive blocks than were then usual – the "sorgozzoni" – such as would be capable of bearing the weight of Michelangelo's scaffold. Their dimensions varied considerably, between 20 cm and 40 cm in height and width, but they were almost invariably about 40 cm deep.

An idea of the structure that Michelangelo supported upon his "sorgozzoni" is provided by the section view of a rapid sketch, identified as a drawing of his scaffold contemporaneously by myself and by Frederick Hartt.[21] It is drawn on the left corner of a well-known study for the figure of the Almighty in the *Creation of Adam,* today in the Uffizi. One can discern a figure putting out his arm as if he were painting, standing on an arched structure, with steps ending at a platform on which a second person lies crouching. The series of curved lines, parallel to the arched structure, which cut through the head and shoulders of the standing figure, refer almost certainly to the ceiling, in section. The sketch is evidently impromptu and diagrammatic, and was probably executed on the spot in order to demonstrate to the foreman of the scaffolders what would happen if he constructed the platform and steps of the scaffold too close to the vault. The fact that the sketch should be done on a preparatory study for the first episode of the second half of the ceiling squares with Vasari's and Condivi's reports of two scaffolds being used rather neatly. The sketch itself has the utilitarian, diagrammatic character of, for instance, the sketches drawn by Michelangelo in 1517 in order to show his servant, who was evidently illiterate, three different menus to serve for parties of different numerical and social composition.

From the drawing it is clear that the scaffolding consisted of an arch stepped on both sides – to enable him to paint the *Prophets* and *Sibyls* – surmounted on top by a platform, from which he could paint the episodes in the centre of the vault and the *ignudi* surrounding them. In the sketch the boarding on which he would paint the lunettes is not shown, because it had no bearing on the problem which he was discussing with the scaffolder, but we may assume that there was a platform resting directly on the "sorgozzoni" or on one of the bearing elements of the scaffold. These bearing elements are not indicated on the drawing, either, but very probably they were just like those illustrated in another sheet in the Uffizi, attributed to Giuliano da Sangallo.[22] This significantly enough once belonged to Vasari;[23] it contains a series of sketches for the building of St Peter's including two little drawings of the system then in use for the centering of vaults. In one, on the upper left, a simple truss supported on a horizontal beam rests on a broad cornice; over the truss is placed the wooden centering on which the vault would be constructed. In the other, the cornice is much smaller, and the bearing surface is broader; inserted into the wall above are two "sorgozzoni" on which rest two horizontal beams, these supporting the truss – which is very probably the system used by Michelangelo in the Sistine Chapel.

According to Vasari, whose accounts, however, are often partisan, the system invented by Michelangelo "was the method that Bramante himself and others took over from him for the centering of a vault soundly and efficiently":[24] in reality the invention probably consisted in adapting for his own needs a method that had been used before for other purposes, and because it had been used for the support of much heavier loads gave him the greatest possible safety and solidity – which would correspond with the notice of Condivi quoted earlier.

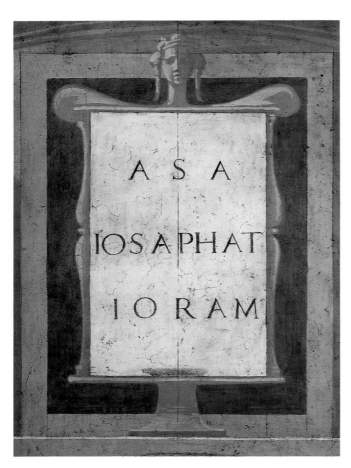

Detail of the tablet of the Asa/Josaphat/Joram *lunette. Each identifying tablet is placed over the head of the window at the apex of the semicircle of the lunette, connecting the groups on each side.*

Opposite page: Michelangelo's palette is not very rich in pigments but his chromatic texture is highly varied. The colour used is sometimes pure, sometimes skilfully mixed to obtain effects of "shimmering shadows". From the absence of blue or green pigments with a copper base (such as azurite and malachite) and the scant use of lead-based colours we may surmise that Michelangelo was well aware of the alterations to which these pigments are subject.

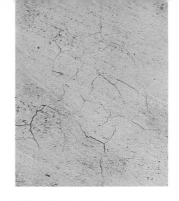

How exactly should we envisage Michelangelo's scaffold once it had been installed in the Sistine Chapel? The most probable hypothesis, taking into account the number of windows in the side walls of the Chapel, is that he constructed a series of six stepped arches, each a little wider than the breadth of the windows, supported by a pair of trusses resting on a pair of "sorgozzoni" inserted opposite each other beside each window. Each arch was connected to the next by a central platform and by boards laid over the steps. These boards were certainly movable, for they would have to be taken up every time Michelangelo went down on to the platform resting on the "sorgozzoni" or on to the structure of beams and trusses over them either to paint the lunettes or, though the viewpoint offered was still far from ideal, in order to check the general effect of the vault he had just been painting. In all probability all the arches had been set up before Michelangelo started painting, so that the artisans responsible could hack down the previous decoration and plaster the *arriccio* layer. One might also suppose that the arches were not set up all together, but in turn, proceeding down the Chapel from the entrance wall, in the direction that Michelangelo would actually paint. Both the removal of the previous work and the re-plastering as far as the *arriccio* would have taken place

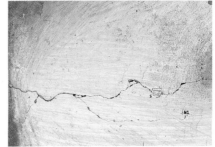

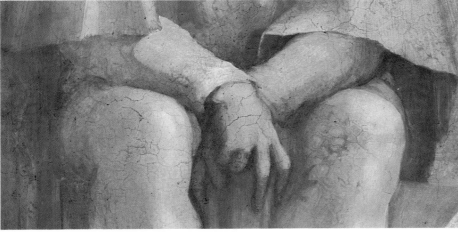

section by section.

The removal of the old decoration would inevitably create a great deal of dust, however, and so there would also be a case for doing it all, for the whole Chapel, at the beginning, so as to avoid the inconvenience or worse that that kind of operation would cause Michelangelo while painting or would occasion for the ceremonies held daily in the Chapel. Paris de Grassis noted significantly in his diary for 10 June 1508 that vespers could not be held that day "because construction is proceeding on the topmost cornices, with a great deal of dust, and the workmen would not stop even when told": he was eventually forced to apply to the Pope who had to send "two successive aides ... to order them to stop work, and they very nearly did not stop even so".[25] If the *arriccio* were not applied in sufficient time beforehand, it could lead to delay in the rest of the work. Andrea Pozzo noted in his *Prospettiva de' Pittori ed Architetti*, though this was written some two centuries later:[26]

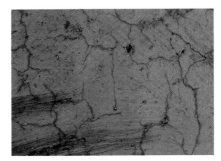

> Here I should warn the Painter, that he should not start working in places where the arriccio *has been laid recently, especially if the places are airless, because besides the moisture, which is unhealthy, the lime gives off an evil smell which is very bad for the head*

ELEAZAR MATTHAN

Details from the Eleazar and Matthan *lunette (see preceding page), on the entrance wall on the left. This is very probably the first lunette Michelangelo painted; as it happens, it was the lunette with which the present restoration began, too. Here, as in the subsequent lunettes, Michelangelo balanced one figure against another, this woman in profile (opposite page) against the three-quarter view of the splendid male figure (details below).*

This young figure exhibits just as much virtuosity and assurance of handling as the more famous ignudi *on the ceiling proper. The weight and mass of his limbs is typically Michelangelesque.*

But besides these considerations of a technical nature the sources and documents provide some significant information on this point. When Paris de Grassis complains on 10 June of the dust produced by the workmen, he gives the impression that the work was proceeding in close proximity to the altar zone. Pietro Rosselli, the man who Michelangelo had hired, at his own expense, not only to "isciarvare la volta ... ariciare e fare quelo bisognerà" – "to hack out the ceiling ... lay down the *arriccio* and make what will be necessary"[27] but also to construct the scaffold (the last payment to him contains the item specifically "for the remainder of the scaffold"), was working for more than two months in the Chapel, because his payments go from 11 May (that is, the day after Michelangelo had received from Cardinal Alidosi, on the Pope's behalf, an advance of 500 ducats) to 27 July. This rather lengthy period would seem to correspond better to the completion of the three operations (hacking down, plastering, making good) throughout the length of the vault, than to work merely on half of it – especially since Paris de Grassis is witness that the men were working until late in the afternoon.

One more note in De Grassis's diary has particular importance in this regard: on 31 October 1512, the day when Michelangelo's frescoes were "unveiled" for the first time, the Master of Ceremonies wrote that "per tres aut quatuor annos tectum sive fornix eius tecta semper fuit ex solari ipsum totum cooperiente" – "for three or four years the ceiling or vault has been covered by the *solari* that enclosed it all",[28] in other words, throughout the period during which work on the ceiling was proceeding, the vault had been completely hidden by a "solaio" or "loft".[29]

The evidence of De Grassis is quite precise and obviously incontrovertible. However, it is partly in contradiction to what we may deduce from another document, in so far as the term "solari" suggests what would appear from below as a continuous floor. We know from the explicit statement of Michelangelo that the scaffold did not cover, or at least was not usable in the whole Chapel, for on 7 September he wrote to his father: "I can tell you that I have coming to me here from

JACOB JOSEPH

Detail of the head of Jacob. These expressive faces are boldly and starkly modelled, and sometimes highly intense. The old man's lifted eyebrow makes it seem he is in reaction to something.

the Pope 50 ducats that I have earned, and another 50 which he should give me for the scaffolding and to continue on the other part of my work. But he has gone, without leaving any orders."[30] If the scaffold was of the nature that is here proposed, it is probable that the movable boards necessary to connect the stepped slopes of the arches were first used by Rosselli and his men during their hacking down and rendering of the entire length of the vault and then set into place only

IACOB

IOSEPH

in the area where the artist had decided to paint, that is, in Condivi's words, "from the door to the middle of the ceiling".[31] During this time the arches were *in situ* in the other half of the Chapel but were not boarded over.

There are essentially two reasons why Michelangelo should have constructed his scaffold only partially. One is simply economic, to save expenditure on wood – the decision could have been Michelangelo's

The Jacob and Joseph *lunette, on the entrance wall on the right. The Joseph is of course St Joseph, husband of Mary, and this is the last lunette of the series. There is something of a paradox in the genealogy, which may explain why the* Ancestors of Christ *were seldom painted: for since Mary conceived without knowing man, Joseph was not exactly the father of Jesus.*

229

Details of the Jacob and Joseph *lunette. Both the field in which they are placed and the necessary seated pose severely limited the possibilities of variation, exploited so fruitfully in the* ignudi. *Nevertheless Michelangelo achieved some dramatic and powerful moments or glimpses, such as this woman's backward glance (opposite page).*

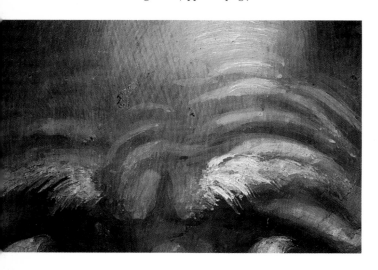

These details show the very brushstrokes of Michelangelo at work, creating the form in comparatively few passes, and without room or time for second thoughts, according to the classic principles of "buon fresco".

or it could have been the Pope's: although the payments to Rosselli show that the construction of the scaffold was certainly Michelangelo's responsibility, we do not know what arrangement was made about the wood required.

The other has to do with the illumination. Given the kind of structure described above, and given that the mouldings of the heads and jambs of the windows were originally much more massive than they are now, it is clear that Michelangelo could not have worked in ideal lighting conditions. Natural light could come in, in effect, only from the upper part of the windows, because it was cut off below by the underflooring, which was provided, as will be shown presently, for reasons of safety and for the sake of appearances. Furthermore, since the central platform was fixed, even the removal of the boards laid across the steps or the provision of some means for reflecting the light would not have made very much difference. At the very best, Michelangelo would have been working in a raking light (ceiling), at worst, the surface on which he was painting would have been thrown into deep shadow by the light streaming through the nearby window (lunettes). Since Michelangelo's technique involved allowing one layer of colour to show through another, and the frequent use of hatching in the modelling, it required good, if not very good, lighting conditions. We have to imagine that he constantly had recourse to artificial light. The light coming in from the windows was hardly sufficient to circulate through the scaffold. But perhaps a second reason for not laying down the boards throughout was to impede no more light than was necessary, to use to the maximum the windows in the half of the chapel that was not being painted.

The conditions in which Michelangelo worked were reproduced on the scaffold that is still in use for the cleaning of the ceiling; this scaffold is in form and structure very similar in section to that which I have supposed used by Michelangelo, even though the materials of which it is made and its engineering are otherwise radically different. There was mention above of an underfloor to the scaffold. Working on the ceiling, Michelangelo had to carry out a whole series of operations (including sometimes perhaps even the preparation of the *intonaco* for the day's work), which were liable to extend their effects to the area beneath – that is, there was always a risk of water or dust falling between the boards, or even of a brush or other tool falling from the hand and down to the floor below. Given these risks, it is difficult to suppose that Michelangelo would not have provided beneath his working area a protective structure of some kind, as light as possible, since it would have no bearing function, of the kind indeed that are used under comparable scaffolds today. This underfloor could only have hung from the beams and trusses of the scaffold and was probably covered over in some material, if indeed it was not made entirely of textile material. An underfloor would also serve to hide the work from those in the Chapel below: for it is difficult to imagine that the Pope, having insisted on a scaffold that would not cause obstruction in the space beneath, would not object to a forest of wood remaining open to view and not masked off in any way. Given such an underfloor, De Grassis's words, and his use of the term "solari" for the scaffolding – implying a structure that appeared flat from below – make much better sense, implying as they do that the vault was completely and not partially covered over during the period of painting. De Grassis obviously had forgotten that on 15 August of

ACHIM ELIUD

The Achim and Eliud *lunette, the first on the left-hand wall of the Chapel facing the altar. Here two figures in profile are balanced against each other, the*

man turning in and the woman turning out. The woman, as usual, has a baby.
(Opposite page) A typically passionate head. The detail shows Michelangelo's modelling in "living colour"; instead of using black or grey for shadows he uses a different shade of the same colour, or even a different colour, creating a vibrant, shimmering effect.

the previous year, after he had fully installed the scaffolding on the second half of the ceiling and had probably taken down everything that was no longer needed, but leaving in position the beams and trusses to which the protective underfloor would once again be attached, Michelangelo "unveiled" for the Pope the half of the ceiling that he had finished.

The examination of the structure of the scaffold leads inevitably to the question of the position in which Michelangelo had to paint, whether it was standing up or lying down. This is perhaps not of the greatest importance and would never have been raised, it may be, had it not been for a remark of Paolo Giovio's that Michelangelo had painted the ceiling "resupinus".[32] In the past the remark has attracted the attention of a number of commentators, and has been used above all in the projection of Michelangelo as a "titanic" figure; it would be as well, if possible, to clear the matter up.

Logically, Michelangelo should have arranged things so that he could stand while working and could be at the best possible distance from the surface he had to paint, both to see it and to apply colours on it.

As far as the central platform is concerned, this distance could not be less than the height of the artist at full stretch, with a brush in his hand: any lesser distance would have inconvenienced the activity not only of the painter but also of the mason who had the task of laying on the *arriccio* or the *intonaco* of the day's fresco, and in any case it would be precisely in the centre of the platform that there would have been the maximum activity and the maximum of coming and going.

The distance from the steps of the scaffold to the ceiling was in large part determined by that between the platform and the ceiling. The crouching figure who appears on this platform in the Uffizi sketch corresponds, as was said, not to reality, but to the hypothetical situation consequent upon the scaffolder setting up the boarding too close to the ceiling.

The idea that Michelangelo could have worked in any other position except upright, lying on his back or, as Milizia suggested,[33] on his knees or on his side, is indeed absurd. It arises from the words of Giovio that Michelangelo painted "resupinus, uti necesse erat", which have been translated in a sense not intended by their author; for Giovio was certainly well informed about events in the Chapel, writing in Rome in 1523–27, and was not a man to make such a gross error. Nor at this time had Michelangelo's fame reached its subsequent proportions of myth.

Everything becomes much clearer if one supposes that Giovio was using the term "resupinus" in the sense in which it was used by Seneca, that is, bent backwards. Then what he says would accord with what Vasari and Condivi also say.

According to Vasari[34]:

> *The work was carried out in extremely uncomfortable conditions, from his having to work with his head tilted upwards*

and Condivi says much the same.[35]

Michelangelo himself drew his own figure upright on the scaffold with his arm stretched out upwards in the act of painting in the well-known sketch appended to the sonnet addressed to Giovanni of Pistoia, a sonnet describing in burlesque fashion and in plentiful detail, designed to place the matter beyond any doubt, the sufferings that the

AZOR SADOCH

artist had to face painting the Sistine Chapel. The text, following the elucidation of Giraldi, amounts to this:[36]

> *I have my beard turned to the ceiling, my head bent back on my shoulders, my chest arched like that of a Harpy; my brush drips on to my face and makes me look like a decorated pavement. My loins are in my stomach and my behind is flattened out so as to balance against the weight of my upside-down body; I cannot see where my feet are. My skin is stretching in front and crumpling behind; I am bent taut like a Syrian bow*

The description is surely quite clear and also explains to a large degree Giovio's choice of the word "resupinus". We might reasonably imagine also that Michelangelo had made use of some kind of support – to which Giovio might again seem to allude – such as that used by Vasari when he was painting the ceiling of the "great rooms of the palace of Duke Cosimo", of which he says:[37]

> *If I had not made a 'chair' on which to rest my head and on which to lie while working, I never would have completed the work*

On 1 November 1512, All Saints' Day, the scaffold was taken down and the vault, "pingi finita", was displayed to the Pope. There also remained visible the bands of *arriccio* which Michelangelo had not been able to paint because the scaffolding was in the way. To finish off that part of the job it would have been necessary to construct a new scaffold, one necessarily different in design, perhaps a moving tower. It was never made, for the same reasons of cost, time and, probably, exhaustion, for which the retouchings *a secco* originally intended for the final embellishment of the vault were also left undone.

THE LUNETTES

The lunettes were the only part of the Sistine ceiling decoration that offered a vertical surface on which to paint; this fact alone sets them apart from the rest of the decoration, both from the point of view of the technique Michelangelo used and from that of their state of preservation.[38]

The surviving lunettes consist of 14 large semicircular areas above the narrow cornice running over the heads of the effigies of the *Popes*, interrupted at their centre by semicircular windows. Each lunette has an average width of 6.5 metres and an average height of 3.4 metres; the windows are on average about 3 metres wide and 1.4 metres high; the semicircular areas painted by Michelangelo vary in width between 1.85 and 1.95 metres.

In the unusually shaped areas provided and on the coves around them Michelangelo did not paint simply ornamental decoration, such as had quite likely been there before, but the monumental images of the 16 families of the genealogy of Christ, according to the list given by St Matthew at the beginning of his Gospel. These included originally the two lunettes on the altar wall, destroyed by Michelangelo himself for the sake of the Last Judgement: their design is recorded in several 16th-century drawings, among them a sketch preserved at Windsor, which is said on the verso to be "by Polidoro (da Caravaggio) after Michelangelo" and a drawing in the Ashmolean Museum in Oxford, in the prints of Giorgio Ghisi and in those of W.Y. Ottley after 16th-century drawings now lost.

When the restoration began, the lunettes were much dirtier than the

(Opposite page) Detail of the bearded man from the Azor and Sadoc lunette (previous page). Particularly in this figure it is tempting to read a kind of self-portrait by the artist; the turn of the head and the gesture recalls Raphael's Heraclitus in the 'School of Athens', taken to be a spiritual portrait of Michelangelo, and the features resemble the artist's. This figure has an extraordinary promptness or momentaneity, to use a term often applied to Impressionist painting; the restoration has revealed that this effect derives partly from the speed of the brush itself. The only good precedent for this kind of work is the fresco technique of Filippino Lippi, painting not long before in Rome in the church of Santa Maria sopra Minerva.

frescoes of the ceiling proper. They were covered with a very thick layer of dirt, soot and glue-varnish, which often rendered invisible not only the individual colours but even the general tone, thus creating, in Tolnay's phrase, their strongly "monochromatic tonality". Their different state of conservation may have several reasons.[39] It is most probable that a difference in temperature between the ceiling and the walls caused the soot produced by candles, oil lamps and braziers to have been deposited in greater quantity on the colder walls. The lunettes would soon have become less legible than the ceiling. But also through the centuries those responsible have not looked on the lunettes in the same way, for while it is clear that the ceiling proper has been subjected to cleanings of greater or lesser intensity, there are no indications that there has ever been any serious attempt to clean the lunettes since they were first painted.

One indication that the lunettes began to darken early is apparent from work on the entrance wall of the Chapel in the years overlapping the pontificates of Pius V (died 1572) and Gregory XIII.[40] The frescoes of Ghirlandaio and Signorelli, the two illusionistic curtains underneath, and the figure of *Pope Marcellus I* were re-painted *ex novo*, though following the original compositions. Probably on this occasion the insertions at the base of the lunettes were also made, in the zone, that is, that Michelangelo himself had been unable to paint because of the presence of the scaffold. These insertions are completely out of tone with the colours of the lunettes (a clear example is the completion of the bag that *Matthan* holds), evidently because the painters had a greatly deteriorated surface in front of them, markedly darker than it had been originally or is now today after cleaning. It is no coincidence that in 1543 so called "mundatores" – "cleaners" – were appointed,[41] lest the *Last Judgement*, completed the year before, should undergo before long the same discoloration that must already have been apparent in the other frescoes of the Chapel.

The application of glue-varnish, perhaps at the time Mazzuoli was at work (1710–1713)[42] or perhaps even earlier, was intended to revive the colours and to improve the legibility of the images, and at the same time to mask the white salt bloom caused by the seepage of water, but it succeeded in fixing the dirt and soot the cleanings had not removed and rendering impossible until now any further restoration to the frescoes beyond mere retouching. It also established the imbalance of tone between the ceiling, which was cleaned by Mazzuoli, and probably by others, and the lunettes, for which almost certainly no cleaning properly speaking was attempted at all. The imbalance was becoming steadily more marked in the years immediately preceding the present restoration.

The lunettes in this way assumed their romantically sombre character – in fact quite foreign to them but determining to an appreciable degree their reception and evaluation, not only artistic but also iconographic. Typical in this regard is the judgement of Tolnay,[43] who based his interpretation of the lunettes and coves partly on their dark colour: they were "the sphere of shadow and death which contrasted to the sphere of light and eternity above it". Not dissimilar, though he did not make the same iconographic inferences, is the comment of Wilde,[44] who speaks of "a darker foil to the display of splendidly lit forms above".

In reality, however, the lunettes did not constitute a darker zone in contrast to the ceiling proper; and their rediscovered luminosity raises

ZOROBABEL ABIUD
ELIACHIM

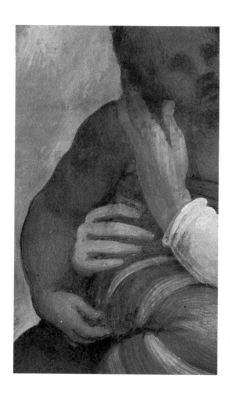

The Zorobabel/Abiud/Eliakim lunette, the second on the left of the Chapel facing the altar. Though the two figures are back to back, they both stare out, it seems, at the same object. These ideal heads by Michelangelo are painted in strokes of the brush that closely resemble the marks of the claw chisel with which he habitually carved out his sculpture. Mother and child are caught in affectionate embrace.

the question of the role they were in fact intended to play in Michelangelo's scheme of decoration. The architectural framework that Michelangelo painted on the ceiling, bearing the monumental images of the *Prophets*, *Sibyls* and *ignudi*, is (contrary even to my own assertions elsewhere) related in no particular to the lunettes or the coves; the one area is simply juxtaposed with the other, just as the lunettes are again juxtaposed without further harmonization to the series of *Popes* painted below. The lunettes, furthermore, are lit differently: in the images on the ceiling the direction of the represented light is decisively from above, through the great openings in which the stories of Genesis and of Noah are represented as if they were visions, while the light is made to fall on the *Ancestors of Christ* consistently from the west, but from lower down, which seems also to be the way in which the *Popes* are lit in the 15th-century fresco below.

If the lunettes are more closely related to the decoration below from the point of view of represented light, so are they again in scale: the height of the *Ancestors* ranges from about 2.1 to 2.4 metres, and is closer to that of the *Popes*, averaging 2.1 metres, than to that of the *Sibyls* and *Prophets*, with the *Delphic Sibyl* at 2.88 metres, *Joel* at 2.83, *Zechariah* at 3.1 metres; and the difference becomes even greater in the second half of the vault where these figures are about half a metre taller again. Viewed from below, as they were certainly painted to be viewed, the *Popes* and *Ancestors* seem all the more clearly related; however, sinde the *Popes* are standing figures and the *Ancestors* are seated, the difference in their proportions is marked, and from this point of

238

JOSIAS JECHONIAS SALATHIEL

view the *Ancestors* are evidently much more with the *Sibyls* and *Prophets*. We may therefore suppose that Michelangelo intended the lunettes as an element serving to provide a transition between the 15th-century decoration and his own ceiling. It is even possible, though it remains to be proven, that the balance between the individual areas constituting the ceiling is determined more by the close proportional relations between the figures than by the architectural framework, especially since the figures strive in a certain sense against their framework; however, the system of proportions can never have been rigidly predetermined, and in many cases, such as those of several *Prophets* and *Sibyls,* was altered or adjusted in the course of execution.

The Josias/Jechonias/Salathiel *lunette, the second on the right of the Chapel facing the altar. Here again Michelangelo achieves variety by making some of the figures respond to some event outside their immediate space; in this case the man on the left turns impulsively, showing a craggy profile, towards the mother and child.*

In this light the fact that in the two surviving studies for the membering of the ceiling, in London and in Detroit, there is no hint whatever of the presence of the lunettes and coves has some significance: these constituted a problem that was largely independent and self-sufficient. However, once he had decided the compositional scheme of the whole, Michelangelo continued his studies for the lunettes and for the ceiling contemporaneously: there are indeed numerous sheets with designs for both zones, and this is particularly clear in the Oxford sketchbook.

240

Having finished the preparations, Michelangelo entered the phase of execution on the walls themselves, beginning, as was logical, with the central episodes or more exactly, as Vasari and Condivi report,[45] with the central episode at the entrance wall end. According to the reconstruction of the scaffolding made above, he next went on to the figures of the *Prophets* and *Sibyls*, immediately beside them, and then moved down finally to paint the corresponding lunettes. We may presume, indeed we may deduce from the sequence of day's works or *giornate*, that the painting was executed in this way throughout the entire Chapel, that is, proceeding from zone to zone, and from the centre of the ceiling to the lunettes, towards the altar wall.

When for the first time Michelangelo went down on to the part of

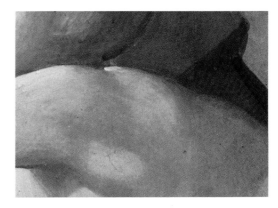

Detail of the shoulder of the child who climbs on the knees of his father.

the scaffold from which he was to paint the lunettes, he found conditions quite different from those of his long and arduous initial months painting the ceiling proper. Above all, he had now acquired and perfected a sophisticated pictorial technique, which, though essentially extremely traditional, was made to produce unprecedented results, thanks to certain very individual variations of his own. Secondly, he had before him a vertical wall and not the curved surface on which he had worked hitherto – which affected his procedure considerably. Finally, for the first time he could stand far enough back

In their turn the mother turns back and the child leaps forward in response to something over the mother's shoulder – perhaps the figure opposite. Usually, however, the pairs of the lunettes do not even appear to be engaged in dialogue among themselves.

241

EZECHIAS MANASSES AMON

from what he was painting to realize what it looked like when seen from a distance.

Technically speaking, the lunettes are all executed in *buon fresco*, according to the principles of the tradition that runs from Cennini to Vasari, with nothing being done *a secco* and without even those retouchings which were normal in order to harmonize the painting when the *intonaco* had dried too quickly or when the colours of one *giornata* differed excessively from those of the previous day. Michelangelo made sure to use only those colours that he knew were suitable to fresco: the reds are almost all ochres (anhydrous oxides), so are the yellows (hydrous oxides); the greens are ferrous silicates; the blues are exclusively lapislazuli, with no trace of azurite; the lilac ground is "morellone" (ferrous sesquioxide), the white is calcium oxide. Further, where there are corrections, the colours of the colouring-over are water-soluble and have mixed into the plaster.

However, though the technique could hardly have been more traditional, one cannot say as much for the use to which it was put. Here the lunettes have individual characteristics, distinct from what we find on the ceiling proper. The figures of the *Ancestors* of Christ, as Wilde had already realized, were all painted without the use of a preparatory cartoon and extremely quickly, and are often unfinished, indeed

The Ezekias/Manasses/Amon *lunette, the third on the left of the Chapel facing the altar. The mother and child are sleeping. Perhaps the almost caricatured figure on the right-hand side of the lunette is also sleeping; the weight and latent power of her relaxed hand is typically Michelangelesque. This hunchback, hook-nosed shrew makes a striking contrast to the epicene beauty of the mother's face (detail opposite page).*

242

typically they are merely sketched out. Their colour is always pure, it has never been mixed beforehand. It was applied very wet, very thinly, and was therefore constantly to some degree transparent, even, in fact especially, in the middle tones. The result is very like watercolour, producing most unusual effects for which there is technically little precedent. However one precedent of great importance can be found in the main apse chapel of Santa Maria Novella in Florence, which was frescoed by Ghirlandaio and his workshop, in which

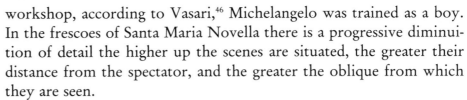

workshop, according to Vasari,[46] Michelangelo was trained as a boy. In the frescoes of Santa Maria Novella there is a progressive diminution of detail the higher up the scenes are situated, the greater their distance from the spectator, and the greater the oblique from which they are seen.

By contrast, however, to Ghirlandaio's practice, which was to assign these upper zones entirely to the workshop, Michelangelo certainly painted the lunettes by himself alone. We can be so certain, not only because of their quality, which can after all be a matter of opinion, but also because of the total absence of any trace of the use of cartoons. The colour is so thin and transparent that if Michelangelo had had

OSIAS JOATHAM
ACHAZ

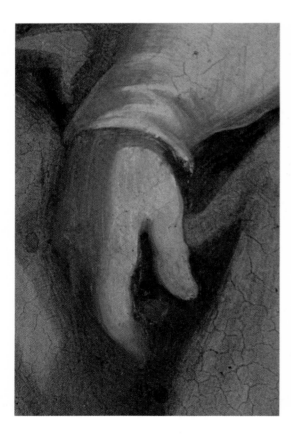

The Ozias/Joatham/Achaz lunette, the third on the right of the Chapel looking towards the altar. The details (above) are of the figure (opposite page) on the left of the lunette. Again the figure has directed attention outside the immediate space; the child points. Increasingly one finds these figures to be the victims of a kind of sloth or malaise; but this is perhaps a by-product of Michelangelo's concern to make them weighty and monumental.

recourse to pouncing or to incision there would be clear traces of it, as there are on other parts of the Ceiling; but what does show through at several points, for example in the head of *Matthan*, is instead a drawing of extremely summary character, done in a dark colour, and intended essentially to outline the mass of an individual figure. This means that Michelangelo must have executed both the drawing and the painting in the time of a single *giornata* (about eight hours), which is all the more surprising when one considers that the lunettes were never painted in more than three *giornate* – one for the central tablet and one each for the areas to the side. The number of *giornate* is still smaller in the second half of the Chapel: in the lunette containing

Roboam, there are no sutures, or joints, visible at all, in the *Asa* lunette the joints are scarcely visible (which means that there was an interruption of only a few hours between the *giornate*), and in the *Aminadab* lunette the only suture that can be seen clearly is that to the left of the tablet.

In order to be able to work as long as possible on these enormous surfaces before the *intonaco* should dry, Michelangelo used a plaster very low in lime, but the absence of sutures in the *Roboam* lunette can be explained only by Michelangelo having worked without stopping until the whole surface was painted, applying the *intonaco* to the next section before the *intonaco* on which he was painting could dry.

The figure on the right side of the *Ozias/Joachim/Achaz* lunette is one of the most extraordinary in the series and has now emerged from the cleaning as even more dramatic. It is shown in quite violent movement, turning it seems in response to the child on the right, who is a little to the rear; but also it possesses a supreme elegance, in the gesture of the hand pulling the cowl, for instance. The putto standing in front has a remote, serene quality, like a creature indeed from a mythical world. But particularly splendid is the figure's face, a severely and intensely characterised face, not easily legible, but full of feeling.

Michelangelo always painted the tablet which contains the inscription identifying the *Ancestors* in that lunette and in the cove above first, for the good reason that the tablet constituted an axial element of the composition determining the symmetry of the whole; and for the same reason he did not draw the tablets freehand (except for their ornament) but incised their verticals and horizontals on to the *intonaco* using various instruments – nails, string, rules – thanks to which he could be certain to remain true to the perpendicular and not to lose sight of the boundaries of the field when he came to paint.

The role of the tablets was crucial also because of their explanatory inscriptions. Furthermore, running round the whole Chapel, like the

ASA JOSAPHAT JORAM

The Asa/Josaphat/Joram *lunette, the fourth on the left-hand side of the Chapel facing the altar. The detail of the right-hand figure (opposite page) shows the children assaulting, or romping, over the* Ancestor, *who turns back in the kind of movement Michelangelo so unflaggingly developed. Her drapery hangs in masses of great weight, like metal.*

The figure on the left-hand side is a kind of cross between an ancient Egyptian scribe and a modern Pierrot; an oriental figure, by his hat, verging on a caricature. But once again the figure has an absorbed presence.

tablets identifying the *Sibyls* and *Prophets* above, and also like the great titles with which the scenes from the *Lives of Christ and Moses* below were adorned (and the *Popes* again have inscriptions, but these are not so prominent), the tablets of the lunettes serve as a unifying element between the various decorations of the Chapel.

In the first half of the Chapel the tablet is almost invariably provided with two lateral mouldings, which disappear in the second half, while the tablet takes on a longer shape, as does its supporting base. This change in shape is accompanied by a change in the *giornate:* in the first half of the Chapel the lunette *giornate* are very irregular and include not only the area of the tablets but also part of the cornice of the lunette and of the extrados of the window, but in the second the *giornata* is always strictly vertical and extends no further than the tablet. Corresponding to the alteration of the shape of the tablet, which becomes slightly narrower, the *Ancestors* move slightly closer to the centre, and become a little taller both in absolute height and in proportion, in a development similar to that of the figures of the ceiling (though there it is much more marked) and perhaps deliberately in order to match them.

Since these changes, both formal and technical, begin exactly at the centre of the ceiling, it is reasonable to suppose that they mark respectively the length of the two scaffolds Michelangelo used, and also that he decided he would make these changes during the enforced interruption to his work between September 1510 and August 1511, with the benefit of the view he had been able to take from below with the "unveiling" of the first half of the vault.

Once he had finished the *giornata* containing the tablet and cut away the superfluous *intonaco,* Michelangelo went on to do the areas at the side, beginning probably on the right. One indication that he did so comes from the *Aminadab* lunette, where the only joint clearly visible is that to the left, and therefore the male figure on this side must have been painted last.

Michelangelo's working procedure was generally the same: after having laid the *intonaco* and waited the necessary time, he designed the figure in very quick, broad strokes, in a very dark brown, at first very summarily and then progressively clarifying the crucial lines, as can be seen very clearly in the head of *Matthan.*

He then laid out the tone of the ground so as to produce a silhouette of the image, and proceeded to model from dark to light, from the voids to the solids, from the shadows to the highlights, with a method, and a confidence, that shows forth the sculptor he was. He worked without *pentimenti* or second thoughts to speak of; should he not be satisfied with what he had done, the consequences were drastic, and involved the complete re-making of the parts that displeased him. For instance, in the *Achim and Eliud* lunette, which presents an anomalous sequence of four *giornate,* two of them have been devoted to the area of the bearded old man to the left. The extraordinary feature is that the joint does not, as it would usually, follow the outline of the old man's head, it cuts right through it: the only possible explanation is that Michelangelo, dissatisfied with what he had first done, cut away the *intonaco* and on the next day, or more probably a few hours later, re-painted from scratch a large part of the figure.

In the absence of traces of pouncing or incision (except of course for the incision of the tablets, but these are incised directly, without an intermediary), the idea that Michelangelo used preparatory cartoons

for the lunettes can be ruled out. However, it is difficult to accept that he could have moved directly, without intermediary stages, from the tiny compositional studies of the sketchbook in Oxford, or even from more detailed drawings like the one in the Uffizi for the male figure in the *Asa* lunette, to the enormous surfaces he had to paint.

Although it is not well recorded, it was probably more common than is generally believed to make preparatory drawings on the *arriccio* or even directly on the wall not only in the 14th and 15th centuries but also later. Drawings of this kind, even though they were very different from the final result, were found in the Vatican when, for reasons of conservation, the fresco of the *putto* holding a papal tiara was detached from the wall of the Sala Clementina, which was decorated by Cherubino and Giovanni Alberti between 1596 and 1600. Quite possibly Raphael also had recourse to the same kind of preparatory drawing, as Winner has supposed with good reason,[47] for the architectural background of his *Coronation of Charlemagne*, in which there is no trace of the use of a cartoon.

The drawing in the lunettes of *Zorobabel* and *Ozias* proved an indication that Michelangelo, too, may have sketched out the figures on the *arriccio*, for in both the joints of the left-hand *giornata* follow the outlines of a seated figure, which would have been impossible to arrange if the artist had not at least sketched out the essential lines of the figures on the *arriccio* below.

It is highly probable that Michelangelo painted first the lunettes on the entrance wall of the Chapel, and that of these two he began with the *Eleazar and Matthan* lunette, with which, quite by chance, the restoration also began. In this lunette the execution is much more careful and refined in detail, which would accord with a trial of the method of procedure; in particular, the ground is much darker here than in other lunettes, in which Michelangelo modified the excess he perceived in this one.

The colour of the ground served to emphasize the caesura between the lunette decoration and the 15th-century work below, and at the same time constituted the tonal base for the building-up of the colours in each individual lunette and the common starting-point from which they all began, like the constantly repeated "line" in a polyphonic composition.

In the lunettes Michelangelo used colour, rather than graphic design, to build up and give substance to his figures. Colour has not a secondary, but a primary, structural role. It is used constantly pure, in order to achieve the maximum tonal intensity, and to enable Michelangelo to anticipate more accurately the eventual effect of the process of carbonation, and perhaps also because in this way, painting entirely "in the wet", improvising as he went along in bad or artificial light, he could keep better control of the differentiation between the planes of the image, as it emerged from the ground into highlight. The modelling is broad, achieving thereby a greater impact and resonance, and made often, if not always, in dense strokes. The contours of the figures are painted with very great freedom, sometimes in the same colour as the planes of the modelling, or more often, particularly in the chiaroscuro of the drapery, in a closely related one. It is not surprising that there is no trace of retouching in tempera, which on the one hand is typical of a much more refined and careful technique than Michelangelo's, and on the other would have created nothing more than opaque marks on the surface of the colour, completely

ROBOAM ABIA

The Roboam *and* Abia *lunette, the fourth on the right of the Chapel looking towards the altar. The woman on the left, as one can tell not only from her belly but from her breasts, is pregnant.*

Michelangelo is painting now with great freedom, without the use of a cartoon, blocking out these great figures with all the strength of a stone mason. The woman on the right (above) hangs in a pose perhaps of abandon, or of resignation.

lacking in resonance and completely opposed to the shimmery, luminous nature of the fresco colours.

For Michelangelo the colour served also to represent the fall of light, thereby increasing the monumental effect and transforming the images of the *Ancestors* into giant polychrome sculptures. Because his colour had this luminous quality, Michelangelo could afford to abandon almost altogether traditional chiaroscuro modelling; his policy of modelling in colour meant in effect the articulation of the image in terms of planes of light, resulting in emphasis on volume and a powerful plasticity. Probably for the sake of this emphasis he chose some violent, and surprisingly modern, juxtapositions, such as green to violet (*Eleazar and Matthan* lunette), violet to green to yellow *(Achim and Eliud)*, red to yellow *(Asa, Josaphat and Joram)*, violet to yellow *(Azor and Sadoc, Ozias, Joatham and Achaz)*, black to red *(Aminadab)*, in which the darker colour is used for the areas in shade and the lighter one for the highlights, and a middle tone is obtained by layering one over the other, thereby creating what Armenini called Michelangelo's "liquidissime ombre", or glittering shadows.[48]

Even in this, however, Michelangelo was hardly doing anything very new technically: the use of such melded colours can be found even in some of the 15th-century frescoes beneath, though its appearance is sporadic and rare, and directed to purely decorative ends (for instance, in the figure of *Pope Calixtus*). What was new was Michelangelo's use of it to model, and creation with it of an apparent fall of light, a very strong light, with its source in the altar end of the Chapel (its iconographical implications, however, are not my present concern), and distinctly non-naturalistic. To study the chiaroscuro effects he achieved in the lunettes Michelangelo probably, as Vasari reports, used models of wax or clay:[49]

> He first for this purpose created models of earth or wax; and from these, which are more solid and stable than life models, he observed the outlines, highlights and shadows

From this point of view Michelangelo's choice of the sculptor Giovanni Michi as his assistant (he approached Michelangelo in July 1508 and entered his shop in the following August, replacing Piero Basso)[50] has a certain significance.

However, it needs to be emphasized that for the *Ancestors* Michelangelo never employed the kind of foreshortenings from below ("di sotto in su") that Bramante had held to be necessary for the decoration of the Chapel, though he did use them in a few instances in the ceiling proper. Vasari hailed Michelangelo as a master of foreshortening "on the flat"[51] and in fact the images of the lunettes are depicted from the point of sight of the painter and not from that of the spectator. The spectator sees them indeed in the kind of oblique, elongated, distorted view that so appealed to the Mannerists and which we find again in Rosso and Pontormo.

One last observation on the technique Michelangelo used is to touch on the question of the "non finito". Given the dimensions of the *giornate* and the extremely short time in which they had to be painted, the execution had to be, as has been said, very quick, broad and sketchy, and though there are many parts that have been worked over with great care, there are details that have deliberately been left in a state of "non finito". However, it does not follow that the quality of the painting diminishes correspondingly, as is the case with the frescoes in Santa Maria Novella which Ghirlandaio handed over

JESSE DAVID SOLOMON

The Jesse/David/Solomon *lunette, the fifth on the left of the Chapel facing the altar. Despite the fame and established iconography for these figures, Michelangelo has eschewed precisely identifiable*

features, indeed his figure on the left (detail opposite page) looks like some Bedouin prince rather than a civic, urban figure like David or Solomon. He is moved by some powerful but inexplicable suspicion – once again animation for the sake of it, but no less splendid for that.

On the right-hand side of the lunette a woman weaves, with a melancholic expression – a weighted gaze, as so often in these lunettes. Again she is hardly identifiable with a known biblical character – certainly not Bathsheba.

SALMON BOOZ OBETH

The anatomical detail of the breast feeding mother has been revealed by the cleaning of the fresco. The comparison between the state of the painting before and after the restoration well illustrates how Michelangelo's use of colour has emerged from centuries of soot and dirt.

entirely to the less expert assistants of his workshop, since they were so far from the spectator that the difference would not be seen; Michelangelo turned the principle on its head and used the lack of finish as a means of achieving greater depth in the figures. In fact he proceeded more or less as if he were adjusting the focus of a camera, in so far as the areas in the forward plane are more "finished" than those in the backward plane, tending therefore to an effect of *sfumato;* the more distant planes are sometimes left simply as sketches.

Even though all the essential elements of Michelangelo's procedure in the painting of the lunettes are already present in the first, the *Eleazar and Matthan* lunette, nevertheless as he worked along the walls of the Chapel he perfected his technique, and he worked increasingly fast, which resulted in a progressive compositional and formal simplification. The effects of this development are particularly evident in the second half of the Chapel. Here Michelangelo painted with fury, so as to leave, for instance, the hairs of his brush imbedded in the *intonaco* of the *Roboam* lunette; he sought all the while to reduce the number of *giornate* required. His fury had certain negative consequences: in this part of the Chapel he tended to start painting while the *intonaco* was still too wet, with the result that his brushstrokes abraded its surface and removed the skin that had formed, and with the consequence also that the first colours he laid on, particularly those of the ground, were subjected to too violent an action of the lime, causing them to become opaque and reducing the sharp gleam of the contours.

Compositionally, the groupings become progressively more compact, the number of figures they contain diminishes (and particularly the number of children), until in the last lunettes (the first in the chronological sequence of the Bible) of *Naasson* and *Aminadab* there are only two pairs of single figures. Their proportions, however, increase, as in the rest of the ceiling, and they become increasingly monumental as they advance to the altar wall. Also their typology

NAASSON

The Naasson lunette, the sixth and last on the left wall of the Chapel facing the altar. In a new variation, the figures are presented both turned in the same direction. While the woman looks into a mirror, the man reads a book, his leg stuck out in a pose of great freedom.

The figure of the woman and even details of her dress relate extremely closely to an antique prototype, one of the nine Muses on a well-known sarcophagus now in the Louvre (see p. 211).

and physiognomy alters, they become more realistic and more expressive, constituting an extraordinary gallery of personages that often seem to have been taken directly from the life and open interesting questions about Michelangelo's iconographic motivations and procedure.

The lunettes are likely to remain the area where the restoration will have had its most dramatic results, such has been the transformation of their colour and legibility. Within Michelangelo's project, as I have said, they have a special position, because of the great differences in their technique and execution. For these differences there seem to have been essentially two reasons: most importantly, having to work on a vertical surface and being able to see the results of his work from a distance, Michelangelo came much more directly to terms with the surface on which he was to work, he was free from the fetter of a preparatory cartoon, and he could treat the surface to be painted much more as he would stone as a sculptor – exploiting to the full the confidence of handling and mastery of form that was second nature to him (or rather, in respect to painting, his first nature).

But also when he began Michelangelo had numerous problems in large part due, as Vasari testifies, to his comparative inexperience as a painter, and in some degree, very probably, due to differences of various kinds, perhaps also of a technical kind, with his workshop – differences which caused one of the assistants he had brought from Florence, Jacopo di Sandro, to leave prematurely in January 1509.[52]

These problems had the effect of delaying the schedule for the project, increasing the difficulties of the artist, facing pressure both from the Pope, who was impatient to see the work finished, and from the court, who certainly found the scaffolding in the Chapel unaesthetic and a nuisance.

By the time that Michelangelo came to paint the sections immediately over the choir, Julius II's impatience was reaching a critical point. Vasari relates:[53]

> Michelangelo himself would sometimes lament the Pope having made him do it in such a hurry, so that he could not finish it in the way he would have liked, but the Pope was always asking him importunately when he would finish. Hence, on one occasion Michelangelo had replied that it would be finished, when he had satisfied himself that it looked as it should. "But it is our desire", the Pope had replied to him, "that you should satisfy our desire to have it finished soon." And he had concluded by saying that if he did not finish it soon he would have him thrown down off the scaffold.

This need to finish the ceiling in a hurry, and the anxiety it caused Michelangelo, are well documented in a letter from the artist dated 24 July 1512 to his brother Buonarroto:[54]

> I have not time to reply to your letter because it is night, and even if I did have time I could not reply to you finally because I do not know how my affairs here will end ... I work more than any man ever did, in ill health and in the greatest discomfort; but still I have the endurance ("pazienza") to achieve the end I long for. So you, too, can endure two more months, being ten thousand times better off than I am

The method of working adopted by Michelangelo in the lunettes was certainly the result of technical and stylistic experience obtained in working on the ceiling proper; but it was also at least partially determined by his need to cut down on the time he was taking – this undoubtedly influenced his decision not to use preparatory cartoons.

AMINADAB

The Aminadab *lunette, the sixth and last on the right wall of the Chapel looking towards the altar. This, now that the lunettes of the altar wall have*

gone, is where the series of Ancestors now starts. The comparatively straightforward, old-fashioned frontal pose of the left-hand figure becomes in this context another sophisticated variation.

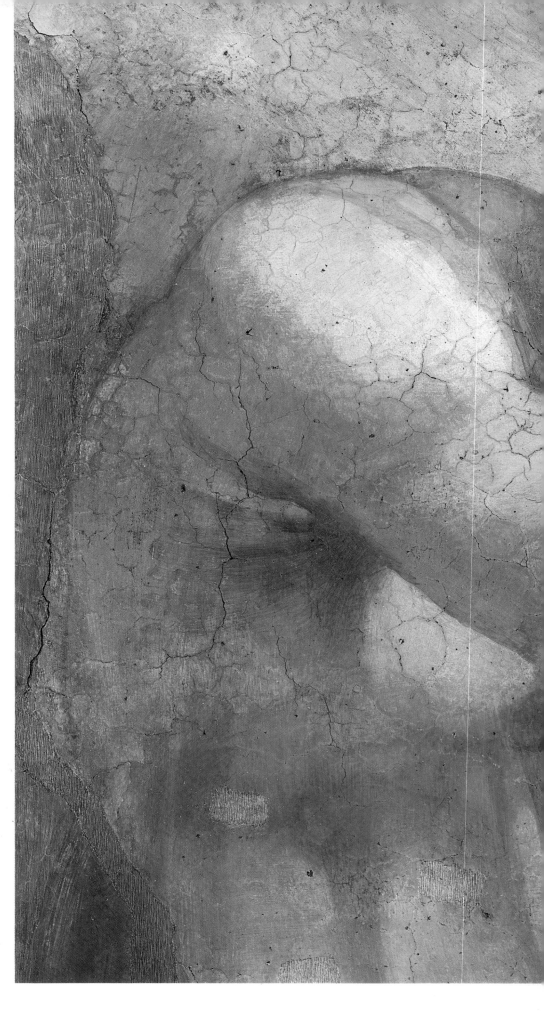

The hairs of the brush left adhering to the *intonaco* of the *Roboam* lunette are eloquent testimony of the furious haste in which Michelangelo was compelled to work.

However, when he moved down on to the part of the scaffolding prepared for the painting of the lunettes, Michelangelo was already

entirely master of his medium and technique, and a long way from the condition in which he had written disconsolately to his father, in January 1509:[55]

> *... and that is the trouble with this job, and anyway it is not my profession*

The detail of the right-hand woman shows Michelangelo's stupendous powers of draughtsmanship, as he sets out the complicated pose of the combing woman in palpable space – palpable, though there is nothing to suggest it except the contour of the woman's arm.

259

APPENDIX

GIANLUIGI COLALUCCI

MICHEL-ANGELO'S COLOURS REDISCOVERED

The activity of restoration can be defined in terms of two overlapping headings, procedure and method. Procedure is fixed and invariable, and consists in the scientific planning and execution of the restoration project, regardless of the material involved.

Method, however, is the department strictly of the action taken in the course of the restoration, and is therefore variable, subject to factors arising from the material, technique and state of conservation of the monument involved.

The adoption of a procedure which governs the progress of the work is characteristic of modern restoration. Under the impetus of a marked development in technological expertise, modern restoration has extended its established and primary func-

tion of conservation for aesthetic ends to include a research capacity, directed towards the work of art considered as an inseparable duality, conceptual and material.

In the past restoration practice aimed at cancelling the effects of time and events on the work of art, termed by Brandi comprehensively its historical aspect;[1] absolute priority was given to its aesthetic aspect, conditioned of course by its contingent situation. The restoration of works of art was therefore entrusted to artists, who were free to introduce personal methods, often secret or private, consistent with the aim of returning the work to its pristine material state, but not necessarily to its original intended state.

In the evolution of the "art" of restoration, the Laboratory for the Restoration of Pictures in the Vatican Museums has had a not insignificant role. Founded in 1922 by Biagio Biagetti according to the latest ideas, and subsequently provided with a Laboratory for Scientific Research, the institute is today directed by Carlo Pietrangeli, who in 1978 established its guidelines in *Rules for the restoration of works of art.*[2]

In June 1980 this laboratory, constitutionally responsible for the restoration of the pictorial patrimony of the Holy See, qualified and informed by its enormous experience, which goes back more than 50 years and has been constantly renewed both technically and in terms of personnel, undertook the most important task it had

yet undertaken in its history, the restoration of the frescoes by Michelangelo in the Sistine Chapel.

In the course of the restoration of the two frescoes by Matteo da Lecce and van den Broeck on the entrance wall of the Sistine Chapel, various checks were run on the lunettes painted by Michelangelo, which ascertained that in several places minute flecks of colour were lifting from the surface, necessitating an immediate restoration. Preliminary preparations, study and research to assess and define the nature of the task were immediately begun, and took

more than six months for the team to complete.[3]

The information available to the researchers at the start, relevant to the state of conservation and the painting technique of Michelangelo's frescoes, consisted partly of reports from written sources and partly of the personal testimony of a few restorers who when very young had taken part in the restoration of the *intonaco* surface in the 1930s; these last were not encouraging, since they spoke of the bad technique of the frescoes, of their being finished off *a secco,* of their perhaps being "varnished" with animal glue and pigment and of their being "burned", a technical term meaning that the colour had been deleteriously affected by an excess of lime in the plaster or by its having dried out too quickly.

However, these were subjective impressions, often mutually contradictory, vitiated by the state of conservation of the frescoes at that time and by the considerable distance from which they were often observed; the notes taken on the previous restorations, including those that had taken place from 1935 to 1938, were no more informative or reliable. This was not surprising, because the true state of the frescoes and their technique could not be perceived even by direct observation at close hand, because of the film over them, corresponding to no known pictorial technique. This very dark, brown, glassy epidermis, consisting essentially of layers of

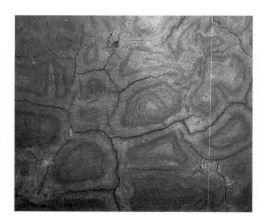

dust and fatty soot and of various substances applied at several different times in the past, concealed not only the quality but even the texture of the colour and so rendered impossible any perception of the artist himself as he should be revealed vividly in his work (and I have in mind particularly the impression made upon me in the course of much work on the *Last Judgement,* and the considerable 'food for thought' it gave rise to). What was clear, however, was that there were innumerable unpleasant and unsatisfactory traces of old restorations. Technical and scientific research, concentrating primarily on an analysis of the pictorial technique, was undertaken on the *Eleazar and Matthan* lunette. By the end of this investigation Michelangelo's use of *buon fresco* was unequivocally vindicated. He had worked in the purest Florentine tradition, using only colours suitable for fresco, avoiding any that would have required application *a secco*. He had worked *a secco*, though to a minimal degree, on the ceiling, but not at all in the lunettes, not even to carry out small alterations as he worked. Nor had he painted the coloured or uncoloured "velature", or glazes containing binder, that some had taken to be not the result of a restoration, as in fact they are, but the later, improvised corrections of Michelangelo himself.

These results were enough to demolish the theory that Michelangelo had never received the kind of training rooted in the workshop tradition, in which art was indissolubly bonded with the rigours of technique. A product of this tradition is the *Libro dell' Arte* of Cennino Cennini, in which the technique of fresco is carefully described in chapter 67, *The method and procedure for working on a wall, that is, in fresco, and for colouring young faces.*[4] In the eleven following chapters he describes in great detail how to paint figures, draperies and colours in fresco, which he dubs "'l più dolce e 'l più vago lavorar che sia" – "the sweetest and most attractive way of working there is". The technique has been

rates and so fixes the pigment of the paint.[5] The technique is clearly very simple but it requires knowledge and experience. Painters lacking in these qualities have made considerable use of retouching or finishings *a secco,* and not only in order to provide the colours that it is inadvisable to use in fresco. Vasari is explicit on this matter[6]:

(Fresco) resists both atmosphere and water and will always withstand any kind of blow, but one has to be careful to avoid having to retouch it with colours bound in animal glue or eggyolk or resin or gum tragacanth, as many painters do; because, besides preventing the fresco from showing forth its natural luminosity, the colours become veiled by the retouchings on top and in a short space of time become black. Therefore, let those who wish to paint on a wall work with courage (virilmente) in fresco and let them not retouch a secco, because, besides being a weak and cowardly thing, it shortens the life of the painting

No such weakling was Michelangelo, whose technique in the lunettes, as was ascertained and confirmed during the restoration, was as orthodox as it could be, indeed it was exceptional for the time in its rigorous maintenance of the principle of *buon fresco.*

Each lunette was painted in only three "giornate" or "day's works" of an absolutely extraordinary size. There was no tracing through from cartoons, which would have used up too much of the time

effect of volume. Michelangelo passed without hesitation from great expanses of wet, thin, flat paint to dense passages of laden brushstrokes marking or emphasizing the projecting surfaces of the figure, just as the sculptor does with the claw chisel. But absolutely unprecedented are the very light veils of pure colour that he laid over modelling in monochrome (mostly over flesh), for which he used a brush that was almost dry "well pressed with the fingers", as Cennini says, in order to open out the bristles. It goes without saying that a technique so refined and so rigorous, arrived at only after the initial difficulties reported by Michelangelo himself,[7] ruled out the possibility of second thoughts, which would have had the same discordant effect as would tempera over a watercolour. There is proof of this in the mild deterioration of certain limited retouchings that he made to the shoulder of *Eleazar* or to the edge of the foot of *Roboam*, where in order to cover the dark colour with a light pigment he had to mix the pigment with white.[8]

Unfortunately, however, Michelangelo's frescoes have suffered insidious attacks from the walls themselves,[9] and above all from the roof, which has too often become leaky and let in the rain.[10] And then there have been constant deposits from the smoke of countless candles used in the liturgy and of braziers used for heating. Large humidity stains had appeared in six lunettes and in five 'pendentives', and of

known since antiquity: founded on a natural chemical reaction, true fresco permits no modifications or transgressions to the rule that the pigments should be mixed with water and applied on a fresh *intonaco*. The *intonaco* may consist of lime and sand or lime and *pozzolana* (a ground volcanic powder) or exceptionally lime and marble dust, reduced to a paste in water. When the *intonaco* starts to dry the calcium hydroxide ($CaOH_2$) rises to the surface where it reacts with the carbon dioxide (CO_2) of the air, creating a crust of calcium carbonate ($CaCO_3$) which incorpo-

available for painting, for this, given that the average size of the *giornate* was about five square metres, was necessarily short. The colours were laid in unmixed one beside another, and were kept very bright by deliberately allowing the ground beneath to show through or by painting them directly over the clear *intonaco*, sometimes enhanced by a thin veil of lime. The nature of the brushwork is very varied (which created some difficulties for the researchers) but perfectly rational, because it was directed, together with the complementary colours, to the creation of an

(Opposite page from left to right):
Saline efflorescence in the Zorobabel *lunette.*
Small flecks of colour that have detached from the wall, held in the restorers' varnish.
An example of silicate deposit disrupting the intonaco *and paint layer.*
(Above) Examples of the application of varnish in order to strengthen the shading of the Delphic Sibyl *and in order to "revive" or bring up an* ignudo.

course in the ceiling, where restoration continues. These stains have been the primary reason for all the successive restorations made to the frescoes. When it passed through the masonry of the vault the water deposited the salts that it carried

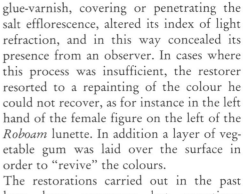

glue-varnish, covering or penetrating the salt efflorescence, altered its index of light refraction, and in this way concealed its presence from an observer. In cases where this process was insufficient, the restorer resorted to a repainting of the colour he could not recover, as for instance in the left hand of the female figure on the left of the *Roboam* lunette. In addition a layer of vegetable gum was laid over the surface in order to "revive" the colours.

The restorations carried out in the past have been numerous but sometimes limited, and the records made have not always been very thorough.[13] They are sufficient, however, with the aid of direct observation, comparison, and scientific analysis, to enable us to reach the conclusion that probably two campaigns of restoration in particular have had the greatest effect on the condition in which Michelangelo's frescoes have appeared until now: these are

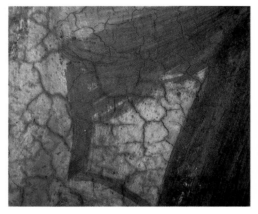

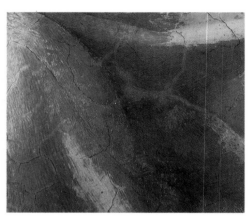

Details of retouchings made to figures of Michelangelo's Sistine Ceiling in the past:
(Above, top) The face of a putto *bearing a tablet beneath a prophet, in which the eyes, nose and mouth have been retouched.*
(Above, left, right and centre) Coarsening retouchings made to the tunic of the prophet Zechariah, attributable to the restorer Mazzuoli, and shadows added to another putto *to make the figure stand out better.*
(Right) The hand of one of the figures of the Roboam *lunette, before cleaning (left), showing the repainting made over disfiguring salt efflorescences, and after cleaning (right).*

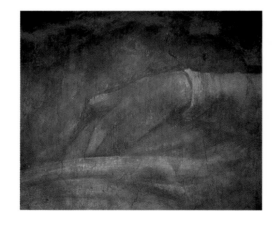

on the painted surface of the *intonaco*, creating whitish stains, and eroding and unsettling the *intonaco* with a consequent "blistering" of the paint layer.[11] These phenomena have attacked the lunettes to a serious degree only here and there, and almost everywhere the paint has not been affected because of the extreme thinness of the pigment, which has allowed the crystals to pass through without resistance. Whitish efflorescences were formed of sulphates and calcium carbonates; dark stains of a circular form were formed by silicates, and these are irreversible; they occur par-

ticularly on the *putti* of the 'pendentives'. Giovio was already writing in about 1547 of Michelangelo's work "being destroyed by saltpetre and cracks". This means that very soon there was required not only a "mundator" responsible for keeping the frescoes clean,[12] but also a restorer proper, who would remove the less adherent salts by mechanical action and treat the more tenacious deposits with quantities of warm animal varnish, sometimes with the addition of a very small proportion of a vegetable oil such as linseed or walnut oil. The treatment was cosmetic, in so far as the

the restorations carried out by Lagi in 1625 and by Mazzuoli in 1710–1713.

Lagi, who held the title "resident gilder", which in fact meant general restorer, was a Florentine painter of brilliant and vivid decorative schemes. A note in a 17th-century manuscript reports of his cleaning of the ceiling frescoes:

... and the procedure used was as follows: that it was cleaned figure by figure, with linen rags the dust was removed with slices of cheap bread or any such lowly stuff, scrubbing hard, and sometimes, when the dirt was more tenacious, the bread was

on the] Vault to the south of the above mentioned Chapel"[15] but also in all likelihood carried out the decorations on the lower edge of the window heads, which have Clement XI's coat of arms on them, and the fascia or band at the base of the lunettes that Michelangelo had left unfinished.

The major impact of the Mazzuoli restoration was on the ceiling, which must have undergone considerable deterioration since the time of Lagi's restoration, because the Mazzuoli were forced to use sponges dipped in Greek wine instead of the blander pieces of bread dipped in water. Evidently in the intervening 85 years the layer of revivifying agents that Lagi almost certainly used, the particles of dirt that had been caught in these and fixed, and the further deposit of soot had become extremely obstinate.

The choice of Greek wine as a solvent, which the painter Carlo Maratti had introduced,[16] must have been determined by its resinous content, which would serve together with its moisture and alcoholic sugar to "nourish" the colours.

From an examination of certain areas where the carbonated surface had become markedly permeable to the liquid, it was deduced that the wine had been allowed to

Tests made on the Asa *lunette, in which the cleaning agent was applied for varying lengths of time. The best results were obtained from an application of three minutes' duration.*
Next page: The head of one of the lunette figures after successive applications of the cleaning agent: before, during and after is shown from left to right.

moistened a little, and so they returned to their previous beauty without receiving any harm

That is as much as it says.[14] The note does not mention at all the use of substances to revive the colours or of glue-varnish, and Lagi would avoid doing so in obedience to the principle dear to restorers of the past of preserving the secrets of their craft. Turning to his method of cleaning, we may note that when Lagi used bits of dried bread to rub across the fresco, thereby obtaining a mild cleaning, it would have had no ill consequences either for fresco or for tempera painting, but resorting to moistened bread when the dirt would not come off in this way makes a great deal of difference, because though water does no harm to a fresco, it has an adverse effect on *secco* painting, and could have been fatal to any tempera finishing, had there been any, if the moistened bread had been applied carelessly. But the documentation reports entirely satisfactory results.

Annibale Mazzuoli, of whose painting very little is known, and his son, not only are reported "to have cleaned and adjusted the Pictures, etc, above the large Cornice [and

acidify beforehand in order that its action should be still more aggressive. This method produced a surface that was subsequently more difficult to clean and considerably hampered by the irregular incidence and varying degrees of thickness

263

and adherence of the substances to be removed.

Experience shows that an attempt to preserve an appreciable stratum of the film of dirt and other substances over frescoes that have been treated in the past with revivifying agents will render the colours dull and flat and lose the chiaroscuro contrasts, because this greyish film, instead of coming away, will shift from one part to another of the surface, achieving a general improvement in the level of dirt, but a lightening of dark tones and a darkening of light tones. In order to obviate this consequence, the Mazzuoli had had recourse to a general and irregular application of revivifying agents and then, on much of the fresco, had introduced patinations, "velature", by going over the chiaroscuro with passages of opaque or transparent paint containing a binder, or had used tempera, sometimes densely cross-hatched and sometimes in parallel strokes, depending on the modelling of the figure beneath. I had observed the same technique, in common use among restorers, particularly in the 18th century, a few years earlier in the Sala del Perseo, the Sala di Amore e Psiche and the Sala Paolina in Castel Sant' Angelo, which had also been restored by Mazzuoli in 1723.[17] The brushstrokes of the Mazzuoli restoration are quite distinct from those of Michelan-

treatment than that described above. Perhaps because they were not so prominently placed, the restorers seem not to have devoted so much attention to them and to have limited themselves on the whole to a more perfunctory and fairly rapid cleaning with a liberal use of glue-varnish to revive the frescoes. In cases where this did not have the desired effect, they repainted the darker areas of the modelling with a thin black paint, and repainted eyes, mouths and nostrils with a rather fatty brown tempera, in order to achieve by this longstanding and approved expedient an illusory effect of cleaning; in this way they re-emphasized the contrasts of the lighter and darker areas. They also completely repainted those areas that had been irretrievably lost to salt efflorescence. But again for the lunettes there is no mention in the documents of the use of glue. The accounts mention only "sponges", "Greek (wine)", *gesso* and colours. At least in the lunettes, the Mazzuoli must nevertheless have used a great deal of glue-varnish for (quite apart from what was found!) only so could Lalande have written in 1768: "The whole ceiling … is monotonous, it colour tends towards dull red and grey".[19] This is unequivocal evidence that there had been applied substances that were now in deterioration, and thereby had muted

preceded and accompanied by research, analysis and record-taking, are partly physical or mechanical, in so far as they are concerned with the consolidation of the *intonaco* layers and the pictorial film of the Ceiling, and partly conceptual, or investigative, in so far as the cleaning is directed towards a recovery of the authentic and historical aspect of the frescoes, with the best available technical and scientific methods.

In this case, both aspects of the restoration centre on the cleaning of the frescoes, which is anyway the most critical activity of the restorer, but which particularly here stands to modify significantly the appearance of one of the most important works of art in the world, which has been criticized, studied, loved and mythologized through the centuries in a form that Michelangelo himself could not have dreamt of: time and human intervention have masked the reality to an almost incredible degree.

The procedure of the cleaning required the use of a solvent and a method that would guarantee the highest margin of safety and would not require either emotional involvement or complex mechanical manipulation on the part of the restorers. In the cleaning of an area of such vast size the employment of several people was in-

gelo, both from the point of view of their draughtsmanship, which is sometimes dense and cloying, sometimes slovenly, and from that of their colourism, which is timid, not venturing beyond the juxtaposition of close tones and having constant recourse to a middle brown, compared to Michelangelo's, which is full of dissonances, "twelve toned" in Argan's words,[18] introducing dark olive on green, dark olive on yellow, red on yellow, dark blue on red, blue on burnt siena, and so on. The lunettes of the Sistine Chapel, however, were subjected to a rather simpler

the colour of Michelangelo's frescoes. In order of time, the last campaign of restoration was that of the Restoration Laboratory of the Vatican Museums in the years 1935–38. It was a limited campaign, directed solely towards the consolidation of the *intonaco* layers of the eastern part of the ceiling and a partial removal of soot and superficial dirt.[20]

The recent restoration, beginning in 1980 with the lunettes,[21] is at present continuing on to the ceiling, and will eventually include the *Last Judgement,* expecting to finish in 1992. Our operations, constantly

evitable, and the homogeneity of the result was a primary objective.

Once the nature and stratification of the substances that in the course of time had become sedimented or been deposited on the pictorial skin of the fresco had been verified, research into the solvents and methods best adapted for their removal followed (a detailed description is in the appendix at the end of this article). The early trials were not carried out on Michelangelo's frescoes but on the fresco by Matteo da Lecce representing the *Conflict over the Body of Moses* on the entrance wall of the

Chapel, which presented a surface of exactly the same nature and stratification. Next the campaign continued on small portions of the *Eleazar and Matthan* lunette. After it had been ascertained that the separate use of solvents designed to affect each kind of constituent substance was contraindicated by the irregularity of the layer to be removed, risking a heterogeneous and therefore unacceptable cleaning, a mixture colour in a vertical-stroke technique.[23] As far as possible, traces of the work of previous restorers were preserved *in situ,* for example the braces of bronze or brass of various kinds that had been applied on several occasions to consolidate *intonaco* layers in danger of detachment, and which still perform their function, or the infills in wax and resin that the painter Carnevali applied to the cracks in the fresco in 1572.[24]

terioration of which would inevitably lead to an equally rapid deterioration of the painting, but to the maintenance and control of the micro-climate of the Chapel.[26]

The four and a half years of work on the lunettes have given the restorers a technical understanding and knowledge of the painting of Michelangelo indispensable for their work on the ceiling proper, which involves

---

GENERAL REPORT ON THE RESTORATION OF THE SISTINE CHAPEL LUNETTES

Michelangelo Buonarroti
(Caprese 1475 – Rome 1564)
The Sistine Chapel ceiling:
the 14 lunettes representing
the *Ancestors of Christ*
Average size of each lunette:
340 × 630 cm

TECHNIQUE OF EXECUTION:
Preparatory:
Arriccio, composed of lime and *pozzolana,* average thickness 15 mm.
Intonaco, composed of lime and *pozzolana,* average thickness 5 mm.
Three *giornate* for each lunette. The first that of the central tablet, the successive *giornata* one for each figure or group of figures. The sutures are visible in the eight lunettes of the eastern section; in the western section less visible and sometimes indiscernible. It is to be supposed that these six were painted each without interruption. The lower fascia of the lunettes, ranging in height between 30 and 40 cm, was left unfinished because it was at the lowest level of the scaffold and its point of attachment.

Means of transfer:
No sign of pouncing or incision from a cartoon. Occasional presence of a schematic drawing in brush in black. Direct incision for the framing of the central tablets and for several vertical or horizontal lines, like those of seats on which figures sit or the lectern of the youth in red in the *Naasson* lunette.

Pictorial skin:
Painting is in *buon fresco,* with colours added. No *pentimenti* proper, except for small corrections made in fresco during the execution. It is to be supposed that instead of making important *pentimenti,* Michelangelo preferred to cut away and remove the *intonaco* altogether (cf the old man in the *Achim and Eliud* lunette, at the top of which there is a small *giornata* with the beginning of the figure, which has been cut at the level of the forehead and continued on a new *giornata*).

STATE OF CONSERVATION:
Mural support:
The state of the mural structure of the Chapel is in the care of the Director General of the Technical Services of the Vatican State.
The mortar of the *arriccio* and the *intonaco* is in a good state of composition and cohesion. The adhesion of the preparatory strata is satisfactory. There are present numerous T and X braces in bronze of various date, introduced to stabilize *intonaci* at risk. The *Aminadab* and *Roboam* lunettes have oblique cracks of some size running across, caused by movement in the wall.

Pictorial skin:
Seepage of rainwater with consequent creation of salt efflorescences, silicates, carbonate crusts and surface corrosion of the *intonaco* had occurred in the following lunettes: *Eleazar, Jacob, Achim, Zorobabel, Roboam, Salmon, Aminadab, Asa, Ezechias.*
The pictorial skin was in perfect preservation almost everywhere, even in the areas attacked by salts. Here there has been light corrosion and modest loss of tonality, also dark round stains and similar stains along the cracks. Over the pictorial skin there was a thin, but very tenacious layer of grey particles, consisting of fatty dusts and soot. There were further layers of some thickness consisting of animal glue-varnish (keratin), which has deteriorated and browned. Over these there were retouchings and repaintings containing binder, and repaintings in a very thin black paint over dark areas and shadows in the figures. Finally there were layers of soot, a slight "veil" of vegetable gum varnish and, everywhere, fatty dusts and soot. But also over the most serious salt efflorescences there were retouchings and repaintings executed with pigments in animal and vegetable binders.

RESTORATION:
Mural support:
Consolidation of areas of the *intonaco* in precarious cohesion with injections of Vinnapas.
Removal of certain *gesso* plasterwork and bronze braces causing particular disturbance to the paintings.
Filling of the gaps with *stucco romano* (lime and marble dust).

Pictorial skin:
Prior consolidation of the less secure pigments or those not so well suited to fresco (blues, reds, greens, etc) by the absorption of acrylic resin, Paraloid B72 diluted to 3% in an organic solvent.
Removal of soot, fatty dust and vegetable glues reversible in distilled water.
Removal of retouchings and repaintings with a mixed gelatinous solvent, consisting of a solution of ammonium bicarbonate, sodium bicarbonate, Desogen (a surf-actant and anti-fungal agent), carboxymethylcellulose (a thixotropic agent), dissolved in distilled water. Mixture acts on contact. The times of application, rigorously measured, were:
First application: 3 minutes, followed by removal and washing with water. Left to dry for 24 hours.
Second application: 3 minutes, followed by removal, washing, and leaving to dry as before. If necessary, and locally only, small applications, followed by plentiful final washing.
In the case of salt efflorescences consisting of calcium carbonate, there was added to the solvent mixture a saturated solution of dimethylformamide.
For the most part, the activity of the solvent was rigorously controlled by the measurement of the length of time of application, though application was repeated until the white crusts had been totally removed; there was absolute respect for the pictorial skin itself.
Final treatment: the thorough, complete and overall application of a solution of Paraloid B72 diluted to 3% in organic solvent, removed from the surface of the pictorial skin by the combined action almost simultaneously of organic solvent and distilled water, which coagulates the surface acrylic resin dissolved by the solvent.
A very limited pictorial retouching was carried out in water colour in the vertical stroke technique.
The restoration began on 10. 6. 1980 and was completed on 13. 10. 1984.

---

of solvents was used, maintained in a gel of PH base, active at the time of application and, as is known by long experience,[22] quite safe to use on fresco. In fact with a rigorous control of the time of contact the cleaning could be rendered gradual and consistent, and yet effective even in those zones where tenacious and frequent salt efflorescence had given poor expectation of a total recovery of the colour underneath.

Since the frescoes were in such a good state, the amount of retouching involved was practically nil; in cases where it was required, the retouching was done in water-

By way of a final treatment, in order to consolidate certain colours that showed a tendency to "lift", acrylic resin diluted to a very small percentage was applied, a method that had been researched with very great care with Michelangelo's frescoes particularly in view, and which both permitted the reinforcement of the cohesion of the pigments in depth and would not leave unsatisfactory "velature", even though transparent, on the surface.[25] In the future the good preservation of the frescoes will no longer be entrusted to protective layers of varnish, the rapid de-

a series of difficulties, and constitutes on a human and emotional level an experience of quite a special order, since one has the privilege of direct and daily contact with the art of Michelangelo: one discovers him centimetre by centimetre, figure by figure, one is able to share and transmit these discoveries, and one is aware, even while enjoying so magnificent a work, of the responsibility that that means.

MICHELANGELO'S WORK: A CULTURAL INHERITANCE FOR MANKIND

I have been asked countless times why a Japanese television company participated in the restoration of Michelangelo's frescoes in the Sistine Chapel. I always give the same answer. I believe that the works should be preserved as a legacy for mankind. In a curious way, there is also something rather apt in our involvement, in that it brings the wheel of fate full circle. Let me explain: In 1549, Francis Xavier reached Japan, and began the first Catholic missionary activity in this country. Forty years later, the first envoys to Europe were sent by Christian feudal lords from southern Japan to be received in audience by the Pope. The ensuing centuries saw ardent proselytizing, the repression of Christianity, the closing of Japan and its reopening, the renewal of religious freedoms, and modernization until, exactly 400 years later, in 1981, the Pope visited Japan for the first time. I was privileged to be granted an audience with His Holiness, perhaps due to Nippon Television's endeavours toward world peace, particularly through the Christian program we have broadcast for over 20 years, "The Light of the Heart". On the occasion of the Pope's historic trip to Japan, we asked for permission to convene and broadcast a gathering of "the Pope with young people", to sponsor "Christian road" and "Vatican" exhibitions, and to contribute to the restoration of the Sistine Chapel frescoes. The restoration work and the recording of it are, for those who love and respect the arts, quite remarkable. The Pope graciously allowed us to participate in this project of the century.

The restoration of the Lunettes is now complete and work has moved to the Ceiling. In the process, new light has been shed on Michelangelo the artist. Many further discoveries should come from the research now in progress on the Lunettes. These newly restored works reveal a Michelangelo who is not simply a great artist, but also a great philosopher and a deeply religious man.

When we think of all those who will see the completely restored frescoes in the Sistine Chapel, we are filled with pride and happiness.

We are using every medium available to record this historic restoration project for the benefit of people around the world and for future generations. This publication, one part of that effort, is the result of international cooperation in the true sense of the word. Japanese handled the camerawork during the restoration, the text represents the combined efforts of the world's top Michelangelo specialists from the United States, Italy, the United Kingdom and France, and editorial professionals from Switzerland, Italy, the United Kingdom and Japan. The final production was handled in Switzerland. The international character of this publication was confirmed when publishers from Japan, the United States, the United Kingdom, Belgium, the Netherlands, Spain, West Germany and France agreed upon simultaneous publication.

I sincerely thank the Vatican for giving a Japanese television company this special opportunity.

Y. Kobayashi

Yosaij Kobayashi
Chairman of Nippon Television Network Corporation

FOOTNOTES

ROME IN THE RENAISSANCE, 1480–1540

1 From the *Diario de' Sebastiana di Branca Tedallini*, quoted by M. Miglio, 'La Rinascita politica dell' antico', in ed. S. Settis, *Memoria dell' antico nell' arte italiana*, (*L' uso dei classici*, vol. 7), Turin 1984.
2 See José Ruysschaert, 'Une Annonciation Inspirée de Roger de la Pasture dans un manuscrit Romain de 1459', *Mélanges d'Archéologie e d'Histoire offerts à Jacques Lavelleye*, Louvain 1978, p. 249.
3 See the contribution of John Shearman below.
4 See L. Ettlinger, *The Sistine Chapel before Michelangelo*, Oxford 1965.
5 See the contribution of John Shearman below.
6 Cf E. and J. Garms, "Mito e realtà di Roma nella cultura europea", in *Storia d'Italia*, vol. 5, Turin 1982.
7 J. de Bellay, *Les Regrets*, Paris 1558, LXXXVII.

THE CHAPEL OF SIXTUS IV

1 Anno domini MCCLXXVIII ... Nicolaus papa III fieri fecit palatia et aulam maiora et capellam (inscription formerly on a garden-wall of the Vatican).
2 Hic ubi sidereum consurgit ad aethera templum
Unde queat propius turba videre deos:
Squalebat senio atque situ, vix nomine phanum,
Vixque ipsis locus is manibus aptus erat.
(Aurelio Brandolini, *De phano quod Sixtus in domo sive palatio condidit).*
3 Tu [Sixtus] sacellum in apostolico palatio parietibus labentibus tecto tabulato et desidenti ex parte omni deformato ... funditus diruisti, dignissimum excitasti novum ... (Andreas of Trebizond, dedicatory preface to a commentary on Ptolemy).
4 Anno domini MCCCCLXXVI di xi kal. dec. Sanctissimus dominus noster Sixtus quartus erexit ecclesiam avinionensem in metropolim: et dedit eidem sufraganeos ecclesias carpentoratensem, cavalisensem et vaxioensem, et assignavit mihi Juliano archiepiscopo petenti nomine eiusdem ecclesie palium in capella maiori in die purificationis post missarum solempnia de eodem anno [i.e. liturgical year] (*Taxae cancellariae apostolicae*, Bibliothèque Nationale, Paris, MS. Lat. 4192 A, fol. 7 r).
5 15 May 1504: Vespers were transferred to Old St Peter's 'quia capella palatii reparabatur per cathenas super voltum superiorem et in voltis inferioribus propter eius rupturam per medium' (Johannes Burchard); and 'quoniam ipsa capella ruinosa erat, et tota conquassata ita ut ibi stare non posset Papa' (Paris de Grassis).
6 Julius II was sending Giuliano da Sangallo to Florence to persuade Michelangelo to undertake the painting of the ceiling, whereupon Bramante said: 'Santo Padre, e' no' sarà nula, perché io òne praticho Michelagnolo asai e àmi deto piue e piue volte none volere atendere a la capela, e che voi li volevi dare cotesto caricho' (Piero Rosselli to Michelangelo, 10 May 1506).

THE THEOLOGY BEHIND MICHELANGELO'S CEILING

I wish to thank Dr. Bernice Davidson, Professors Kathleen Weil-Garris Brandt and John Shearman, who read earlier versions of this essay and offered valuable suggestions.

1 Vasari, *Le vite dei più eccellenti pittori, scultori e architetti*, ed. Carlo L. Ragghianti, 4 vols, Milan–Rome (Rizzoli) 1947–1949, vol. 3, p. 430. English translations are by George Bull (Middlesex: Penguin Books, 1965).
2 Ibid.
3 Ibid., pp. 430–431.
4 For a review of opinions up to 1964, see Ettore Camesasca's appendix in Roberto Salvini, *The Sistine Chapel*, 2 vols, New York (Harry N. Abrams) 1965, I, pp. 178–230. Among the more important studies since then are Esther Gordon Dotson, 'An Augustinian Interpretation of Michelangelo's Sistine Ceiling,' *The Art Bulletin*, lxi, 1979, pp. 223–256, 405–429; Frederick Hartt, *Michelangelo*, New York (Harry N. Abrams) 1965; Lutz Heusinger and Fabrizio Mancinelli, *All the Frescoes of the Sistine Chapel*, Florence (Scala) 1973; Howard Hibbard, *Michelangelo*, 2nd ed., New York (Harper and Row) 1985; Edmund R. Leach, 'Michelangelo's *Genesis:* Structuralist Comments on the Paintings on the Sistine Chapel ceiling,' *Times Literary Supplement*, March 18, 1977, pp. 311–313; Rudolf Kuhn, *Michelangelo: Die Sixtinische Decke*, Berlin (W. de Gruyter) 1975; Charles Seymour, Jr., *Michelangelo: The Sistine Chapel Ceiling*, New York (W. W. Norton) 1972; Staale Sinding-Larsen, 'A Re-Reading of the Sistine Ceiling'; *Institutum Romanum Norvegiae*, iv, 1969, pp. 143–157; Johannes Wilde, *Michelangelo: Six Lectures*, ed. John Shearman and Michael Hirst, Oxford (Clarendon Press) 1978, esp. pp. 48–84; Edgar Wind, 'Michelangelo's Prophets and Sibyls', *Proceedings of the British Academy*, li, 1965, pp. 47–84.
5 Ascanio Condivi, *Vita di Michelangelo*, in edd. Paolo D'Ancona, et al., *Michelangelo: Architettura-Pittura-Scultura*, Milan (Bramante) 1964, p. 204. English translations are by Alice Sedgwick Wohl, Baton Rouge (Louisiana State University Press) 1976.
6 See e.g. Dotson, "Augustinian Interpretation," p. 230; Kuhn, *Michelangelo*, pp. 52–58; Wind, 'Prophets', pp. 78–81.
7 See Frederick Hartt, *'Lignum Vitae in Medio Paradisi:* The Stanza d'Eliodoro and the Sistine Ceiling,' *The Art Bulletin*, xxxii, 1950, pp. 115–145, 181–218, esp. 129–134.
8 Ed. Giovanni Poggi, Paola Barocchi, and Renzo Ristori, *Il Carteggio di Michelangelo*, 5 vols, Florence (Sansoni) 1966–1976, III, pp. 10–11 (DXCV).
9 Charles De Tolnay, *Michelangelo*, 5 vols, Princeton (Princeton University Press) 1943–60, vol. 2 (1945). See also Kuhn, *Michelangelo*, pp. 84–148.
10 See Eugenio Garin, "Thinker," in *The Complete Works of Michelangelo*, ed. Mario Salmi, New York (Reynal and Company) 1964, pp. 517–530.
11 Leach, cit. note 4.
12 See Dotson, cit. note 4, and Hartt, cit. note 7.
13 See Edgar Wind, 'Sante Pagnini and Michelangelo: A Study of the Succession of Savonarola,' *Gazette des Beaux-Arts*, 6th ser., xxvi, 1944, pp. 211–246.
14 Wind, "Sante Pagnini," p. 212, n. 4.
15 See e.g. Salvatore Camporeale, *Lorenzo Valla: Umanesimo e Teologia*, Florence (Istituto Nazionale di Studi sul Rinascimento) 1972; Remo L. Guidi, *Aspetti religiosi nella letteratura del Quattrocento*, 5 vols, Rome–Vicenza (L.I.E.F.) 1973–83; John W. O'Malley, *Giles of Viterbo on Church and Reform*, Leyden (E. J. Brill) 1968; id., *Praise and Blame in Renaissance Rome*, Durham (Duke University Press) 1979; id., *Rome and the Renaissance*, London (Variorum) 1982; id., 'Egidio da Viterbo and Renaissance Rome', in *Egidio da Viterbo, O.S.A., e il suo tempo*, Rome (Analecta Augustiniana) 1983, pp. 67–84; Eugene F. Rice, Jr., *Saint Jerome in the Renaissance*, Baltimore and London (The Johns Hopkins University Press) 1985; Charles L. Stinger, *Humanism and the Church Fathers*, Albany (State University of New York Press) 1977; Charles Trinkaus, *"In Our Image and Likeness"*, 2 vols, Chicago (University of Chicago Press) 1970; Ronald G. Witt, *Hercules at the Crossroads: The Life, Works and Thought of Coluccio Salutati*, Durham (Duke University Press) 1983. For the more general context, see Stinger, *The Renaissance in Rome*, Bloomington (Indiana University Press) 1985.
16 See Charles L. Stinger, 'Greek Patristics and Christian Antiquity in Renaissance Rome', in *Rome in the Renaissance*, ed. P. A. Ramsey, Binghamton (Center for Medieval and Early Renaissance Studies) 1982, pp. 153–169; John W. O'Malley, 'The Feast of Thomas Aquinas in Renaissance Rome: A Neglected Document and Its Import', *Rivista di Storia della Chiesa in Italia*, xxxv, 1981, pp. 1–27.
17 See O'Malley, *Giles of Viterbo*, cit. note 15 esp. pp. 67–99, and Jerry H. Bentley, *Humanists and Holy Writ*, Princeton (Princeton University Press) 1983, pp. 1–69.
18 See O'Malley, *Praise and Blame*, cit. note 15, and Hanna Holborn Gray, 'Renaissance Humanism: The Pursuit of Eloquence', *Journal of the History of Ideas*, xxiv, 1963, pp. 497–514.
19 See Hellmut Wohl, 'Papal Patronage and the Language of Art', in *Umanesimo a Roma nel Quattrocento*, ed. Paolo Brezzi and Maristella De Panizza Lorch, Rome and New York (Istituto di Studi Romani, Barnard College) 1984, pp. 235–246; Thomas Martone, 'Interpretation of the Sistine Ceiling', *The Art Bulletin*, lxiv, 1982, pp. 484–485; Esther Gordon Dotson, 'Interpretation of the Sistine Ceiling: Reply', ibid, pp. 655–657.
20 See O'Malley, *Praise and Blame*, cit. note 15, p. 159.
21 'Convivium religiosum', in *Opera omnia*, Amsterdam (North Holland Publishing Company) 1972, I/3, p. 254.
22 See e.g. Wind, 'Prophets', cit. note 4, and André Chastel, *Art et Humanisme à Florence au temps de Laurent le Magnifique*, Paris (Presses universitaires de France) 1961, pp. 236–240.
23 See e.g. John W. O'Malley, 'Fulfillment of the Christian Golden Age under Pope Julius II: Text of a Discourse of Giles of Viterbo, 1507', *Traditio*, xxv, 1969, pp. 265–338; id., 'The Discovery of America and Reform Thought at the Papal Court in the Early Cinquecento', in *First Images of America*, ed. Fredi Chiappelli et al., 2 vols, Berkley (University of California Press) 1976, I, pp. 185–200; and Jean Delumeau, *La peur en Occident (XIVe–XVIIIe siècles): Une cité assiegée*, Paris (Fayard) 1978.
24 Condivi, *Vita*, ed. cit. note 5, pp. 208–210.
25 See the "Unde et memores" of the Canon of the Mass, *Missale Romanum.*
26 See Marcia B. Hall, 'Michelangelo's *Last Judgment:* Resurrection of the Body and Predestination', *The Art Bulletin*, lviii, 1976, pp. 85–92.
27 See Wind, "Prophets," cit. note 4, pp. 49–57.
28 See e.g. Dotson, cit. note 4, pp.415–418.
29 See O'Malley, *Praise and Blame*, cit. note 4, pp. 132–133.
30 See ibid., 132–136, and Seymour, *Michelangelo*, cit. note 4, pp. 83–84, 132–141.
31 Vasari, *Vite*, ed cit. note 1, III, p. 431.
32 Ibid., p. 432.
33 Ed. Enzo Noé Girardi, *Rime*, Bari (Laterza) 1960, pp. 60–61 (# 106). English translation by Creighton Gilbert, *Complete Poems and Selected Letters of Michelangelo*, New York (Random House) 1963, p. 76 (# 104); see also pp. 284–85.
34 See e.g. Hartt, *'Lignum Vitae'*, cit. note 7, pp. 190–191.
35 See Stinger, 'Greek Patristics', cit. note 16, p. 161.
36 See O'Malley, *Praise and Blame*, cit. note 15, pp. 55–56, 83, 105, 139–140, 146.
37 See Wind, 'Prophets', cit. note 4, pp. 61–64.
38 See Edgar Wind, 'Maccabean Histories in the Sistine Chapel: A Note on Michelangelo's Use of the Malermi Bible', in *Italian Renaissance Studies*, ed. E.F. Jacob, London (Faber and Faber) 1960, pp. 312–327. See also e.g. Kuhn, *Michelangelo*, cit. note 4, pp. 58–69.
39 See e.g. Kathleen Weil-Garris, 'On Pedestals: Michelangelo's *David*, Bandinelli's *Hercules and Cacus* and the Sculpture of the Piazza della Signoria', *Römisches Jahrbuch für Kunstgeschichte*, xx, 1983, pp. 378–414.
40 *Vita*, ed. cit. note 5, p. 213.
41 Ibid., p. 204.
42 See O'Malley, *Praise and Blame*, cit. note 15, p. 141, and, more broadly, pp. 137–52. See also Leo Steinberg, *The Sexuality of Christ in Renaissance Art and Modern Oblivion*, New York (Pantheon) 1983.
43 Ibid.
44 See the "Deus, qui humanae substantiae" of the Order of the Mass (Offertory), *Missale Romanum.*
45 See O'Malley, *Praise and Blame*, cit. note 15, p. 150.
46 See the *Summa theologiae*, II/II, 26, 6.
47 See O'Malley, *Praise and Blame*, cit. note 15, pp. 165–166.
48 Ibid., pp. 168–169; *De officiis*, 1.7.22: "... non nobis solum nati sumus ortusque nostri partem patria vindicat, partem amici."
49 See e.g. William J. Bouwsma, 'Renaissance and Reformation: An Essay in Their Affinities and Connections', in *Luther and the Dawn of the Modern Era*, ed. Heiko A. Oberman, Leyden (E.J. Brill) 1974, pp. 127–49; Bernd Moeller, 'Piety in Germany Around 1500', in *The Reformation in Medieval Perspective*, ed. Steven Ozment, Chicago (Quadrangle Books) 1971, pp. 50–75; Thomas N. Tentler, *Sin and Confession on the Eve of the Reformation*, Princeton (Princeton University Press) 1977.
50 See e.g. Dotson, 'Augustinian Interpretation', cit. note 4, p. 418.

FIRST REACTIONS TO THE CEILING

1 A. Luzio, "Federigo Gonzaga ostaggio alla corte di Giulio II", *Archivio della Reale Società Romana di Storia Patria*, ix, 1886, pp. 540–41.
2 Ed. G. Milanesi, Giorgio Vasari, *Le Vite ...*, Florence 1906, vol. V, p. 456.
3 See A. E. Popham, *The Italian Drawings at Windsor Castle*, London 1949.
4 Ed. P. Barocchi, *Scritti d'Arte del Cinquecento*, Milan–Naples 1971, vol. 1, p. 10.
5 Ed. cit. note 2.
6 Ed. cit. note 2.
7 Bartsch XIV, 2; B. XIV 464; B. XIV, 5 a.
See Evelina Borea, "Stampe da modelli fiorentini nel Cinquecento", in *Il Primato del Disegno*, Florence 1980.
8 Michal and R.E. Lewis, *The Engravings of Giorgio Ghisi*, catalogue raisonné. Introduction by S. Boorsch, New York 1985.
9 Not in Bartsch; an example is preserved in the Marucelliana.

MICHELANGELO'S LAST JUDGEMENT

1 J. Wilde, *Italian Drawings ... in the British Museum. Michelangelo and his studio*, London 1953, p. 99.
2 Edd. P. Barocchi, R. Ristori, *Il Carteggio di Michelangelo*, Florence 1979, IV, p. 18, no. cmx.
3 Cf notably A. Gotti, *Vita di Michelangelo Buonarroti narrata con l' aiuto di nuovi documenti*, Florence 1875, p. 225; E. Steinmann, *Die Sixtinische Kapelle*, Munich 1905, II, p. 479. Michelangelo attests to the meeting with Clement VII in a 'ricordo' published by G. Milanesi, *Le Lettere di Michelangelo*, Florence 1875, p. 604: 'nel mille cinquecento trentatre. Ricordo come oggi a dì 22 di settembre che andai a Santo Miniato al Tedesco a parlare a papa Clemente che andava a Nizza; e in tal dì mi lasciò frate Sebastiano del Piombo un suo cavallo'.
4 Ed. P. Barocchi, Giorgio Vasari, *La Vita di Michelangelo*, Milan–Naples 1962, I, p. 10: '... volentieri se ne sarebbe stato a Roma, poi che senza cercarla gli era venuta questa occasione per non tornare più a Fiorenza, avendo molta paura del Duca Alessandro, il quale pensava gli fusse poco amico ...'.
5 See L. von Pastor, *Geschichte der Päpste seit dem Ausgang des Mittelalters*, Freiburg 1907, IV, p. 567, note 2.
6 Ed. K. Frey, A. Condivi, *La Vita di Michelangelo Buonar-*

roti, Berlin 1887, p. 150: "in questo mezzo papa Clemente mancò e fu creato Paolo Terzo, il quale mandò per lui e lo ricercò che stesse seco. Michelangelo, che dubitava di non essere impedito in tale opera [la "Sepoltura" di Giulio II], rispose non poter ciò fare, per essere egli ubligato per contratto al duca d'Urbino, finchè avesse finita l'opera che aveva per mano. Il papa se ne turbò e disse: Egli son già trenta anni che io ho questa voglia; et ora che son papa non me la posso cavare? Dove è questo contratto? Io lo voglio stracciare" – "meanwhile Pope Clement died and Paul III was made Pope. The new Pope sent for Michelangelo and besought him to stay with him. Michelangelo, who did not wish to be diverted from the Tomb of Julius II, replied that that was impossible, since he was under contractual obligation to the Duke of Urbino and would not be released until he had finished the work he was doing. The Pope took this ill and said: 'I have been wanting this for 30 years now; and now that I am Pope can I not have it? Where is this contract? I am going to tear it up!" Condivi's story is taken up by Vasari, ed. cit. note 4, I p. 71.

7 Ed. cit. note 4, I, p. 71: "Fece dunque Michelagnolo fare, che non vi era prima, una scarpa di mattoni, ben murati e scelti e ben cotti, alla facciata di detta cappella, e volse che pendessi dalla sommità di sopra un mezzo braccio, perchè né polvere né altra bruttura si potessi fermare sopra". – Vasari's account had been doubted, but was vindicated by Biagetti's technical examination: see D. Redig de Campos, B. Biagetti, *Il Giudizio Universale di Michelangelo,* Rome 1946, p. 136.

8 Ed. cit. note 4, III, pp. 1384–86. "As was said, Bastiano was greatly loved by Michelangelo. However, it is also true that at the time when Michelangelo was engaged in painting the wall of the Pope's Chapel, where indeed his *Last Judgement* is now to be seen, there was some bad feeling between them, because Sebastiano had persuaded the Pope that Michelangelo should be made to do it in oils, even though Michelangelo himself was not prepared to do it except *a fresco.* But Michelangelo said nothing about it, either yes or no, and let them prepare the wall in the way that Fra Sebastiano wanted, then passed several months without putting his hand to the work at all. Being finally urged, he eventually said that he was not prepared to do it except *a fresco,* and that this *colorire* in oils was a way of doing it for women and for people of leisure who were workshy like Fra Bastiano. And so, having had demolished the surface that had been prepared on Sebastiano's orders, and having had it plastered correctly for painting *a fresco,* Michelangelo set to work, without forgiving what seemed to him the injury done to him by Fra Sebastiano ..."

9 Ibid.
Id, I, p. 70; see also the commentary, III, pp. 1157f.:
"... Clement wanted him to paint a *Last Judgement* on the main wall, where the altar is, and on the other, directly opposite, [the *Fall of the Rebel Angels,]* when Lucifer through his pride was cast out of Heaven and precipitated into the midst of Hell together with all the angels who had sinned with him."

10 For example, F. Hartt, 'The meaning of Michelangelo's Medici Chapel', in *Beiträge für Georg Swarzenski,* Berlin 1951, p. 152; C. de Tolnay, *Michelangelo,* Princeton 1960, V, p. 19.

11 Cf Wilde, cit. note 1, pp. 87f.

12 The drawing in Casa Buonarroti, Florence, no. 65F.

13 On this question see now A. Chastel, *Il Sacco di Roma, 1527,* Turin 1983.

14 Id, p. 189.

15 See in particular C. de Tolnay, 'Le Jugement Dernier de Michel Ange – Essai d'interpretation', *Art Quarterly,* iii, 1940, p. 126; id, *Michelangelo,* Florence 1951, p. 74f.

16 The phrase is from J. Wilde, *Michelangelo – Six Lectures,* Oxford 1978, pp. 162–63: "nor is the painting an illusionistic extension of the chapel space: it opens up the view of a second reality behind it and independent of it. We face this reality as something opposed to us, as a world that is governed by its own rules". I do not, however, believe that there are good grounds for Wilde's hypothesis that Michelangelo originally intended to divide the *Last Judgement* into tiers coordinated with those of the side walls.

17 On this question see the exemplary remarks in Redig de Campos, Biagetti, cit. note 7. Their observations on the technical condition of the fresco seem to confirm Vasari's phrase 'sì unitamente dipinta e condotta' (ed. cit. note 4, I, p. 78; commentary at III, p. 1370), a quality that Vasari praises nowhere else in Michelangelo's work.

18 Matthew 24, 29–31; 25, 31–34.

19 See Condivi, ed. cit. note 6, p. 80. The Pope asked, "Questa tua statua, dà ella la benedizione o maledizzione?" To which Michelangelo: "Minaccia, Padre Santo, questo popolo se non è savio". "It threatens".

20 In particular British Museum no. 1895-9-15-517. Cf Wilde, cit. note 1, pp. 91f.

21 Cf M. Hall, 'Michelangelo's Last Judgement: Resurrection of the Body and Predestination', *Art Bulletin,* lviii, 1976, p. 86.

22 Cf Vasari, ed. cit. note 4, l, p. 76: "Evvi Cristo, il quale, sedendo, con faccia orribile e fiera ai dannati si volge maledicendogli, non senza gran timore della Nostra Donna che, ristrettasi nel manto, ode e vede tanta rovina". Condivi (ed. cit. note 4, p. 166) has the Virgin "separata e prossima al Figliuolo ... timorosetta in sembiante e quasi non bene assicurata de l' ira e secreto de Iddio, trarsi quanto più può sotto il Figliuolo".

23 Against such an interpretation see in particular C. Lanckoronska, 'Appunti sulla interpretazione del *Giudizio Universale* di Michelangelo', *Annales Institutorum,* v, 1932–33, p. 125; Tolnay, *Jugement,* cit. note 16, p. 132; L. Steinberg, 'Michelangelo's *Last Judgement* as Merciful Heresy', *Art in America,* lxiii, 1975, p. 52.

24 Condivi, ed. cit. note 6, pp. 160f.

25 Steinberg, cit. note 24, had affirmed that a 'material' Hell was missing.

26 Published in Pastor, cit. note 5, V, p. 842.

27 Vasari, ed. cit. note 4, I, p. 75: "... Michelangelo had already three quarters finished the work, when Pope Paul went to see it, and asked his Master of Ceremonies, Biagio da Cesena, a very scrupulous man, who was there with him, what he thought of it; Biagio replied that in such an honoured place it was a great shame to have so many nudes who shamefully showed their pudenda, and they did not belong in a papal chapel, but in public baths or brothels. This did not endear him to Michelangelo, who resolved to have his revenge. As soon as he had gone, he drew his portrait, even though he had had no better sitting of him than that, in Hell, in the figure of Minos, with a great serpent wrapped round his legs, in a heap of devils. Nor was any pleading on Biagio's part of the slightest effect, either to Michelangelo or to the Pope: he would not remove it, and left it there as a lesson to him, where it can still be seen."

28 The text is in E. Steinmann, H. Pogatscher, 'Dokumente und Forschungen zu Michelangelo', *Repertorium für Kunstwissenschaft,* xxx, 1906, p. 491: "... as a Christian, I feel shame and offense to my soul at the liberty you have taken in giving form to that Judgement to which every part of us looks forward in the unshakable conviction of our Faith. The Michelangelo of such stupendous fame, the Michelangelo known for his wisdom and sense, the admirable Michelangelo – is he the one who would show to the world not just perfection in painting but also sacrilegious irreverence? How is it possible that you, the divine Michelangelo, above the society of men, should have done such a thing in God's greatest temple? Over the foremost altar of Jesus? In the greatest chapel in the world, where the Cardinals of the Church, its reverend priests, and the Vicar of Christ himself confess, contemplate and worship in catholic ceremony, in holy order, in divineprayer, the Body and Blood and Flesh of Christ? ... even the pagans, in sculptures not of chaste, clothed Diana, but of naked Venus, had had her cover with her hand those parts that need covering; but you, a Christian, with more consideration, however, for your art than for your Faith, present as a royal spectacle a sight entirely remote from martyrs and virgins, indeed such a fervent display of genital organs as would cause even a brothel to blink. Such painting belongs in a voluptuary bath house, not in the choir of the supreme pontiff. It would have been better if you had been a pagan, than to have diminished in this way, as a Christian, the Christianity of others."

29 Ibid ...
"Because our souls have greater need of the spirit of devotion than of spiritedness in design, God inspired St Paul, and inspired in particular St Gregory, who preferred to strip Rome of her proud statues of idols than for their sake to do irreverence to the humble images of the Saints."

30 "And apparently the origin of it all stems from that inventor of bestialities, more concerned for his art than for his faith, Michelangelo Buonarroti, whom every painter and sculptor of today imitates in these Lutheran amusements. The result is that they paint or sculpt today for our holy churches nothing except figures that serve to smother faith and devotion", in G. Gaye, *Carteggio inedito di artisti,* II, Firenze 1840, p. 500.

31 Published and dated to 1549 by K. Behrath, *Rivista Cristiana,* ii, 1900, p. 293: "per avere tu patito e patire una pictura così obscene et sporca come quella di Michel Angelo nella Cappella, ove si hanno da cantare li offitii divini, la quale molto meglio servirebbe in un teatro o scena comica ove qualche cosa obscena se havesse da recitare" – "for having permitted and permitting a picture as dirty and revolting as Michelangelo's in the Chapel where divine offices are sung, when it would be much more suitable in a theatre or in a setting for a comedy where something obscene were performed".

32 *A. Catharini Commentaria in omnes divi Pauli et alias septem canonicas epistolas,* Venice 1551, p. 645: 'Est pictor et sculptor nostra aetate egregius, Michael Angelus, qui admirabilis est in exprimendo nuda hominum corpora et pudenda. Comendo artem in facto: at factum ipsum vehementer vituperor et detestor. Nam haec membrorum nuditas indecentissima in aris et praecipuis Dei sacellis ubique conspicitur. Verum annumeretur et hic cum caeteris multis et magnis abusis, quibus foedatur Ecclesia Dei sponsa Christi'.

33 *Due Dialoghi di M. Giovanni Andrea Gilio da Fabriano. Nel primo ... Nel secondo si ragiona degli errori de' pittori circa l' istorie. Con molte annotazioni fatte sopra il Giudizio di Michelangelo et altre figure tanto de la vecchia quanto de la nuova Cappella; et in che modo vogliono esser dipinte le sacre imagini,* Camerino 1564.

34 Vasari, ed. cit. note 4, I, p. 97.

35 The pictures in the Apostolic Chapel should be covered over, and those in other churches should be destroyed, if they display anything obscene or clearly false. (Decision of January 21, 1564).

36 For subsequent 'emendations' see in particular the commentary of Barocchi to Vasari, ed. cit. note 4, III, p. 1377; and R. De Maio, *Michelangelo e la Controriforma,* Bari 1978, pp. 37f.

37 *Dialogo della Pittura di Lodovico Dolce intitolato l'Aretino,* Venice 1557.

38 See particularly P. Barocchi, 'Schizzo di una storia della critica cinquecentesca sulla Sistina', *Atti dell' Accademia Toscana di Scienze e Lettere: La Columbaria,* viii, 1957, pp. 197f; ed. P. Barocchi, *Trattati d'Arte del Cinquecento,* Bari 1960, I, p. 316.

39 Vasari, ed. cit. note 4, I, pp. 78–79; commentary, III, pp. 1370–77.

40 A full survey of such reactions is in Barocchi's commentary to Vasari, ed. cit. note 4, III, p. 1254.

41 See above, notes 23 and 24. The attitudes of Christ, the Virgin and the saints were the particular objects of criticism of such as Gilio.

42 The Romantic interpretation still lives on, indeed is still persuasive, even if today some of its more one-sided and anachronistic elements are clear to see and must be dismissed. In itself the persistence of the Romantic reading of the fresco would be a fertile ground for art historians – though the field has not been tackled with any perseverance; it might also lead us to consider that despite its very slight historical foundation and its proven distortions, the Romantic interpretation of Michelangelo's fresco might serve to bring us closer to the heart of the problem and might be revealed to correspond in some ways with the contemporary reactions to the fresco that can be historically validated.

43 A survey of the doctrines read into the frescoes is in Barocchi's commentary, ed. cit. note 4, III, pp. 1287f: since then, there have been notably D. Redig de Campos, *Il Giudizio Universale di Michelangelo,* Milan 1964; H. von Einem, *Michelangelo,* London 1973; Steinberg, cit. note 24; Hall, cit. note 22; De Maio, cit. note 35; M. Calì, *Da Michelangelo all' Escorial,* Turin 1980.

44 See now De Maio, cit. note 35; Calì, cit. above.

45 Ed. E. N. Giraldi, Michelangelo, *Rime,* Bari 1960, no. 66, lines 9–11.

46 Ed. cit. above, no. 33, lines 7–12.

"IL MODO DELLE ATTITUDINI"

1 *I Ricordi di Michelangelo,* ed. L. Bardeschi Ciulich and P. Barocchi, Florence 1970, pp. 1–2.

2 *Il Carteggio di Michelangelo,* ed. P. Barocchi and R. Ristori, Florence, I, 1965, p. 16.

3 *Il Carteggio ...,* I, p. 57.

4 *Il Carteggio ...,* I, pp. 64–5.

5 *I Ricordi ...,* pp. 2–3.

6 The best text of the Diary in E. Steinmann, *Die Sixtinische Kapelle,* Munich 1905, II, Appendix II, p. 699, edited by H. Pogatscher.

7 *Il Carteggio ...,* I, p. 77.

8 *Il Carteggio ...,* I, p. 80.

9 *Il Carteggio ...,* I, pp. 88–9.

10 *Il Carteggio ...,* I, p. 106.

11 *Il Carteggio ...,* I, p. 108.

12 *Il Carteggio ...,* I, p. 116.

13 Steinmann, *op. cit.,* p. 722.

14 For the viewing, Steinmann, cit. note 6, pp. 735–6; for the letter, *Il Carteggio ...,* I, p. 137.

15 H. Wölfflin: "Die Sixtinische Decke Michelangelo's" in *Repertorium für Kunstwissenschaft,* XIII, 1890, pp. 264–72.

16 See, for example, C. de Tolnay, *The Sistine Ceiling,* Princeton 1945, pp. 111–2.

17 See my comments below. For the text, *Il Carteggio di Michelangelo,* ed. P. Barocchi and R. Ristori, Florence, III, 1973, pp. 7–9; the other draft, *ibid.,* pp. 10–11.

18 J. Wilde, *Michelangelo, Six Lectures,* Oxford 1978, pp. 66ff.

19 A. Condivi, *Vita di Michelagnolo Buonarroti,* ed. A. F. Gori, Florence 1756, p. 27.

20 For this, see F. Mancinelli in *Apollo,* May, 1983, p. 364; the fact already noted by Wilde, cit. note 18, p. 68.

21 *Il Carteggio ...,* III, p. 8.

22 Ibid.

23 K. T. Parker, *Catalogue of the Collection of Drawings in the Ashmolean Museum,* II, Oxford 1956, p. 143.

24 The leaves of Pontormo's so-called Corsini sketchbook measure approximately 21.5 by 15.5 cm, a scale almost exactly equalled by Bambaia's sketchbook in Berlin.

25 An attempted identification of the original study in Tolnay, *Corpus,* I, no. 166 *recto* fails to take into account the reversal of the image caused by offsetting.

26 For this mis-identification, Tolnay, *Corpus,* I, no. 171 *verso,* and for a comparable one, no. 166 *recto.*

27 *Il Carteggio ...,* I, p. 121.

28 See W.Y. Ottley, *The Italian School of Design,* London 1823, p. 29, and J.C. Robinson, *A Critical Account of the Drawings by Michel Angelo and Raffaello in the University Galleries, Oxford,* Oxford 1870, p. 30.

29 G. Vasari, *Le Vite ...,* ed. G. Milanesi, Florence 1878, I, p. 174.

30 Uffizi 233F *recto,* Tolnay, *Corpus,* I, no. 37 *recto.*

31 The sheet is Haarlem, Teyler Museum Inv. A27 *verso,* Tolnay, *Corpus,* I, no. 136 *verso,* made after the 1510–11 interruption.

32 This concession to illusionism seems not to have been noted in the literature.

33 The drawing is Casa Buonarroti 24F *recto;* Tolnay, *Corpus,* I, 160 *recto,* there wrongly described as preceding the Oxford studies.

34 There is some evidence that the relief's design was known in the Bandinelli circle.

35 For Leone Leoni's dispatch of four examples to Michelangelo, see his letter of 14 March 1561, in *Il Carteggio ...,* V, Florence, 1983, pp. 244–5. For the medal, see E. Plon, *Leone Leoni ...,* Paris 1887, pl. XXXIII.

36 The Casa Buonarroti drawing is 33F *recto,* Tolnay, *Corpus* 146 *recto.*

37 J. Wilde, in *Mitteilungen des Kunsthistorischen Instituts in Florenz,* IV, 1, 1932, p. 63.

MICHELANGELO AT WORK

1 J.J. de la Lande, *Voyage en Italie*, Paris 1769.
2 C.H. Wilson, *Life and Works of Michelangelo Buonarroti*, London 1876; B. Biagetti, 'La Volta della Cappella Sistina', *Rendiconti della Pontificia Accademia Romana di Archeologia*, xii, 1936, p. 220; J. Wilde, 'The Sistine Ceiling', in *Michelangelo. Six Lectures by Johannes Wilde*, Oxford 1968, p. 68.
3 Text by André Chastel, published by Kodansha Publishers, Tokyo.
4 H. Wölfflin, 'Die Sixtinische Decke Michelangelo's', *Repertorium für Kunstwissenschaft*, xiii, 1890, p. 264 f.
5 C. de Tolnay, *Michelangelo II. The Sistine Chapel Ceiling*, Princeton 1945, pp. 105–111, 187, and especially p. 108.
6 Wilde, cit. note 2, 63–71.
7 Ed. G. Milanesi, G. Vasari, *Le vite …*, Florence 1881, VII, p. 176.
8 Ed. P. D' Ancona, A Condivi, *Michelangelo. La Vita*, Milano 1928, p. 113.
9 For the hypotheses put forward about the structure of the scaffold see E. Camesasca's appendix in R. Salvini, *La Cappella Sistina in Vaticano*, Milan 1965, p. 183.
10 C. Gilbert, 'On the Absolute Dates of the Parts of the Sistine Chapel Ceiling', in *Art History*, xiii, 2, 1980, pp. 159–81.
11 P. Joannides, 'On the Chronology of the Sistine Chapel Ceiling', in *Art History*, iv, 3, 1981, pp. 250–53.
12 F. Hartt, 'The Evidence for the Scaffolding of the Sistine Ceiling', in *Art History*, v, 3, 1982, pp. 273–86.
13 F. Mancinelli, 'Il ponte di Michelangelo per la Cappella Sistina', *Rassegna dell' Accademia Nazionale di San Luca*, 1–2, 1982, pp. 2–9.
14 Ed cit. note 8, p. 177.
15 Ed cit. note 7, VII, p. 174.
16 Ibid.
17 Ibid.
18 Ed cit. note 8, p. 178.
19 L. Grassi, M. Pepe, *Dizionario della Critica d' Arte*, Turin 1978, II, p. 552.
20 Published by E. Steinmann, *Die Sixtinische Kapelle*, Munich 1905, II, p. 699. The "diary" of Paris de Grassis relative to the years 1504–21 was published by E. Müntz, *Gazette des Beaux-Arts*, 1882.
21 Mancinelli, cit. note 13, p. 4; Hartt, cit. note 12, p. 280.
22 Kindly brought to my notice by Arnold Nesselrath.
23 L. Collobi Ragghianti, *Il "Libro de' Disegni" del Vasari*, Florence 1975, p. 101, pl 153, fig. 293.
24 Ed. cit. note 7, VII, p. 174.
25 See Steinmann, cit. note 20, II, p. 699.
26 A. Pozzo, 'Breve istruzione per dipingere a fresco', in *Prospettiva de' Pittori ed Architetti*, Rome 1693–1702, part II.
27 Steinmann, cit. note 20, II, p. 698.
28 Ibid., II, p. 736.
29 'Solari' = *solaio*, or in old Italian *solaro*. Hartt, cit. note 12, p. 279, has a different interpretation of the term.
30 Steinmann, cit. note 20, II, pp. 716–17; edd. P. Barocchi, R. Ristori, *Il Carteggio di Michelangelo*, Florence 1965, I, p. 108.
31 Ed. cit. note 8, p. 113.
32 Ed. P. Barocchi, *Scritti dell' Arte del Cinquecento*, Milan–Naples 1971, I, p. 10.
33 F. Milizia, *Le vite de' piu celebri architetti d' ogni nazione e d' ogni tempo*, Rome 1768.
34 Ed. cit. note 7, VII, p. 178.
35 Ed. cit. note 8, p. 115.
36 Ed. E. N. Giraldi, Michelangelo, *Rime*, Bari 1960, pp. 158–59.
37 Ed. cit. note 7, p. 174.
38 On the restoration of the lunettes and its results see also: C. Pietrangeli, 'I recenti restauri nella Cappella Sistina', in *Rassegna dell' Accademia Nazionale di San Luca*, 1982, 1–2, pp. 8–15; F. Mancinelli, 'Die Restaurierung der Lunettenbilder Michelangelos in der Sixtinischen Kapelle', in *Kunstchronik*, xxxvi, 3, 1983, pp. 121–25; Id, 'The technique of Michelangelo as a painter: a note on the cleaning of the first lunettes in the Sistine Chapel, in *Apollo*, cxvii, 255, 1983, pp. 362–67; G. Colalucci, 'Scheda del catalogo della Mostra Restauri in Vaticano', in *Monumenti Musei e Gallerie Pontificie, Bollettino IV*, 1983, pp. 144–60.
39 On past restorations and on Michelangelo's colour see F. Mancinelli, G. Colalucci, 'Vero colore di Michelangelo: le lunette della Cappella Sistina', in *Critica d' Arte*, 1, 6, 1985, pp. 72–89.
40 F. Stasny, 'A note on two frescoes in the Sistine Chapel', in *Burlington Magazine*, cxxi, 1979, pp. 777–83.
41 The text of the motuproprio of Paul III was published by D. Redig de Campos, *Il Giudizio Universale di Michelangelo*, Milan 1964, pp. 93–94.
42 The documents for 18th-century restoration, particularly by Mazzuoli, are in course of publication, edd. E. Cicerchia, A. M. de Strobel, in the forthcoming bulletin of *Monumenti, Musei e Gallerie Pontificie*.
43 Cit. note 5, pp. 77–92.
44 Cit. note 2, p. 68.
45 Ed. cit. note 7, VII, p. 176; ed. cit. note 8, p. 112.
46 Ed. cit. note 7, VII, pp. 137–41.
47 M. Winner expressed this opinion at a seminar held in May 1983 at Villa I Tatti, Florence. On the *Coronation of Charlemagne* and its restoration see F. Mancinelli, 'Raphael's Coronation of Charlemagne and its cleaning', in *Burlington Magazine*, cxxvi, 976, 1984, pp. 404–08; Id, 'L'Incoronazione di Francesco I nella Stanza dell' Incendio di Borgo', in *Raffaello a Roma. Il Convegno del 1983*, Rome 1986; A. Nesselrath, 'La progettazione dell' Incoronazione di Carlomagno', ibid.
48 G. B. Armenini, *Dei veri precetti della pittura*, Ravenna 1587.
49 Ed. cit. note 7, I, pp. 177–78.
50 See the letters in *Il Carteggio*, cit. note 30, of Michi to Michelangelo, 22.7. 1508, of Michelangelo to his brother Buonarroto, 29.7. 1508, and of Buonarroto to Michelangelo, 5.8. 1508, pp. 73, 75–76, 79, 376; Steinmann, cit. note 20, II, pp. 702–05.
51 Ed. cit. note 7, VII, p. 177.
52 Cf. Michelangelo to his father, *Carteggio*, cit. note 30, 27. 1. 1509, pp. 82–89; Steinmann, cit. note 20, II, p. 710.
53 Ed. cit. note 7, p. 177.
54 *Il Carteggio*, cit. note 30, p. 133; Steinmann cit. note 20, II, p. 731.
55 Ibid. p. 88 and II, p. 710 respectively.

MICHELANGELO'S COLOURS REDISCOVERED

1 C. Brandi, *Teoria del Restauro*, Rome 1963.
2 *Norme per il restauro delle Opere d' Arte*, Rome 1978.
3 The team consisted of Dr Fabrizio Mancinelli, Inspector of Byzantine, Medieval and Modern Art, director, Dr Nazzareno Gabrielli, who ran the research laboratory, and Gianluigi Colalucci, chief restorer of the Laboratory, assisted by restorers Maurizio Rossi and Piergiorgio Bonetti. The supervisor of this, as of all the restoration undertaken by the Laboratory, was Professor Carlo Pietrangeli, Director General of the Pontifical Monuments, Museums and Galleries; Consultant for the restoration was Professor Pasquale Rotondi, former Director of the Central Institute of Restoration, Rome.
4 Ed. A. Brunello, C. Cennini, *Il libro dell' Arte*, Vicenza 1971: El modo e ordine a lavorare in muro, cioè in fresco, e di colorire o incarnare viso giovanile.
5 See P. Mora, L. Mora, P. Philippot, *La Conservation des Peintures Murales*, Bologna 1977, pp. 13–15.
6 Ed. G. Milanesi, G. Vasari, *Le Vite …*, Florence 1906, I, ch. V, p. 182.
7 Cf his letter to his father of 27. 1. 1509, quoted in E. Steinmann, *Die Sixtinische Kapelle*, Munich 1905, II, p. 710.
8 See C. Maltese, *Le tecniche artistiche*, Milan 1973, pp. 321–22.
9 For such damage cf L. von Pastor, *Storia dei Papi dalla fine del Medioevo*, Rome 1929, vol. 8, p. 81; E. Steinmann, *Die Sixtinische Kapelle*, Munich 1905, vol. 2, pp. 780–83.
10 The roof was completely reconstructed in 1903 and recently repaired and reconstructed in 1978.
11 See S. Augusti, *Natura e cause delle effluorescenze bianche che si producono sugli affreschi*, Naples 1948.
12 See E. Camesasca, *La Cappella Sistina in Vaticano*, Appendice, Milan 1974, p. 187, where he also quotes the sentence of Giovio.
13 See F. Mancinelli, G.L. Colalucci, 'Vero colore di Michelangelo. Le lunette della Cappella Sistina', in *Critica d' Arte*, series 4, 1, no. 6, July–September 1985, p. 72 f, and bibliography.
14 See Vatican Library, Vat. Capponiano 231, f. 238 and Chigiano G. III. 66, f. 108. The text quoted goes: 'e l'ordine che si tenne fu questo, che spolverata figura per figura, con panno lino se gli levava la polvere con fetti di pane a baiocco o altro più vile, stropicciando diligentemente, e tal volta, dove la polvere era più tenace, bagnavano un poco detto pane e così ritornano alla pristina bellezza senza ricever danno alcuno'.
15 See A.M. De Strobel, E. Cicerchia, 'Documenti inediti dell' Archivio Segreto Vaticano sui restauri delle Stanze di Raffaello e della Cappella Sistina all' epoca di Clemente XI,' in *Monumenti, Musei e Gallerie Pontificie*, Bollettino vi (forthcoming).
16 Cf G.P. Bellori, *Vite di Guido Reni, Andrea Sacchi e Carlo Maratti. Trascritto diplomatico dal Manoscritto MS 2506 della Biblioteca Municipale di Rouen*, Rome 1942, p. 147.
17 See F. Aliberti Gaudioso, 'Il restauro degli affreschi'; and G.L. Colalucci, 'Relazione sul restauro della volta della Sala Paolina', in *Gli affreschi di Paolo III a Castel Sant' Angelo 1543–1548. Progetto ed esecuzione* (exhibition catalogue), Rome 1981. I am grateful to Bruno Contardi for courteously informing me about the Mazzuoli in Castel Sant' Angelo.
18 G.C. Argan, 'Quel pennello furioso', in *L'Espresso*, 24. 1. 1982.
19 M. de la Lande, *Voyage en Italie*, Paris 1768.
20 See B. Biagetti, 'La volta della Cappella Sistina', in *Rendiconti della Pontificia Accademia Romana di Archeologia*, xiii, 1936. Further information is in the *Diari di Restauro* in the archive of the Vatican Restoration Laboratory.
21 See F. Mancinelli, G.L. Colalucci, 'Mostra Restauri in Vaticano', in *Monumenti, Musei e Gallerie Pontificie*, Bollettino iv, 1983, pp. 143–60.
22 Cf Mora, Mora and Philippot, cit. note 5, pp. 400–01.
23 See Brandi, cit. note 1, pp. 45 and 105.
24 Cf B. Nogara, 'Restauri degli affreschi di Michelangelo nella Cappella Sistina', *Arte*, ix, fasc. iii, 1906, p. 229.
25 Cf G.L. Colalucci, 'Mostra Restauri', cit. note 21, pp. 159–60.
26 A study of the micro-climate of the Sistine Chapel was prepared by Professor Dario Camuffo of the Istituto di Chimica e Tecnologia dei Radioelementi of Padua. See D. Camuffo, A Bernardi, 'Dinamica del microclima e scambi termoigrometri tra pareti e atmosfera interna nella Cappelle Sistina', in *Monumenti, Musei e Gallerie Pontificie*, Bollettino vi (forthcoming).

PICTURE CREDITS

INDEX